COLLINS FIELD GUIDE

LAND SNAILS

OF BRITAIN &
NORTH-WEST EUROPE

M P KERNEY
R A D CAMERON
ILLUSTRATED BY GORDON RILEY

HarperCollins*Publishers*

HarperCollins*Publishers*

Originally published by William Collins Sons and Co Ltd.
London · Glasgow · Sydney · Auckland
Toronto · Johannesburg

ISBN 0 00 219676 X

First published 1979
Reprinted 1987
Reprinted 1994

Filmset by Jolly and Barber Ltd., Rugby
Reproduction by Adroit Photo-Litho Ltd., Birmingham
Produced by HarperCollins Hong Kong

Contents

Colour plates

Preface

Of all the many recent books on the land Mollusca of western Europe, only the classic, but dated *Die Tierwelt Mitteleuropas II* (1) *Weichtiere, Mollusca* of Ehrmann (1933) covers an area outside the confines of a single nation. With increasing interest in land slugs and snails, there is a need for a single work covering the fauna of the whole area. This we have attempted to do, restricting ourselves, for reasons explained in the text, to N.W. Europe only. All the species known to occur within this area are described, and all but a very few are illustrated.

Many people have helped with this book. We are particularly indebted to Dr E. Gittenberger and to Dr L. Lloyd-Evans for their substantial assistance with the families Chondrinidae and Succineidae. Help was also received from Professor H. Ant, Dr W. Backhuys, Mr J. R. M. de Bartolomé, Dr M. J. Bishop, Professor A. J. Cain, Dr June Chatfield, Dr H. Chevallier, Miss Stella M. Davies, Mr A. E. Ellis, Dr N. J. Evans, Dr L. Forcart, Dr F. Giusti, Mr J. Heath, Dr W. Klemm, Mr J. G. J. Kuiper, Dr P. B. Mordan, Dr H. Nordsieck, Mr A. Norris, Dr O. Paget, Mr J. F. Peake, Mr and Mrs D. Rands, Dr Günter Schmid, Professor F. W. Shotton, Dr B. Verdcourt and Dr A. Wiktor. The value of the distribution maps was considerably enhanced by much unpublished information kindly provided by Dr L. Hässlein, Dr J. H. Jungbluth, Dr I. Valovirta, Dr Hildegard Zeissler, and above all Dr H. W. Waldén, who placed at our disposal his unrivalled knowledge of the Mollusca of Scandinavia; Dr Waldén advised us additionally on a number of taxonomic problems. We should also like to thank those many friends who lent or gave us shells from their collections or who undertook special searches for living material for illustration.

We are also indebted to the museums which lent us material from their collections: British Museum (Natural History), London; Naturhistoriska Museet, Göteborg; Muséum d'Histoire Naturelle, Bâle; National Museum of Wales, Cardiff; Muséum National d'Histoire Naturelle, Paris; University Museum of Zoology, Cambridge; Leeds City Museums; Rijksmuseum van Natuurlijke Historie, Leiden; and Naturhistorisches Museum, Wien.

All the illustrations, both colour and line, are the work of Gordon Riley, to whom we owe an immense debt, not only for the superb quality of the pictures, but also for his pertinent comments and assistance with finding specimens.

The preparation of this book was divided in the following way: most of the introductory matter was written by R.A.D.C., together with the sections on the following families: Arionidae, Milacidae, Limacidae, Testacellidae, Bradybaenidae, Helicidae. The remaining families were treated by M.P.K., who also compiled the maps and all data concerning geographical distribution and nomenclature. The index was kindly prepared by Mr A. E. Ellis. We are of course responsible for any imperfections and deficiencies, and should be grateful for suggestions towards remedying these.

7

How to use this book

On the **plates** and **line-drawings** are illustrated all the species of land slug and snail found in northern Europe (see pp. 10–11 for details of area covered). In general, the illustrations are of adult specimens, and, where identification requires it, there may be two or three views of the same specimen, and of common colour and pattern variants. *Always pay attention to the scale of each illustration.*

The caption gives the name of the species and in the case of the plates, references to description in the text and to the general account of the family to which it belongs. Read the account of the family first, before trying to identify your specimen.

In the **main text**, each family is given a brief introduction, and then each species in it is described, and its habitats, range and distribution are briefly noted. There are **distribution maps** for most species, but remember that these are based on much less information than similar maps for birds or plants; you are quite likely to find a species some way outside its presently known distribution. Map reference numbers relate both to European maps, pp. 226–256, and British maps, pp. 260–288.

For most of the species in this book, external features of the body or shell, examined with the naked eye, or with a hand lens and a ruler graduated in millimetres, are sufficient for correct identification. For a few species, however, a binocular microscope is an advantage, and for a few others, dissection, to see internal characters, is necessary. Where internal characters are used, this is indicated in the family account, and also under the species descriptions, and figures of the internal differences are provided. Read the section on identifying slugs and snails (p. 31) before you start. Juvenile specimens, and old, empty shells are often difficult to identify, so try to find living, adult, specimens or very fresh shells for your first attempts.

There is a **glossary of terms** used on pp. 37–8, a **check-list of species** on pp. 39–47, and a **list of further reading** on pp. 213–14. The accounts of each species in the text use the following conventions.

*: species living in British Isles.

Synonyms: common ones only given, esp. those used in modern standard works.
Descriptions: Based on fresh, mature shells. Sizes are for, first, *height*, and then *breadth*. If only a single figure is given, this is for *height*; if breadth, this is specified. Sizes given are for normal range in N.W. Europe; occasionally extremes are given separately. For geographically very variable species only the form occurring in N.W. Europe is described. In some cases this may be untypical, e.g. an unusual subspecies; if so, a rider to this effect may be added.
Habitat: only within N.W. Europe, and may be different elsewhere (e.g., different elevational ranges in the eastern Alps).
Range: total world range.
Distribution: i.e. in N.W. Europe.
Colour: white (colourless) forms found in most species – not usually specified.

Introduction

Land slugs and snails are a small part of the great animal phylum Mollusca, which, with about 80,000 known species is second in size only to the phylum Arthropoda, which includes insects, spiders and crustaceans. The range of size, shape and form in molluscs is immense, but they can generally be distinguished from other animals by possessing a muscular *foot*, a *mantle* covering the internal organs, and, usually, but not always, by possessing a shell which covers all or part of the body.

Land slugs and snails all belong to the class Gastropoda, which have a well-developed foot, and, primitively, a single coiled shell into which the animal can withdraw. Other molluscs include the Bivalvia (mussels, oysters, cockles etc), the Cephalopoda (octopus, squid, cuttlefish), Scaphopoda (tusk shells) and Amphineura (chitons or coat of mail shells). All except the Gastropoda are completely aquatic, and the great majority even of the Gastropoda are found in the sea.

Originally, all gastropods had both a shell and gills, and were aquatic. Over the course of their evolution, some species have lost either or both of these features.

Species which have lost, or appear to have lost, their shell are usually referred to as slugs. However, the dividing line between slugs and snails (gastropods which have *not* lost their shells) is impossible to draw precisely, because all the intermediate stages in the process of shell reduction and loss can be found in living species.

In the area covered by this guide there are three families of slugs with no *external* shell (but there is a small one inside in most species) (Plates 4, 5, 12–14) and one with a very small external shell (Plate 14) into which the whole animal could not possibly fit. Some snails have very small shells, proportional to the size of their body (*Daudebardia*, Plate 11) or have shells that are partly covered by the body when the animal is crawling (Vitrinidae, Plates 6, 7). We call all those animals which cannot fit inside their shells slugs, and those that can, snails. The word snail, is however, often used much more loosely – it may refer to all gastropods, or all terrestrial gastropods including slugs.

Land snails are easy to recognize as such, because they all have a spirally coiled shell, unlike any other land animal. Many are missed by the unobservant, either because of their small size (the smallest are about 1.5 mm wide and 1.0 mm high) or because of their peculiar shape (e.g. the Clausiliidae). Slugs can be more difficult, and may be mistaken for worms or insect larvae. They are, however, very easily distinguished by their *tentacles* and by the presence of a *mantle* with a breathing pore. They are not segmented like earthworms and insect larvae.

Just as people who study insects are called entomologists, and those who study birds, ornithologists, so there is a name, in fact two names, for those who study molluscs: conchologists or malacologists. Both of these words mean 'studiers of shell-fish', but there were times in the past when the two names had rather different implications, and might even be used as a term of abuse for one whose methods of study were disapproved of. In the past, and to some extent still, most amateur students of molluscs collected and studied sea-shells – these being the most abundant, the largest, and superficially the most attractive. Some rare or beautiful species consequently acquired considerable commercial value, and the building up of a collection of rarities became an end in itself. Land snails, being smaller, and usually less strikingly coloured, were until recently of interest only to specialists and a small but dedicated band of amateurs.

Happily, this is no longer true. More and more general naturalists want to identify and study the slugs and snails they come across. The total number of species is not large, and most of them can be identified in the field with the aid of a hand-lens and a ruler.

At present, however, there is no single book to help the naturalist in N.W. Europe. There are many good guides to the slugs and snails of individual countries, but some of these are now rather out-of-date, or so massive as to be works of reference only. There are also formidably specialist works on particular groups of snails. This book is designed to provide a single, compact guide to the identification of all the species of land slug and snail in N.W. Europe. Although we hope it will be of use to the specialist, it is aimed mainly at those with little or no previous experience.

The area covered by this guide

The map opposite shows the boundaries of the area covered by this guide. The boundaries follow national frontiers, for convenience, with the exception of France, where we have omitted the departments of Alpes Maritimes, Basses Alpes, Var, Bouches du Rhône, Vaucluse, Drôme, Ardèche, Gard, Hérault, Aude and Pyrénées Orientales, which lie in the Mediterranean zone.

To the south and east of our area, the number of species increases rapidly, and many of them are ill known or poorly described. Even within our area, there are difficult species over which experts disagree – outside it there are far more. It is for these reasons that we have omitted considering Eastern and Mediterranean Europe.

Some minor biogeographical anomalies have resulted from this. Two should be mentioned. Several Italian species are included which occur only within a small area of S. Switzerland (Ticino). Secondly, a number of east Alpine species extend just into the mountains of S.E. Germany. Further research will undoubtedly reveal more species living in the south and east of our area, and it is possible that you may find there species not described in this book. Conversely, many of the species described in this book occur widely outside our area, especially in Poland and western Russia.

All 279 known species native or naturalized in our area are included in this book, plus a selection of those found only in greenhouses. In general, the fauna increases in richness from north to south. Iceland and the northernmost parts of Scandinavia have only 25–30 species, southern Britain and N. Germany about 100 species, and parts of S. Germany and France over 130 species. Many local endemic species are found in the southern areas, particularly in mountains, whereas the northern countries (e.g. Britain) have none. This is because their faunas were largely destroyed during the glacial period, the molluscs now living there being the descendants of immigrants from the south, allowing insufficient time for the evolution of new species *in situ*.

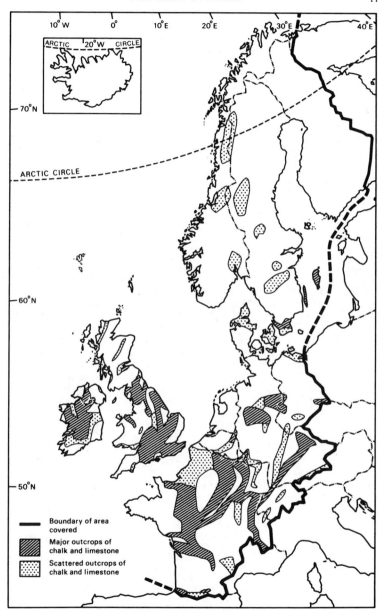

Boundary of area covered

Major outcrops of chalk and limestone

Scattered outcrops of chalk and limestone

The biology of slugs and snails

Although they live successfully even in deserts, slugs and snails are not so thoroughly adapted to life on land as insects and spiders, and they are not nearly so numerous or diverse. They retain a wet skin, and use a method of moving which loses water through mucus, and their only defence against dry conditions is to become inactive. Their proverbially slow movement, and comparatively large size make them vulnerable to predators. It is the needs to avoid desiccation and predation which have the greatest influence on their structure and habits.

STRUCTURE

The shell

A hard, spirally coiled shell, into which the animal can withdraw is a characteristic and original feature of gastropods. In some marine shells (e.g. limpets) the shell has uncoiled, and is a cone, while in slugs it is reduced, buried or lost. In the sea, where snails originated, the shell protects the animal from predators, and in some cases from wave action. In the intertidal zone, and on land, it serves the additional function of protecting its occupant from drying up – it is nearly impermeable to water.

The shell is in some ways a very cumbersome means of protection. It is heavy and unjointed, unlike the hard cuticle of an insect, and it provides maximum protection only when the animal is withdrawn. On the other hand, the pattern of spiral growth means that the shell can be enlarged continuously without much alteration in shape – there is no need to moult, something all insects do, and which is a period of considerable danger for them.

The growth of the shell is not completely regular and even. A newly hatched snail already has a shell, formed inside the egg, the *protoconch*. This will form the apex of the shell of the adult. It is often smoother and thinner than the rest, and it can usually be distinguished from the rest with a lens.

During the growth period, the rate may also slow down or stop, for example in winter, or during a drought, and then speed up again. This often leaves irregular radial growth-lines. In large snails, taking several years to reach maturity, there may be several such lines at different points on the shell.

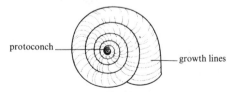

Top view of shell showing protoconch and growth-lines

12

When the snail becomes adult, the pattern of growth changes. The shell does not get larger, but the area round the mouth may be strengthened with a rib or lip and with various other thickenings (see below).

The shell has two distinct layers: the thick, inner *ostracum* made mostly of calcium carbonate (chalk) with some protein, and the outer *periostracum*, which is proteinaceous, horny and transparent. Its effect on the appearance of the ostracum is similar to that of a coat of varnish – it creates a smoother and more glossy surface, and brightens the colours in the ostracum.

The periostracum is soon worn from empty shells, and may be partly eroded in living snails, especially in sand dunes where there is much abrasion. Such shells appear matt and faded.

The shell itself is dead and inert, and so as it is made the periostracum must be laid down first. In juvenile snails the leading edge of the shell is often much thinner and more transparent than the rest – the ostracum has not yet been deposited.

Details of shell shape, size, colour etc., are of great importance in identifying snails. All the main details needed are described and illustrated below – a few special features found only in single families are dealt with in the accounts of the families concerned.

With only very rare exceptions, the direction of coiling is always the same for each species. Coiling is *dextral* when the mouth is on the right when the shell is held facing you, and *sinistral* when it is on the left.

The spiral of the shell creates an internal *columella*, which may be hollow or solid. Each successive coil of the spiral is a *whorl*; all the whorls except the *last* or *body whorl* form the *spire*, the tip of which is the *apex*. The line of contact between the whorls is the *suture*. On the underside, the last whorl circles the *umbilicus*, which may, however, be sealed off in some species.

Method of counting whorls

Characters of these parts of the shell are much used in identification. The number of whorls in a shell is sometimes useful. The count starts at the line of the diameter of the semicircle at the apex (see figure). Passing round the whorls, one whorl is added to the count each time the extension of the line is passed; any 'remainder' of the last whorl is estimated to the nearest quarter, and the final count is expressed with a whole number and a fraction – in this case 2¼ whorls. The shape of the whorls, and the rate at which they expand and descend, determine the overall shape of the shell. The spire may be *sunken*, below the level of the last whorl; it may be flat, or raised to varying degrees. If raised, it may be *conical* or *convex*, or more or less *cylindrical* or *fusiform* until near the apex.

Whorls may expand *rapidly* or *slowly*. They may be convex or rather flattened.

The body whorl may be smoothly rounded, or it may be *angled* or *shouldered* at, or just above the *periphery*, or it may even be *keeled*. The suture may be *deep* or *shallow*.

The size and shape of the shell are also important, and are best determined by measurement. The key measurements are shell *breadth* and *height*. Shells are not completely circular, and the breadth is always the largest diameter. Occasionally it is useful to measure the heights of the body whorl and spire separately, also the mouth.

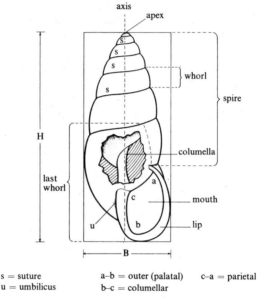

s = suture   a–b = outer (palatal)   c–a = parietal
u = umbilicus   b–c = columellar

Nomenclature of shell (*Ena montana*)

Characters of the *mouth* and *mouth-edge (peristome)* are often very important, and these characters are only fully developed in adult shells. In some species, the shell ends in a simple peristome, without any thickenings or changes in shape. Even here, the shape and angle of the mouth may be important. Most species, however, have at least a *thickened internal rib*, just behind the peristome. In transparent or translucent shells, it may show on the outside as a more opaque band. Alternatively, or in addition, the peristome may be thickened into a *lip*, which is often somewhat everted.

Within the mouth, there may be other thickenings or folds, generally known as *teeth*. In order to describe teeth and other features round the mouth accurately, the inside of the mouth and the peristome around it are divided into distinct areas. The mouth is divided into the *parietal*, the *columellar* and the *palatal* regions, as indicated in the figure. Teeth and other thickenings are described by the region of the mouth in which they are found. The peristome round the palatal region is *outer*, that round the parietal and columellar regions is *inner*.

There are also finer structural characters of the shell which may be useful. Some shells are *hairy* – the hairs being extensions of the periostracum. They frequently are lost by abrasion, but leave little pits or scars visible under the microscope. Stiffer, larger extrusions of the periostracum are called *spines*. The shell surface is frequently ribbed. These *ribs* are usually transverse (radial) (occasionally spiral as well) and may vary in size and regularity of disposition. Other species may have minute grooves or *striae* in the surface, and others still may have a fine *sculpture* of *reticulations*, which often give a dull and hazy lustre to the surface when viewed with the naked eye. A binocular microscope is usually needed to see the pattern clearly. Many species, though, have very smooth and glossy surfaces with none of these features.

Shell colour and translucency also vary. These characters are based on the ostracum – the thinner and less calcareous the ostracum, the more translucent the shell becomes – some have a glass-like transparency, and are very fragile. Such shells soon turn milky white when empty. Colour is rather a variable character within the species, and by itself is not very reliable. Quite a number of species are polymorphic for shell colour and pattern, especially amongst the Helicidae (p. 175) (see below). Besides the ground colour of the shell, there may be different coloured bands, blotches or flecks, and the lip or peristomal rib may also be distinctively coloured.

Shell variation within species
The size, shape and colouration of shells can vary considerably within a species. Variation in size and shape is usually continuous – i.e. the whole range between the extremes may be found. In general, this variation does not complicate identification; where it can cause difficulties this is mentioned in the text. Very rarely, one comes across monstrosities – highly aberrant shapes or sizes which may be inherited, or may be caused by accident or disease.

Variation in colour and pattern, by contrast, is usually discontinuous – i.e. there are no intermediates between the various forms. This variation is almost always inherited. Its simplest form is seen in the occurrence of *albino* shells amongst normally coloured ones. This is found in many species.

In the largest snail family, the Helicidae (p. 175), many species have a much greater range of colour and pattern variation. Apart from the ground colour of the shell, there is variation in the number, colour and arrangement of spiral bands and blotches; in consequence, some species have hundreds of distinct varieties. Where a single local population of a species contains many variants, it is said to be *polymorphic*, and the occurrence of different distinct variants in a single population is *polymorphism*. Usually, the proportions of different variants alter from one local population to another. Much work has been done to explain such variation. Sometimes, it is the most camouflaged varieties which predominate in each place, but this is by no means always true.

The body

External Features
The bodies of slugs and snails are soft and wet, being coated in a layer of mucus or slime, which is usually thicker and more copious in slugs. All the major external features of the body are seen when the animal is active and fully extended.

At the front end is the *head*, armed, in the more primitive prosobranch and basommatophoran families (see p. 26) with one pair of *tentacles*, and in most stylommatophorans with two. In the more primitive snails, with one pair of tentacles, there is an eye-spot near the base of each; the tentacles can be contracted, but

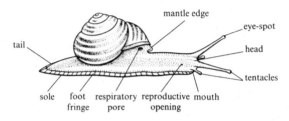

External morphology of snail

not inverted. In those with two pairs of tentacles, there are eye-spots at the tips of the upper (posterior) pair, which are longer than the lower (anterior) pair. The tentacles are withdrawn by being inverted like the finger of a glove being pulled inside out. The *mouth* can be seen in front, and the *jaw* on the upper lip can be seen when the animal is feeding.

Just behind the tentacles on the right hand side (on the left in sinistral snails) lies the *common reproductive opening* (a few species have separate male and female openings). This is not always visible, but can always be seen during courtship and mating, when the distal reproductive organs are extruded through it (see below).

The surface on which the animal crawls is the *foot* consisting of the *sole* surrounded by a *foot-fringe*. If a slug or snail is made to crawl on a glass plate, the method of movement can be seen from underneath – waves of muscular contraction pass forward up the sole, carrying the animal with them. The foot is lubricated with mucus, which leaves a characteristic slime trail behind the animal.

The upper parts of the body are, for obvious reasons, rather different in slugs and snails. In snails, much of the body remains permanently inside the shell. At the shell mouth is the *mantle*, which encloses the mantle cavity or lung, and there is a *respiratory pore* through which air passes in and out. The rear part of the body, behind the shell, is the *tail*.

When the snail withdraws inside the shell, the whole body is hidden behind the mantle, which then fills the shell mouth. When it re-emerges, the foot is extruded between folds of the mantle. If a snail remains inactive for some time, it usually secretes a film of mucus over the shell mouth, which dries to form an *epiphragm*. The epiphragm may be stretched over the shell mouth, with only a small hole for air circulation, or it may connect the rim of the shell mouth to the object on which the snail is resting. In some species, the epiphragm may be strengthened with chalky granules – it is then thick and opaque. Such epiphragms are most often found in hibernating snails. Prosobranch snails (see p. 26) do not make epiphragms – they have a permanent door or *operculum*, carried on the tail when the snail is crawling, which seals the mouth of the shell when the animal has withdrawn. It is horny or calcareous, and is built up in concentric rings or spirally added increments to match the mouth of the shell during all stages of growth.

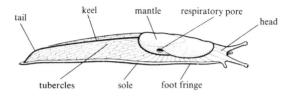

External morphology of slug (*Milax*)

Slugs with external shells (Testacellidae, Plate 14) resemble snails in their general structure, except that most of the body lies in front of the shell and mantle. In slugs without external shells, the mantle covers part of the front half of the body; it is a distinct raised area with the respiratory pore on the right hand side. The tail is long, and in some species carries a raised *keel* along the mid-line.

The skin of slugs and snails is roughened with small bumps or *tubercles*; these are generally larger and more prominent in slugs. The skin is usually pigmented, and in slugs there may be diagnostic bands and blotches. The upper skin, like the sole, is coated in mucus. In some slugs the mucus of the upper parts is different in colour and consistency from that of the sole. Skin colour and pattern can show polymorphic variation like that seen on shells, and some slugs are very variable (e.g. *Arion ater*, Plate 4).

Internal Features

This book is not the place for a detailed systematic account of internal anatomy, but some knowledge of the internal structure and functioning of slugs and snails helps us understand their way of life, and is also useful in the identification of the few species which cannot be reliably identified on the external features alone. Dissection of larger species to examine the internal organs is extremely simple, and instructions for doing this are given on p. 32.

The figure shows, in a diagrammatic way, the body of *Helix aspersa* dissected to show the major organs of the body. Some of the organs have been unravelled and displaced to make their structure clear.

The alimentary canal is long and much looped. The *mouth* opens directly into the *buccal mass*, the muscles of which operate the *radula*, a mobile chain of minute horny teeth which is moved back and forth like a rasp over the food. There are many thousands of these teeth, arranged in transverse rows, and their shape and size vary from the middle to the sides, and from species to species. The radula lies on the floor of the mouth; at the front of the roof is mounted the horny *jaw*, which also cuts and scrapes the food.

From the buccal mass, there is a thin *oesophagus* leading to a wider crop, which is overlain by *salivary glands* which open into the buccal mass. The crop in turn leads to the long and thin intestine, much looped, which terminates in the *anus* which is situated very close to the respiratory pore. Much of the body-space is occupied by the large, multi-lobed *digestive gland* in which much of the digestion takes place – it opens into the intestine.

The blood of snails is more or less colourless, although it contains a blood

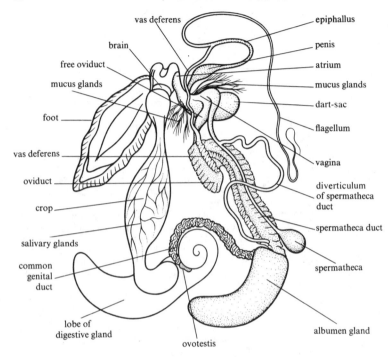

Anatomy of snail (*Helix aspersa*)

pigment, *haemocyanin*, which, like the red *haemoglobin* in our own blood, enables oxygen to be carried in the blood at higher concentrations than would otherwise be the case. There is a heart (which can be seen beating in species with thin, transparent shells) which pumps blood along a few major vessels, especially to the lining of the mantle cavity which acts as a lung. There is not a capillary system however, and much of the blood circulates in the general body cavities, bathing the organs directly. Besides transporting food, waste materials and oxygen around the body, the blood serves as a hydrostatic skeleton. The pressure of blood in different parts of the body can be altered by muscular contraction, and this allows for rapid changes in shape, and also enables the snail to evert organs like the tentacles and distal reproductive organs. When pressure drops, these organs become flaccid, but would not retract – this is achieved by retractor muscles.

Excretion is performed by the *kidney*, which lies close to the heart. Snails, always liable to lose too much moisture, extract it from their waste products very effectively, and most of the urine is solid uric acid.

Slugs and snails have a well-developed nervous system, with a *brain* of many fused ganglia surrounding the buccal mass. Most of the muscles of the body are concentrated in the foot, but there is one very important muscle, the *columellar*, which spirals round the columella of the shell – this muscle pulls the body rapidly into the shell when the animal retracts.

It is details of the reproductive organs which are most often used as internal diagnostic characters, and so the reproductive system is here described in some detail. *Helix aspersa* has one of the most complex systems.

The Pulmonate slugs and snails are hermaphrodite – both male and female in the same individual. When they mate, each partner transfers sperm to the other. As far as is known, no snails or slugs reproduce asexually, but some are capable of self-fertilization.

At the *proximal* end (where the system starts) is the *ovotestis* which produces both eggs and sperm. The eggs and sperm travel down a *common duct* to the *albumen gland*, which secretes the albumen round each egg to supply the embryo with food. Thereafter, eggs and sperm travel different paths, the eggs down the wide and lobed *oviduct*, the sperm down the narrower but partly glandular *vas deferens* which lies on the oviduct for much of its length. The organs between this point, where the oviduct and vas deferens part, and the final opening to the outside are known as the *distal genitalia*. Diagnostic features are usually found in this region, and not further up.

In the male part, the vas deferens lies free for a part of its length, then joins the *epiphallus*, which has a long blind *flagellum* proximally, and leads distally to the thicker, muscular and evertible *penis*, which in turn opens into the atrium, the common end-point of the whole system. The penis is everted by blood-pressure, but retracted by the strong *retractor muscle* at its proximal end.

In the female part, the oviduct leads to the *vagina*, which in turn leads to the atrium. Joining the vagina are the branched *mucus glands*, the *dart-sac* and the *spermatheca duct*, which leads to a long blind *diverticulum* and to a spherical *spermatheca* or *bursa copulatrix*. Inside the large, muscular dart-sac is the *love dart* discharged during courtship.

Mating is preceded by courtship, during which the partners circle one another, touching often, and leaving a large platform of accumulated slime. Eventually, the love-darts are discharged – these may protrude for a while through the atria, or they may actually lodge in the body of the partner. During mating itself, which may last several hours, the snails align themselves so that their common reproductive openings are contiguous; the penis of each is everted and inserted in the vagina of the partner. Sperm is transferred in a long, thin package, the *spermatophore*, which is formed in the flagellum beyond the epiphallus. The intact spermatophore is passed into the blind diverticulum of the spermatheca duct of the partner receiving it, where it is broken down. The liberated sperm are stored in the spermatheca until required. They then swim up the oviduct, and fertilize the eggs in the region of the albumen gland. Sperm may be stored for more than a year, but egg-laying usually takes place about a fortnight after mating.

The pattern of reproductive bahaviour and anatomy described above for *Helix aspersa* is broadly similar in other species, but there are minor modifications. Many species lack some or all of the accessory organs – dart and dart-sac, mucus glands, diverticulum, flagellum. Some species have more than one dart-sac, and the proportions and size of the essential organs also differ between species. All these features can be used in identification.

None of our slugs have a dart or dart-sac, but several species have developed other organs with a similar, stimulating role. These organs are living tissue, and are not discharged and then replaced like darts, but are withdrawn into the body. It has frequently been noticed that closely related species have characteristic differences in the shape or texture of their stimulating organs, be they darts or not. These differences may serve to prevent mating with a partner of a different species, but this has not been proved.

LIFE-HISTORY, GROWTH AND MORTALITY

After mating, slugs and snails lay eggs, usually in clutches in small holes made in the soil, or in cracks in rotting wood or under logs and stones. The number of eggs in a clutch varies greatly, often 20–50 in larger species, but sometimes 100 or more. The eggs are usually round. In some species, they are rather soft and transparent; in others they have a hard, opaque, calcareous shell. The rate of development depends on temperature, but most hatch within 6 weeks. More than one clutch may be laid in a season.

Full details of breeding are known for few species. In general, egg-laying occurs in summer and autumn, and not in winter, but this is not always true. Many slugs, and some snails living in dry and exposed habitats, have their main breeding season in late autumn, when the risk of drying out iş less than in midsummer.

Newly hatched young are very like miniature adults; their development is direct, and there is no metamorphosis or moulting. The young grow by adding material to the leading edge of the shell, adding more whorls to the shell as they grow. Most species reach maturity in about a year, although the largest slugs and snails may take 2–4 years. In snails, adulthood is usually marked by a halt in growth, and by the formation of a lip or rib at the mouth of the shell. Some species lack these features, as, of course, do slugs, and size or evidence of mating are the best indicators of adult status.

Mortality is heaviest in the very early stages of life. The eggs are not guarded by the parent – many dry out, or are found and eaten by predators; some are parasitized by flies. The small young are also vulnerable to climate and enemies, and it is quite usual for 5 per cent or less of eggs laid to reach adulthood. In small species, most adults die soon after breeding, so that the life-span is little more than a year. Some may survive a second season. In large species, only half, or less of the adults die each year, and some individuals may live 8–10 years, and possibly longer.

Many deaths are caused by predators and parasites. The best known predator is the song thrush, which often feeds on the larger species. The song thrush has a special technique for breaking the shell, picking it up by the mouth and hammering it on a stone. One song thrush will use the same stone again and again, and soon this 'anvil' is surrounded by a litter of broken, empty shells.

Other birds also eat snails, swallowing juveniles and small species whole, or smashing larger shells with their beaks (only rather large birds can do this). Swallowed shells are not always completely digested, and their whitened remains may be found in droppings underneath a roost. Slugs are not taken so readily – their slime is stickier, and birds will often wipe a slug on the ground, presumably to remove some of it.

Shrews and hedgehogs also eat snails, as do some rodents. A small mammal nibbles away at the shell, starting at the lip or elsewhere. Such shells may be found in mouse-runs, or piled under a log where a mammal has been feeding.

Many smaller animals also attack slugs and snails. Carnivorous snails frequently

attack other species, but beetles, and especially their larvae, are especially important. The best known is the glow-worm *Lampyris noctiluca*, the larvae of which
depend entirely on snails. Snails and their eggs may also be parasitized by flies,
whose larvae develop inside the body and eventually kill the host.

GENERAL HABITS AND FEEDING

Slugs and snails are restricted in their habits by the need to avoid drying up.
Consequently, they are, as a rule, most active at night or in wet weather. Being
nocturnal has another advantage, for they escape predators which hunt by sight – in
the daylight a snail once discovered has little chance of escape.

Most small species live permanently near the soil surface. Some climb vegetation
or on rocks, and some, especially slugs, may climb a long way up trees, usually to
graze the lichens and algae growing on the bark.

In shady and cool conditions, most snails stay out of sight when resting – under
logs and stones, in leaf litter, under clumps of vegetation, or buried just below the
soil surface. The few that remain in the open – on tree-trunks or rocks, are usually
well camouflaged. In very hot sunny conditions, in open habitats, this is not always
true, because the soil surface is too hot – many snails will climb some way up plants,
where it is cooler. Such snails often have thick white shells, which reflect a lot of
sunlight.

The shells of snails are nearly waterproof, and when they retreat inside it, only
the mantle is exposed, and the mantle is better at conserving water than the rest of
the body. A resting snail, protected in addition by its epiphragm, can withstand dry
conditions well – the larger species can survive for several months of a dry summer
in a state of suspended animation or *aestivation*. Many species also *hibernate*; very
few are active at temperatures below freezing.

Slugs appear to be at a disadvantage, lacking a shell, but this is offset by their
greater ability to burrow deep into the soil, or into cracks and crevices in rocks and
logs – without a large rigid shell, they are more manoeuverable. Slugs may burrow
down more than a metre into the soil in dry weather – hence they can then be very
hard to find.

Most species of slug and snail feed on rotting vegetation, fungi, algae and lichens;
healthy green plants are not much attacked – although flowers, fruit and seed, and
underground storage organs like potatoes or carrots are taken. No herbivorous
snail or slug is known to have a restricted diet – nearly all of them can be successfully reared on a variety of artificial diets – lettuce, carrots, porridge oats etc. Unlike
many herbivorous animals, they can digest cellulose – damp paper and cardboard
are eaten.

A few species are pests. Many of the plants we grow are softer and more
nutritious than wild ones, and attract species that normally eat decaying matter.
Most of these pests are slugs, but a few snails can become pests. Large scale control
of these pests is very difficult.

Many species will eat carrion, but only a few are actively carnivorous. *Testacella*
slugs (Plate 14) feed on earthworms, while carnivorous snails in the Zonitidae
(Plates 8–11) and Vitrinidae (Plates 6, 7) frequently eat other species of snail and
their eggs. Some other species e.g. *Limax maximus* (Plate 13) can be voraciously
carnivorous in captivity, but do not appear to be so in the wild.

HABITATS

Since most slugs and snails have rather mixed diets, it is the climate and structure of a habitat which affects them, rather than the presence or absence of particular food plants. Soil conditions are also important. Most species do better on lime-rich, alkaline soils; and in very acid soils, e.g. on moorland, there are very few species to be found.

The need for lime is partly, for snails, due to its use in making the shell – the shells of individuals living on acid soils are often very thin and fragile, although not smaller than those elsewhere. But lime has other effects – changing the character of soil and litter so that it is more suitable for snails to live in. Consequently, lime-rich areas have the greatest numbers of species and individuals. A few species, *calcicoles*, are found only in lime-rich areas, and many more are much commoner there than elsewhere.

Climate is of great importance, but it is the climate at ground level, and not the broader features of climate that we experience which is crucial. In general, high temperatures are favourable to slugs and snails, as can be seen in the increasing diversity of species as one moves from the Arctic to the Mediterranean, but in exposed habitats high temperatures can be dangerous, both by being directly lethal (exposed ground in direct sunshine may reach 70°C) and, more importantly, because it tends to lower humidity, and increases the risk of drying out.

Most slugs and snails do best in conditions where the humidity rarely falls very low for long, but a few are well adapted to hot dry environments. They can survive long periods of inactivity by aestivation, and they may burrow very deep to rest, or alternatively climb up vegetation to escape the great heat at ground level. Often, they have thick, white shells, which reflect more of the sunlight.

The structure of the habitat is also important. Although species do differ in their food requirements, there are also differences in the places where they shelter or are active – in litter, on rocks, on logs or up trees or on smaller plants. The greater the variety of microhabitats of this sort there are in a site, the greater the number of species you are likely to find.

Finally, amongst these general features, there are the effects of man and his animals. Man has cleared most of the forests, and drained most of the wetlands of Europe, creating many drier and more open habitats. There are many more subtle effects too, which tend to reduce the variety of species found. In woods, forestry activities remove rotting timber and trample the ground; in open habitats the trampling and grazing of farm animals makes the soil unsuitable for many species; the effect of ploughing is similar. On the other hand, some of the habitats created by man have proved very suitable for a few species, which have increased their geographical range by spreading into man-made habitats such as gardens, parks and hothouses far outside their natural limits. Some have become pests.

As the land in N. Europe has become drier and more open due to man's activities, it has given rise to a number of habitats suitable for few of the existing woodland species. Consequently, there are many open-country species in the north of our area which have spread from the south in comparatively recent times – many have been accidentally transported by man.

The range of climate in N. Europe is very great, and there are many disturbed or changing habitats due to man's activities. It is not surprising therefore, that it is rather difficult to be precise about the habitats in which any particular species may be found. Many of the species with wide ranges live in completely different habitats in, say, N. Scotland to those in C. France. Consequently, the description of habitat of many species in this guide is rather broad, but in any one area they will not usually be found in the whole range given. Near the edges of their geographical ranges, many species become more restricted in habitat, and often become more dependent on lime.

In spite of these complications, there are several rather wide categories of habitat in which one expects to find a certain kind of molluscan fauna.

Woodlands are undoubtedly the richest of all habitats. They represent the original, natural cover of most of Europe, they have damp and equable climates, and plenty of different sites for feeding and shelter. A rich wood – relatively undisturbed, with lime-rich soil and rock outcrops – may yield forty or more species. Acid soils and forestry reduce the diversity, and a tally of ten species in a new conifer plantation on very acid soil would be very good.

Many woodland snails are found elsewhere – in hedges, gardens, long grass, thickets and scrub, and also in screes, where they can survive in the cool, damp space between the stones. In very wet climates – along the N.W. seaboard, or in the mountains, they may be found in completely open areas.

Wetlands are another distinct habitat type. The soil is nearly always waterlogged, which inhibits burrowing, but reduces the need for heavy plant cover – humidity will always be high. Base-rich wetlands – fens and some pond and river margins – have a very characteristic fauna, of which many species are rarely found elsewhere. Acid wetlands are very poor; often there may be one or two species only. Remember when you search in wetlands that there will be freshwater snails around too, and dead shells of land and freshwater species may well be found side by side.

Grassland, especially short grazed turf on chalky soil, has also a special fauna of species capable of withstanding drought and high temperatures. Excessive trampling by grazing animals may damage the fauna, unless there are rocks or other shelter. *Sand dunes* may have a rather similar set of species, but the damper hollows behind the main dunes may have some wetland species as well – hollows or 'slacks' often flood in winter.

Rocks, cliffs and screes, especially if made of limestone, harbour a set of characteristic species. Some are also woodland species – living on trees; others may be found on rocks only, but do not mind shade or sunshine. Many of the rockloving species are much longer than they are wide – at rest the shell is held close to the rock surface, but some of the largest and more conventionally shaped species live here too – hiding in fissures in dry weather. Several rock-loving species have spread onto walls, new road cuttings etc.

The faunas of man-made habitats – such as hedges, roadside verges, gardens and parks – are usually a mixture of species found normally in woodland and grassland, the balance depending partly on accidents of colonization, and partly on the extent to which the habitat resembles either of the originals. Introduced and man-dependent species will also be found in the richer places.

Habitats in high mountains (especially the Alps and Pyrenees) may have rather unusual faunas, because there are many very local species which are not found elsewhere.

The names and classification of slugs and snails

Names

Very few species of slug and snail have genuine English names, and some of the few names used apply to more than one species. Rather than invent a large number of names, we have decided to use only the Latin scientific names for all the species in this book.

Beginners may find the names hard to remember at first, but it is well worth the trouble. All keen conchologists (or malacologists!) use them, and you will find them in every article or book about snails. There are many good foreign books on snails which you may want to use – even if you cannot understand the text, the illustrations and the Latin names may be very useful. To make things easier, we give below a very short and simple guide to the way scientific names work.

The scientific name of a species of animal has a standard form laid down by the International Commission on Zoological Nomenclature (I.C.Z.N.), in the hope that people all over the world will always use the same name for the same species.

The name is always in Latin, and is always two words. The first is the generic name, placing the species in a *genus* of closely related species. The second is the *specific* name, defining the species within the genus. The generic name always starts with a capital letter, the specific name never. Large or unusually variable genera are additionally sometimes divided into *subgenera*. Subgeneric names form no essential part of the binominal Latin name and in practice are not very often used, but occasionally they will be found (always placed in round brackets) immediately following the name of the genus (e.g., as in the formal check-list on p. 39)

When the name is given in full, the name of the person who first published a description of it, and gave it its name is added at the end, and the date of publication is also added. For example, the full scientific name of what, in England, is called the garden snail is:

Helix aspersa Müller 1774

This full scientific name is given for each species in this book both in the check-list and at the head of the description of each. In many books or articles this full name is given only once, or not at all (the reader being referred to another book for the information), and the garden snail is then referred to as *Helix aspersa*, or, where it is quite clear which genus is meant, as *H. aspersa*.

Every scientific name must be unique. However, species in different genera may have the same specific name – e.g. *Cepaea hortensis* (a large snail) and *Arion hortensis* (a slug).

Unfortunately, but inevitably, even the strict rules of the I.C.Z.N. have not prevented muddles occurring, nor have they prevented the names of species being changed from time to time.

First, opinions change as to how and which species should be placed in a particular genus. The earliest workers made very large genera, and sometimes defined them in ways now thought to be wrong. There isn't any absolute definition of a genus, and so this situation will always be with us.

Consequently many species (most of those in this book) are now put into a different genus than the one they started with. When this happens, the generic name is altered, but the specific name is not, except in gender, if that of the genus has changed. In the full name, the name of the original describer is now put in brackets, to show that he did not give it that generic name. For example, the common brown-lipped snail was originally called *Helix nemoralis* Linné 1758. It has now been put in another genus and is called *Cepaea nemoralis* (Linné 1758).

Much more confusing are difficulties which arise because of poor communication, or through inaccurate or incomplete descriptions. The rules of the I.C.Z.N. say that the correct name is the first properly published one since 1758. Unfortunately, not all workers see all the results or material of others, so that two or more names are given to animals which turn out to be the same species. Once this is discovered, the oldest name alone should be used, but in practice many species are known by a variety of names for some time.

Similarly, new work may reveal that what were regarded as a number of species are simply variants of one, or conversely, that what was thought to be one species is in fact several. In the latter case, older records may be unidentifiable.

In general, names which have been used for a species, but which are incorrect, are called *synonyms*. A list of all the synonyms used for all the species in this book would completely fill it and more besides. We have, however, given a few of the most commonly used ones, to help you make the best use of older books which may use them. Most of the reference books on national faunas given in the Bibliography have much fuller lists of synonyms.

This is not a book designed solely for specialists, and so we cannot go into the details of cases where the correct name is disputed. British readers familiar with local books will find many changes in generic names; French readers will find that we have regarded many of the species once recognized in France as synonymous with others.

Although slugs and snails have received a lot of attention from professional taxonomists, they have never had the huge amounts of work expended on them as has been on birds, or butterflies. Consequently, new species are still being found in W. Europe, and new records of species known only outside our area are being made within it. In particular, now that more attention is being paid to internal features (most snails were described only by their shells), many new species of slug are being discovered, and would-be slug enthusiasts must keep their eyes on articles in the journals we list at the end.

Members of the same species never look exactly alike. Where variation is geographical, i.e. where one form occurs in one part of the species' range and another elsewhere, the forms may be described as *subspecies*. Subspecies are given a third Latin name. This is an added complication of little use in field identification, and we have only very rarely mentioned subspecies in this book.

Where variation occurs between individuals from the same place, the more conspicuous variants are often also given Latin varietal names. You may, therefore, come across names like *Helix aspersa* var. *exalbida*, which is a yellow variant of the common garden snail. Again, we have not used these old varietal names, but in species which are particularly variable, the commonest kinds of variant are described in the text, and shown in the plates. Some kinds of variation found in many species are discussed in more detail on page 15.

Classification

All slugs and snails are in the class Gastropoda of the phylum Mollusca (see introduction). Below the level of class come other divisions, carrying on down to genus and species mentioned above. Two subclasses of Gastropoda contain all the species in this book.

The subclass Prosobranchia is represented by only one of its orders, the Mesogastropoda, of which three families are found in N.W. Europe: the Cyclophoridae (p. 51), Pomatiidae (p. 53), and Aciculidae (p. 53). Most prosobranch snails are marine, and the few which occur on land that have made this change have done so independently of those in the other subclass, the Pulmonata. There are many internal differences between the two subclasses, but the most noticeable difference is that prosobranchs retain an operculum, or permanent door to the shell, which is held on the tail when the snail is crawling, but seals the mouth when the animal withdraws inside its shell. This operculum is hard to see in the minute Aciculidae.

The subclass Pulmonata lacks an operculum. Pulmonates are so called because they have a lung inside the mantle cavity. There are two orders – the Basommatophora, nearly all freshwater snails, with eyes at the base of the tentacles, and the Stylommatophora which are terrestrial, with eyes at the tips of the tentacles. In N.W. Europe, only one basommatophoran family, the Ellobiidae (p. 57), has terrestrial species. All the remaining families in this book are Stylommatophora.

Altogether 28 families of land slug and snail are found in our area, two of which are found only as introductions in greenhouses. Although families are further divided, we have not given details of these divisions except for some of the largest families – notably the Zonitidae, Clausiliidae and Helicidae. The descriptions of species in each family are preceded by a short account of the family as a whole. Most families are defined on internal characters which are too specialized to go into here, but members of a family generally have some similarity in size and shape, and are fairly easily recognized.

A warning

At present, there is no single work which lists all European snails in a systematic way. In the two centuries since Linnaeus started the binomial names of species outlined above, there have been many ideas about how a species should be defined, and some of the most eccentric have been held by people studying snails. There is therefore no generally accepted list of species living in N.W. Europe, and experts still disagree about the status and naming of some forms.

Anybody producing such a check-list for experts to use would therefore be expected to justify his list with arguments for every entry over which there was any dispute. Such arguments are inappropriate here, and in any case, some forms are so poorly known that there is no material to argue with.

Consequently, the list of species in this book is provisional. We have done our best to take into account all the evidence which is available, and have taken advice from experts in most of the countries in our area. Where there are still serious doubts about the status of certain forms, we have made this clear in the text.

This warning is of particular concern to those of our readers who identify slugs and snails from the Alps, and from the southern and eastern borders of Germany. In the Alps, there are many very local forms, whose status is doubtful, and in S.E. Germany species so far known only from further east may possibly be discovered.

Finding, collecting and preserving slugs and snails

There are two stages in successful snail-hunting. The first is choosing the right sites, and the second is the conduct of the search itself. Some slugs and snails may be found in almost any situation, but if you want to get a good idea of all the species living in an area, it is necessary to be selective, and to pick a range of sites which will include most of the likely finds.

The key to choosing the right places to search lies in remembering what features of the environment favour slugs and snails, as outlined in the habitats section. Areas of chalk or limestone are likely to be rich, as are any areas of old woodland and fen. If the area is unfamiliar, a geological map is a great asset; even better, if you can get one, is a geological drift map, which shows where the underlying rock is deeply buried by other deposits – many limestone areas are less promising than they look, because covered with peat or clay.

After a bit of experience, choosing sites with the aid of a map, or even spotting likely sites as you walk around, becomes easier – you will get a 'feel' for the right kind of place.

Searching presents a new set of problems. There is a large range of size in slugs and snails, from about 2 mm up to 45 mm for snails; some slugs may be 100 or 200 mm long, and it is impossible to use the same technique successfully for all species. For larger snails – say 5 mm or more, and slugs, a search by eye is usually sufficient, but, of course, in daytime most are inactive, and will be found under logs and stones, in litter, or on the ground amongst the bases of plants. It is almost always necessary to get down on hands and knees for a good search, and to have gardening gloves to protect yourself from nettles or brambles. Try to damage the habitat as little as possible, and replace anything turned over. Depending on the weather and the habitat, fifteen minutes to an hour will usually reveal all the common large snails. Slugs are a bit more difficult. If the weather has been dry for a long time, they may be a long way below ground. Damp weather in autumn is usually best for them.

If you go out at night, or at dawn, or in rainy weather, you will find more active animals, but even in summer the light inside a wood during a rainstorm is not good, and things will be missed.

Almost certainly, you will find some, maybe most, of the smaller species if you search for them in the same way, but with your eye closer to the ground. Small white shells, like *Carychium tridentatum* (p. 58) show up well against the brown background, but many small species are dull brown and easily overlooked. The best way of finding these is to collect some leaf litter and surface soil and take it home in a polythene bag. It can then be spread out on paper and examined closely under a bright light. Much the easiest way of handling these minute snails is with a slightly moistened small watercolour paint-brush; if you handle them with your fingers you will inevitably damage some. If you collect a lot of litter and soil, you will find that this sorting takes rather a long time, and you can speed it up a bit by sieving it (when dry) through a mesh of 3 or 4 mm, which will hold back the larger pieces of rubbish.

27

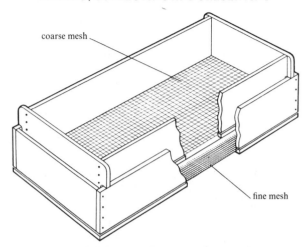

coarse mesh

fine mesh

Wooden field sieve, showing method of construction

Alternatively, you can take a sieve with you into the field. Copper mesh soil sieves (with 3 mm and 0.5 mm mesh apertures) are adequate, but expensive, and it is possible to make your own sieve from wood and nylon mesh. The figure shows the appearance and construction of such a sieve which has been used successfully in the field. It consists of two interlocking frames, the upper one of which has wide mesh nylon (Nybolt 10GG 2000) and the lower the smaller mesh (Nybolt 30GG 670). Large bits of rubbish get held by the upper sieve, while dust falls through the lower, on which the smaller species will be found. Nybolt mesh can be obtained from J. Staniar & Co., Manchester Wire Works, Sherborne St, Manchester 3.

Small snails in wetlands can be collected by placing a small white tray or dish underneath tussocks of vegetation, and then shaking the leaves and stems over it. Small snails (and much else besides) may fall onto the dish for you to examine.

Another useful place to look is in flood-debris deposited by rivers. There are often rich deposits of shells washed down and deposited in such debris, which should be taken home and sieved.

If you don't collect soil and litter, but search for the smallest snails by eye, then it is sensible to have a small penknife or a small pair of forceps to pick up your finds. Fingers can be very clumsy – especially when wet and cold. A small hand-rake is useful for turning over litter and debris.

There will be many occasions when you will want to collect specimens – either to make sure of their identification, or to examine them in more detail, or to add to a reference collection of species you have found. Most of the very small species are much easier to identify indoors – you can control the light, and there is no wind or rain to blow the specimen away.

When collecting, be conservation minded. Common species will not suffer from the removal of a few individuals, but never collect more than you need. If you want a specimen of a rare species, try to find a fresh empty shell, before taking a live one.

In fact, you are much more likely to harm a species by thoughtless destruction of habitat while searching – wetland vegetation is particularly vulnerable, and you should always cause the absolute minimum of disturbance.

When you set out on a snail-hunt, be prepared. Always have a notebook handy to record the details of the sites you visit, and to list the species you have seen at each. For collecting, use small glass or plastic tubes for small species of snail, and polythene bags for larger snails and slugs. Always put some vegetation or damp paper in the polythene bags, and take great care that they don't get crushed. Tubes and polythene bags are air-tight, so do not leave the catch in them for more than a few hours: snails can be kept alive in dry cardboard boxes for a while, slugs must always be kept damp and should be kept in a non-airtight container with damp paper. Remember that some species are carnivorous.

It is very important to label your tubes and bags, either with numbers which can be matched with site numbers in your notebook, or with full details. Remember, though, that slugs and snails eat cardboard and paper, especially when they are wet. *Labels must be on the outside of the container.*

Since most snails are identifiable by their shells, most people keep collections of shells alone. Whole animals can be preserved by pickling in alcohol (industrial methylated spirit). Slugs can be preserved in this way, but they shrink considerably, and their colours change. Since they are large, a photographic record of living specimens is not too difficult to make, and this is much more useful and attractive.

Empty shells can be kept in any containers you have handy – specimen tubes, small cardboard boxes etc. Standard sized glass specimen tubes are best. Tubes each 65 mm long and 12 or 18 mm wide can be stacked neatly in drawers for easy care of your collection. For very small species, gelatine capsules (used as swallowable containers for medicines) are handy, and you may also be able to get unused pill boxes. Do not use completely air-tight containers. Museums display shells in small glass-topped boxes, but these are very expensive. The colour of shells fades if

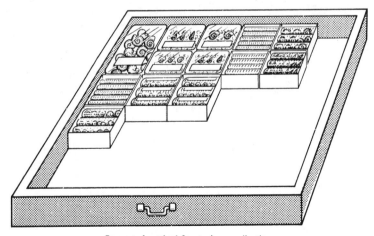

Suggested method for storing a collection

Clausilia bidentata (Ström)
Among limestone rocks,
Cheddar Gorge, Somerset.
(Grid ref: ST 47254·3)
J. Smith leg. 10·Ⅴ·1976

Specimen tube, with label

they are continuously exposed to light – keep your collection in a drawer or cabinet when not in use.

If you have living specimens, you will need to dispose of the bodies. Snails are instantly killed by immersion in boiling water, and for the larger species, the body can be extracted with a bent pin (like extracting a winkle from its shell to eat). For smaller species this is difficult to do without breaking the shell, and the body frequently breaks in large ones, leaving some flesh at the top of the spire. Leave such specimens in a damp sealed container until the flesh has rotted – it can then be dislodged by a fine jet of water aimed into the mouth. If newly empty shells are to be stored in watertight containers, make sure they are absolutely dry inside and out – otherwise there will be condensation and discolouration.

For the very small species, extracting the body is not practical; simply let them dry out very thoroughly, and preferably keep them in small tubes stoppered with cotton wool. Do not keep specimens in corked or stoppered tubes – any dampness will cause discolouration.

Always keep your collection fully labelled. Each tube or box should contain only one species collected from one locality, and in each there should be a label giving details of species, site (with a map reference if possible), habitat and date of collection, with the name of the collector and of the person who identified it, if different. If the identification was confirmed by dissection, that should be added.

Many of the larger species can be kept in captivity very easily, and given the right conditions will breed successfully. Plastic lunch-boxes or small fish-tanks are ideal; put soil, or soft absorbent paper in the bottom and keep it damp. Lids must be arranged so as to let air in, but not the slugs and snails out. Most species will eat such things as carrot peelings, porridge oats, outer leaves of lettuce and cabbage. Slugs *must* be kept damp all the time. Snails can tolerate dry conditions for some time, depending on species – the large ones will easily survive for a month in a dry, cool cardboard box while you are on holiday. In general, the containers will need to be cleaned out if there is a lot of mould developing – this happens much more rapidly in hot conditions. Some foods – e.g. potato peelings, rot very quickly and can kill the snails. Captive snails give you lots of opportunity to observe behaviour, breeding and development, all of which are rather difficult to do in the field.

Identifying slugs and snails

For most of the species in this book, the only equipment needed for identification is a good hand-lens ($\times 12$ or $\times 15$) and a ruler calibrated in millimetres. A few species need to be dissected to be absolutely sure of their identification – instructions are given below. However, for the smallest species, a low power binocular microscope is greatly superior to a hand-lens – quite apart from greater magnifications, it enables you to work in comfort, and with good light. They are, alas, expensive, but no more so than the bird-watcher's binoculars or the photographer's camera. Sturdy metal measuring callipers, capable of measuring to 0.1 mm with a vernier scale are also much better than a simple ruler, especially for small species.

Snails

Most snails are identified by characters of the shell – all of which are explained on pages 12–15. Size and shape are the most important characters to get your specimen to the right family. The descriptions in the text, and the plates and figures, are of fresh, adult shells. These are much easier to identify than old worn shells, which lose the periostracum and much of their colour or than juveniles, which lack many adult characters. Try to find living, adult, specimens for your first attempts.

Characters in and around the shell mouth and umbilicus may be difficult to see if the animal will not withdraw inside the shell. They will usually do so if prodded gently with a grass-stalk or twig.

If you do get into difficulties with a specimen, check first that you have noted the characters correctly. Make sure any measurements have been made in the right way (p. 14). If you are still in trouble, it is possible that you have a juvenile or an unusual variant. Variation in colour is very common, and colour alone is not a very reliable character. Occasionally, you may come across a shell coiled the wrong way; only the family Clausiliidae, two species of *Vertigo* and *Jaminia quadridens* are regularly sinistral. Occasionally, too, one comes across monstrous distortions of the usual shape, but both these and reversed coiled shells are *very* rare.

With practice, juveniles and even old, broken shells can often be identified, especially when they can be compared with fresh adult specimens under a binocular microscope. Characters like the size and shape of the protoconch, surface ribbing or sculpture, and the relative size and rate of expansion of the whorls are useful here.

Only a very few snails need dissecting – this is always indicated in the text.

Never record an identification as definite if you have doubts. Be particularly cautious at first where *similar species* are noted in the description. Keep doubtful specimens, and try to check them against known specimens, or show them to an expert – once identified they form a useful part of your reference collection. Even experts find some shells impossible, so there is no need to be disappointed if you cannot identify every specimen you find.

Slugs

Most slugs lack an external shell, and it is external features of the body which matter most. Size, the presence or absence of a keel, the texture of the mantle and the position of the respiratory pore are the main characters used to identify the right genus. Specific differences relate to colour and banding patterns, size and shape of tubercles, characters of the sole, and the colour and consistency of the mucus or slime. Internal characters are given for most slugs, but this does not mean that dissection is always necessary. Use external characters first – dissect if in doubt.

A quick guide to dissection

There are a few species in this book which can only be identified with certainty by dissecting the animal to examine the reproductive organs. It is, of course, necessary to kill the animal to do this, and so it should be done only when absolutely necessary and on as few specimens as possible. Juveniles should not be dissected; their reproductive systems are not fully developed.

Dissection is simply cutting open the body to reveal the internal organs. For the beginner, this sounds a complicated and difficult thing to do but in the case of slugs and the larger snails it is very easy, and the whole operation may last only 5–10 minutes when you have had some practice.

The equipment needed is a small scalpel with disposable blades, fine and coarse forceps, a box of small pins and a couple of mounted needles. Fine dissecting scissors are an advantage, but not strictly necessary. A small dish with sides at least 1 cm high, with some wax or plasticine stuck firmly on the bottom is also required.

Since it is usually the reproductive organs which need examining, adult specimens are necessary. The animal must be killed. This can be done quickly by

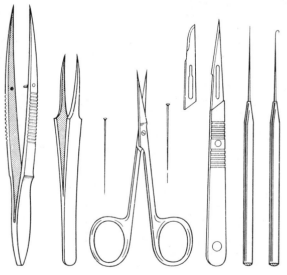

Dissecting equipment for molluscs

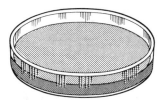

Glass dissecting dish, containing black wax

immersion in boiling water, or in alcohol, but for the beginner there is some advantage in drowning the animal by leaving it in a full, sealed tube of deoxygenated water overnight. (Freshly boiled and cooled water has lost most of its oxygen). This leaves the animal relaxed and fully extended, in which condition it is easier to dissect.

Snails must be removed from their shells. It may be possible to extract them intact with a pin. Insert pin into foot and pull round spirally (not straight). Often the shell must be broken away in small pieces with the coarse forceps. Slugs are ready for dissection the moment they are dead.

Pin the body to the wax or plasticine with pins between the tentacles, and near the tail, stretching it out straight, but not with too much force, or the body will break round the pins. Fill the dish with water until it covers the specimen.

The reproductive system ends at its opening to the outside just behind the right tentacles. Remember this, and be careful to avoid cutting through it.

First, remove the mantle, by cutting round the edge from the respiratory pore,

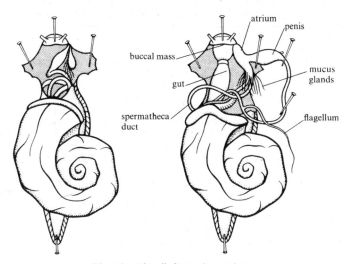

Dissection of snail, first and second stages

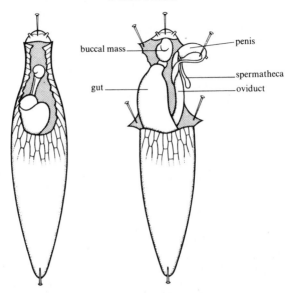

Dissection of slug, first and second stages

freeing the whole upper surface and removing it. Then make a small cut in the skin in the mid-line, and extend it backwards to the back of the mantle, and forward to the head. Always cut with the sharp side of the blade pointing upwards, and be careful not to damage organs underneath. Then make similar cuts across the body at both ends of the existing cut, and pin down the two flaps of skin thus created.

The internal organs behind the head are now exposed. There may still be a thin, transparent layer of tissue over them – if so, cut it away. Examine the organs as they lie, and identify as many of them as you can. Then tease them out gently with fine forceps and a mounted needle, cutting through small muscles and connective tissue once you are sure that they are not vital organs. Spread the reproductive system out to expose as much of it as possible, and hold them in place with pins.

You should now be able to find all the diagnostic characters with the aid of a hand-lens or binocular microscope. Use the small diagrams in the text in conjunction with the general dissection diagram on p. 18.

For *Succinea* (p. 58) the jaw is sometimes used as an identification character. It is found on the upper surface of the mouth, and can be found by cutting open the buccal mass, and then removing the jaw from its attached muscles.

Practice dissection on large species – try *Helix aspersa* and *H. pomatia* for snails, and *Arion ater* for slugs. Many books and leaflets give more information on dissection and internal anatomy – they are listed in the bibliography. If you want to preserve a dissection, put the specimen in a tube in 70 per cent alcohol. Often, though, a simple drawing or diagram of your specimen is a more useful aid to memory.

Mapping schemes

In spite of nearly two centuries of recording, the distribution of most species of land molluscs is still only rather roughly known. This is particularly true of the commoner species.

Mapping schemes are now being undertaken in several European countries. They involve the use of gridded maps, such as the Ordnance Survey maps of Britain bearing the metric National Grid. The information is collected by visiting a spectrum of the habitats available within each grid square (e.g., a wood, a marsh, rocky ground, etc.) and marking off the species observed on a specially-printed field card. The size of the grid unit chosen may vary from 1 × 1 or 2 × 2 km if mapping a small area, to 10 × 10 km or larger if conducting a national survey. The presence of a species is then shown by a conventional symbol placed within each square of a

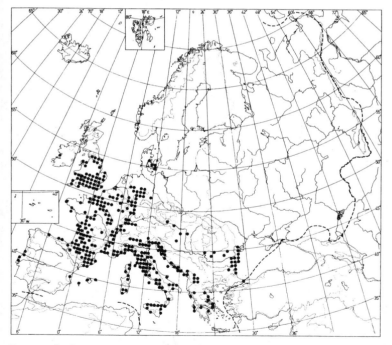

European distribution map of *Pomatias elegans*. Each dot represents a 50-kilometre square

base map. The resulting distribution patterns are sufficiently detailed to show correlations with physical, geological, climatic or other factors. An atlas of maps showing the distributions of all British species on a basis of 10 km squares has already been published (see Bibliography, p. 213).

Anyone interested in helping with a mapping scheme should write in the first place to the national society or other organization responsible; addresses may be obtained from the Secretary, European Invertebrate Survey, c/o Biological Records Centre, Monks Wood Experimental Station, Abbots Ripton, Huntingdon PE17 2LS.

For making distribution maps of the whole of Europe, 50 × 50 km squares of the international U.T.M. (Universal Transverse Mercator) Grid are used. An example of such a map is included here. Obviously it will be many years before enough information can be collected to produce similar maps for all species. This work is being co-ordinated by an international committee of the Malacological Union (*Unitas Malacologica*).

Glossary of shell terms

APEX. First-formed end of shell, usually pointed (Fig., p. 14).

AXIS. Imaginary line through apex around which whorls are coiled (Fig., p. 14).

BASAL CREST. External angulation at base of last whorl.

CALLUS. Smooth interior lining of pale shelly matter, frequently obvious within the mouth, e.g., as a coating on the parietal area.

CHANNELLED. Sharply sunk below general surface (e.g., channelled suture).

CLAUSILIUM. Spoon-shaped flexible plate that functions as an operculum in Clausiliidae (Fig., p. 152).

COLUMELLA. Solid or hollow pillar surrounding axis in coiled shells, formed by the inner walls of the whorls (Fig., p. 14).

COLUMELLAR. Referring to that part of the interior surface of the shell, comprising the columella (Fig., p. 14).

DENTICLE. Small round or oval prominence on interior surface of shell, often on or just within the mouth-edge.

DEXTRAL. Right-handed coil; mouth on observer's right when apex is directed upwards, and with mouth facing observer (cf. SINISTRAL).

DISCOIDAL. Approaching a disc in form; axially compressed.

EPIPHRAGM. Dry mucus sheet, temporarily used to close mouth. In large snails, may be thickened with lime and consequently opaque.

FOLD. Spiral ridge on interior of shell wall.

FUSIFORM. Spindle-shaped (e.g., Clausiliidae).

GROWTH-LINES. Surface markings left in former positions of the mouth-edge.

INNER. Referring to that part of the mouth-edge from the base of the columella to the suture, and consisting of columellar and parietal parts.

LAMELLA(E). Thin plate; generally applied to spiral structures on interior of shell wall, especially in the Clausiliidae.

LAST WHORL ('BODY WHORL'). Last-formed complete turn of shell (Fig., p. 14).

LIP. Thickened or reflected mouth-edge, present only in adult shells of some species (Fig., p. 14).

MOUTH. Opening of shell, providing outlet for soft parts (Fig., p. 14).

MOUTH-EDGE (or PERISTOME). Shell edge round mouth.

OPERCULUM. Horny or calcareous plate carried by foot and serving to close the mouth when the animal is withdrawn into the shell.

OUTER. Referring to that part of the mouth-edge from the suture to the base of the columella (Fig., p. 14).

PALATAL. Referring to that part of the interior surface of the shell within the outer mouth-edge, from the suture to the base of the columella.

PARIETAL. Referring to that part of the interior surface of the shell between the columella and the suture – in effect, formerly the external surface of earlier-formed whorls (Fig., p. 14).

PERIOSTRACUM. Horny organic coat covering the calcareous inner shell or ostracum.

PERIPHERY. Part of whorl furthest from the axis.

PROTOCONCH. Apical whorls of shell (Fig., p. 12); in land molluscs that part formed within the egg.

REFLECTED. Turned outwards at margin – referring to mouth-edge.

RETICULATE. Forming a network of obliquely intersecting sculptural elements.

RIB. Projecting ridge on shell, usually transverse (on external surface unless otherwise indicated).

SCULPTURE. Relief pattern on shell surface.

SHOULDER. Angulation near upper margin of whorl.

SINISTRAL. Left-handed coil; mouth on observer's left when apex is directed upwards, and with mouth facing observer (cf. DEXTRAL).

SINUS. Indentation at margin of mouth.

SPIRAL. Passing continuously around whorls, parallel to the suture (cf. TRANSVERSE).

SPIRE. Visible part of all the whorls except the last (Fig., p. 14).

STRIA(E). Fine incised groove on shell surface.

SUTURE. Continuous spiral line on shell surface where whorls adjoin (Fig., p. 14).

TOOTH. General term for shelly prominence on interior surface of shell (see DENTICLE, FOLD, LAMELLA).

TRANSVERSE. Crossing direction of shell growth, usually parallel with growth-lines (cf. SPIRAL).

UMBILICATE. With an umbilicus.

UMBILICUS. Cavity surrounding axis, opening at base of shell (Fig., p. 14).

WHORL. Any complete coil of shell (Fig., p. 14).

Systematic check-list of the land mollusca of N.W. Europe.

† = greenhouse aliens

Subclass PROSOBRANCHIA

Order MESOGASTROPODA

Family **CYCLOPHORIDAE**

Cochlostoma *(Cochlostoma)* **septemspirale** (Razoumowsky 1789)
Cochlostoma *(Obscurella)* **obscurum** (Draparnaud 1801)
Cochlostoma *(Obscurella)* **crassilabrum** (Dupuy 1849)
Cochlostoma *(Obscurella)* **partioti** (Saint-Simon 1848)
Cochlostoma *(Obscurella)* **nouleti** (Dupuy 1850)
Cochlostoma *(Obscurella)* **apricum** (Mousson 1847)
Cochlostoma *(Auritus)* **patulum** (Draparnaud 1801)

Family **POMATIIDAE**
Pomatias elegans (Müller 1774)

Family **ACICULIDAE**

Acicula *(Acicula)* **fusca** (Montagu 1803)
Acicula *(Acicula)* **lineata** (Draparnaud 1801)
Acicula *(Acicula)* **lineolata** (Pini 1884)
Acicula *(Platyla)* **cryptomena** (Folin & Bérillon 1877)
Acicula *(Platyla)* **polita** (Hartmann 1840)
Acicula *(Platyla)* **gracilis** (Clessin 1877)
Acicula *(Platyla)* **dupuyi** (Paladilhe 1868)
Renea *(Pleuracme)* **veneta** (Pirona 1865)

Subclass PULMONATA

Order BASOMMATOPHORA

Family **ELLOBIIDAE**
Carychium minimum Müller 1774
Carychium tridentatum (Risso 1826)

Order STYLOMMATOPHORA

Family SUCCINEIDAE

Catinella *(Quickella)* **arenaria** (Bouchard-Chantereaux 1837)
Succinea *(Succinella)* **oblonga** Draparnaud 1801
Succinea *(Succinea)* **putris** (Linné 1758)
Oxyloma pfeifferi (Rossmässler 1835)
Oxyloma sarsi (Esmark 1886)

Family COCHLICOPIDAE

Azeca goodalli (Férussac 1821)
Cochlicopa lubrica (Müller 1774)
Cochlicopa lubricella (Porro 1838)
Cochlicopa nitens (Gallenstein 1848)

Family PYRAMIDULIDAE

Pyramidula rupestris (Draparnaud 1801)

Family VERTIGINIDAE

Columella edentula (Draparnaud 1805)
Columella columella (Martens 1830)
Columella aspera Waldén 1966
Truncatellina cylindrica (Férussac 1807)
Truncatellina callicratis (Scacchi 1833)
Truncatellina costulata (Nilsson 1823)
Truncatellina claustralis (Gredler 1856)
Truncatellina monodon (Held 1837)
Truncatellina arcyensis Klemm 1943
Vertigo *(Vertigo)* **pusilla** Müller 1774
Vertigo *(Vertigo)* **antivertigo** (Draparnaud 1801)
Vertigo *(Vertigo)* **substriata** (Jeffreys 1833)
Vertigo *(Vertigo)* **pygmaea** (Draparnaud 1801)
Vertigo *(Vertigo)* **heldi** Clessin 1877
Vertigo *(Vertigo)* **moulinsiana** (Dupuy 1849)
Vertigo *(Vertigo)* **modesta** (Say 1824)
Vertigo *(Vertigo)* **ronnebyensis** (Westerlund 1871)
Vertigo *(Vertigo)* **lilljeborgi** (Westerlund 1871)
Vertigo *(Vertigo)* **genesii** (Gredler 1856)
Vertigo *(Vertigo)* **geyeri** Lindholm 1925
Vertigo *(Vertigo)* **alpestris** Alder 1838
Vertigo *(Vertilla)* **angustior** Jeffreys 1830

Family **ORCULIDAE**

Orcula *(Orcula)* **dolium** (Draparnaud 1801)
Orcula *(Orcula)* **gularis** (Rossmässler 1837)
Orcula *(Sphyradium)* **doliolum** (Bruguière 1792)
Pagodulina pagodula (Des Moulins 1830)
Pagodulina subdola (Gredler 1856)

Family **CHONDRINIDAE**

Granopupa granum (Draparnaud 1801)
Granaria frumentum (Draparnaud 1801)
Granaria illyrica (Rossmässler 1837)
Granaria variabilis (Draparnaud 1801)
Granaria stabilei (Martens 1865)
Granaria braunii (Rossmässler 1842)
Abida secale (Draparnaud 1801)
Abida pyrenaearia (Michaud 1831)
Abida occidentalis (Fagot 1888)
Abida partioti (Saint-Simon 1848)
Abida bigerrensis (Moquin-Tandon 1856)
Abida polyodon (Draparnaud 1801)
Chondrina avenacea (Bruguière 1792)
Chondrina megacheilos (Cristofori & Jan 1832)
Chondrina bigorriensis (Des Moulins 1835)
Chondrina tenuimarginata (Des Moulins 1835)
Chondrina clienta (Westerlund 1883)
Chondrina ascendens (Westerlund 1878)
Chondrina centralis (Fagot 1891)

Family **PUPILLIDAE**

Pupilla *(Pupilla)* **muscorum** (Linné 1758)
Pupilla *(Pupilla)* **alpicola** (Charpentier 1837)
Pupilla *(Pupilla)* **triplicata** (Studer 1820)
Pupilla *(Pupilla)* **sterri** (Voith 1838)
Leiostyla *(Leiostyla)* **anglica** (Wood 1828)
Lauria *(Lauria)* **cylindracea** (da Costa 1778)
Lauria *(Lauria)* **sempronii** (Charpentier 1837)
Argna ferrarii (Porro 1838)

Family **VALLONIIDAE**

Vallonia costata (Müller 1774)
Vallonia suevica Geyer 1908
Vallonia pulchella (Müller 1774)
Vallonia enniensis (Gredler 1856)

Vallonia excentrica Sterki 1892
Vallonia declivis Sterki 1892
Acanthinula aculeata (Müller 1774)
Spermodea lamellata (Jeffreys 1830)
Planogyra sororcula (Benoit 1857)
Zoogenetes harpa (Say 1824)

Family **PLEURODISCIDAE**

†**Pleurodiscus balmei** (Potiez & Michaud 1838)

Family **ENIDAE**

Chondrula *(Chondrula)* **tridens** (Müller 1774)
Jaminia *(Jaminia)* **quadridens** (Müller 1774)
Ena *(Ena)* **montana** (Draparnaud 1801)
Ena *(Ena)* **obscura** (Müller 1774)
Zebrina *(Zebrina)* **detrita** (Müller 1774)

Family **ENDODONTIDAE**

Punctum *(Punctum)* **pygmaeum** (Draparnaud 1801)
†**Helicodiscus** *(Helicodiscus)* **parallelus** (Say 1821)
Helicodiscus *(Hebetodiscus)* **singleyanus** (Pilsbry 1890)
Discus *(Discus)* **ruderatus** (Férussac 1821)
Discus *(Discus)* **rotundatus** (Müller 1774)
Discus *(Discus)* **perspectivus** (Mühlfeldt 1816)

Family **ARIONIDAE**

Geomalacus maculosus Allman 1843
Arion *(Arion)* **ater** (Linné 1758)
Arion *(Arion)* **lusitanicus** Mabille 1868
Arion *(Mesarion)* **subfuscus** (Draparnaud 1805)
Arion *(Carinarion)* **fasciatus** (Nilsson 1823)
Arion *(Carinarion)* **circumscriptus** Johnston 1828
Arion *(Carinarion)* **silvaticus** Lohmander 1937
Arion *(Kobeltia)* **hortensis** Férussac 1819
Arion *(Kobeltia)* **intermedius** Normand 1852

Family **VITRINIDAE**

Vitrina *(Vitrina)* **pellucida** (Müller 1774)
Vitrinobrachium breve (Férussac 1821)
Semilimax *(Semilimax)* **semilimax** (Férussac 1802)
Semilimax *(Semilimax)* **kotulae** (Westerlund 1883)
Semilimax *(Semilimax)* **pyrenaicus** (Férussac 1821)

Eucobresia diaphana (Draparnaud 1805)
Eucobresia nivalis (Dumont & Mortillet 1852)
Eucobresia pegorarii (Pollonera 1884)
Phenacolimax *(Phenacolimax)* **major** (Férussac 1807)
Phenacolimax *(Gallandia)* **annularis** (Studer 1820)
Phenacolimax *(Insulivitrina)* **glacialis** (Forbes 1837)

Family ZONITIDAE

†Hawaiia minuscula (Binney 1840)
Vitrea *(Vitrea)* **diaphana** (Studer 1820)
Vitrea *(Vitrea)* **subrimata** (Reinhardt 1871)
Vitrea *(Crystallus)* **crystallina** (Müller 1774)
Vitrea *(Crystallus)* **contracta** (Westerlund 1871)
Aegopis verticillus (Férussac 1822)
Nesovitrea *(Perpolita)* **hammonis** (Ström 1765)
Nesovitrea *(Perpolita)* **petronella** (Pfeiffer 1853)
Aegopinella pura (Alder 1830)
Aegopinella nitidula (Draparnaud 1805)
Aegopinella nitens (Michaud 1831)
Aegopinella minor (Stabile 1864)
Aegopinella epipedostoma (Fagot 1879)
Aegopinella ressmanni (Westerlund 1883)
Retinella *(Retinella)* **hiulca** (Albers 1850)
Retinella *(Retinelloides)* **incerta** (Draparnaud 1805)
Oxychilus *(Oxychilus)* **draparnaudi** (Beck 1837)
Oxychilus *(Oxychilus)* **cellarius** (Müller 1774)
Oxychilus *(Oxychilus)* **mortilleti** (Pfeiffer 1859)
Oxychilus *(Oxychilus)* **hydatinus** (Rossmässler 1838)
Oxychilus *(Ortizius)* **alliarius** (Miller 1822)
Oxychilus *(Ortizius)* **helveticus** (Blum 1881)
Oxychilus *(Ortizius)* **clarus** (Held 1837)
Oxychilus *(Morlina)* **glaber** (Rossmässler 1835)
Oxychilus *(Riedelius)* **depressus** (Sterki 1880)
Daudebardia rufa (Draparnaud 1805)
Daudebardia brevipes (Draparnaud 1805)
Zonitoides *(Zonitellus)* **excavatus** (Alder 1830)
†Zonitoides *(Zonitellus)* **arboreus** (Say 1816)
Zonitoides *(Zonitoides)* **nitidus** (Müller 1774)

Family MILACIDAE

Milax *(Milax)* **gagates** (Draparnaud 1801)
Milax *(Milax)* **nigricans** (Philippi 1836)
Milax *(Milax)* **sowerbyi** (Férussac 1823)
Milax *(Milax)* **rusticus** (Millet 1843)
Milax *(Milax)* **budapestensis** (Hazay 1881)
Boettgerilla pallens Simroth 1912

Family LIMACIDAE

Limax *(Limax)* **maximus** Linné 1758
Limax *(Limax)* **cinereoniger** Wolf 1803
Limax *(Limax)* **tenellus** Müller 1774
Limax *(Limacus)* **flavus** Linné 1758
Limax *(Limacus)* **pseudoflavus** Evans 1978
Limax *(Lehmannia)* **nyctelius** Bourguignat 1861
Limax *(Lehmannia)* **marginatus** Müller 1774
Limax *(Lehmannia)* **macroflagellatus** (Grossu & Lupu 1962)
†**Limax** *(Lehmannia)* **valentianus** Férussac 1821
Deroceras *(Deroceras)* **laeve** (Müller 1774)
Deroceras *(Deroceras)* **sturanyi** (Simroth 1894)
Deroceras *(Malino)* **caruanae** (Pollonera 1891)
Deroceras *(Agriolimax)* **agreste** (Linné 1758)
Deroceras *(Agriolimax)* **reticulatum** (Müller 1774)
Deroceras *(Plathystimulus)* **rodnae** Grossu & Lupu 1965

Family EUCONULIDAE

Euconulus *(Euconulus)* **fulvus** (Müller 1774)
Euconulus *(Euconulus)* **alderi** (Gray 1840)

Family FERUSSACIIDAE

Cecilioides *(Cecilioides)* **acicula** (Müller 1774)
Cecilioides *(Cecilioides)* **jani** (De Betta & Martinati 1855)
Cryptazeca monodonta (Folin & Bérillon 1876)

Family SUBULINIDAE

†**Subulina octona** (Bruguière 1789)
†**Subulina striatella** (Rang 1831)
†**Lamellaxis** *(Allopeas)* **clavulinus** (Potiez & Michaud 1838)
†**Opeas** *(Opeas)* **pumilum** (Pfeiffer 1840)
Rumina decollata (Linné 1758)

Family CLAUSILIIDAE

Laminifera *(Neniatlanta)* **pauli** (Mabille 1865)
Cochlodina *(Cochlodina)* **laminata** (Montagu 1803)
Cochlodina *(Cochlodina)* **fimbriata** (Rossmässler 1835)
Cochlodina *(Cochlodina)* **costata** (Pfeiffer 1828)
Cochlodina *(Cochlodina)* **comensis** (Pfeiffer 1849)
Cochlodina *(Paracochlodina)* **orthostoma** (Menke 1830)
Itala itala (Martens 1824)

Charpentieria diodon (Studer 1820)
Ruthenica filograna (Rossmässler 1836)
Fusulus varians (Pfeiffer 1828)
Erjavecia bergeri (Rossmässler 1836)
Macrogastra ventricosa (Draparnaud 1801)
Macrogastra lineolata (Held 1836)
Macrogastra densestriata (Rossmässler 1836)
Macrogastra badia (Pfeiffer 1828)
Macrogastra plicatula (Draparnaud 1801)
Macrogastra rolphii (Turton 1826)
Clausilia parvula Férussac 1807
Clausilia bidentata (Ström 1765)
Clausilia dubia Draparnaud 1805
Clausilia cruciata Studer 1820
Clausilia pumila Pfeiffer 1828
Neostyriaca corynodes (Held 1836)
Neostyriaca strobeli (Porro 1838)
Laciniaria *(Laciniaria)* **plicata** (Draparnaud 1801)
Laciniaria *(Alinda)* **biplicata** (Montagu 1803)
Bulgarica *(Strigilecula)* **cana** (Held 1836)
Bulgarica *(Strigilecula)* **vetusta** (Rossmässler 1836)
Vestia turgida (Rossmässler 1836)
Balea perversa (Linné 1758)

Family **TESTACELLIDAE**

Testacella *(Testacella)* **maugei** Férussac 1819
Testacella *(Testacella)* **haliotidea** Draparnaud 1801
Testacella *(Testacella)* **scutulum** Sowerby 1821

Family **STREPTAXIDAE**

†**Gulella** *(Huttonella)* **io** Verdcourt 1974

Family **BRADYBAENIDAE**

Bradybaena *(Bradybaena)* **fruticum** (Müller 1774)

Family **HELICIDAE**

Candidula unifasciata (Poiret 1801)
Candidula intersecta (Poiret 1801)
Candidula gigaxii (Pfeiffer 1850)
Cernuella *(Cernuella)* **virgata** (da Costa 1778)
Cernuella *(Cernuella)* **aginnica** (Locard 1894)
Cernuella *(Xerocincta)* **neglecta** (Draparnaud 1805)
Helicella *(Helicella)* **itala** (Linné 1758)

Helicella *(Helicella)* **obvia** (Menke 1828)
Helicella *(Helicella)* **bolenensis** (Locard 1882)
Helicella *(Xerotricha)* **conspurcata** (Draparnaud 1801)
Helicella *(Xerotricha)* **apicina** (Lamarck 1822)
Trochoidea *(Trochoidea)* **elegans** (Gmelin 1791)
Trochoidea *(Xeroclausa)* **geyeri** (Soós 1926)
Helicopsis *(Helicopsis)* **striata** (Müller 1774)
Cochlicella acuta (Müller 1774)
Cochlicella barbara (Linné 1758)
Monacha *(Monacha)* **cartusiana** (Müller 1774)
Monacha *(Monacha)* **cantiana** (Montagu 1803)
Ashfordia granulata (Alder 1830)
Zenobiella subrufescens (Miller 1822)
Perforatella *(Perforatella)* **bidentata** (Gmelin 1788)
Perforatella *(Monachoides)* **incarnata** (Müller 1774)
Perforatella *(Monachoides)* **glabella** (Draparnaud 1801)
Perforatella *(Monachoides)* **vicina** (Rossmässler 1842)
Perforatella *(Monachoides)* **umbrosa** (Pfeiffer 1828)
Perforatella *(Pseudotrichia)* **rubiginosa** (Schmidt 1853)
Pyrenaearia carascalensis (Férussac 1821)
Hygromia cinctella (Draparnaud 1801)
Hygromia limbata (Draparnaud 1805)
Trichia *(Trichia)* **hispida** (Linné 1758)
Trichia *(Trichia)* **plebeia** (Draparnaud 1805)
Trichia *(Trichia)* **suberecta** (Clessin 1878)
Trichia *(Trichia)* **striolata** (Pfeiffer 1828)
Trichia *(Trichia)* **montana** (Studer 1820)
Trichia *(Trichia)* **caelata** (Studer 1820)
Trichia *(Trichia)* **clandestina** (Hartmann 1821)
Trichia *(Trichia)* **graminicola** Falkner 1973
Trichia *(Trichia)* **villosa** (Studer 1789)
Trichia *(Trichia)* **biconica** (Eder 1917)
Trichia *(Petasina)* **unidentata** (Draparnaud 1805)
Trichia *(Edentiella)* **edentula** (Draparnaud 1805)
Ponentina subvirescens (Bellamy 1839)
Euomphalia *(Euomphalia)* **strigella** (Draparnaud 1801)
Ciliella ciliata (Studer 1820)
Drepanostoma nautiliforme Porro 1836
Helicodonta obvoluta (Müller 1774)
Helicodonta angigyra (Rossmässler 1835)
Trissexodon constrictus (Boubée 1836)
Elona quimperiana (Férussac 1821)
Arianta arbustorum (Linné 1758)
Helicigona lapicida (Linné 1758)
Chilostoma *(Campylaea)* **planospira** (Lamarck 1822)
Chilostoma *(Cingulifera)* **cingulatum** (Studer 1820)
Chilostoma *(Chilostoma)* **squamatinum** (Moquin-Tandon 1856)
Chilostoma *(Chilostoma)* **desmoulinsi** (Farines 1834)
Chilostoma *(Chilostoma)* **zonatum** (Studer 1820)

Chilostoma *(Chilostoma)* **achates** (Rossmässler 1835)
Chilostoma *(Delphinatia)* **glaciale** (Férussac 1821)
Chilostoma *(Delphinatia)* **alpinum** (Férussac 1821)
Isognomostoma isognomostoma (Schröter 1784)
Isognomostoma holosericum (Studer 1820)
Theba pisana (Müller 1774)
Eobania vermiculata (Müller 1774)
Cepaea *(Cepaea)* **vindobonensis** (Férussac 1821)
Cepaea *(Cepaea)* **nemoralis** (Linné 1758)
Cepaea *(Cepaea)* **hortensis** (Müller 1774)
Cepaea *(Cepaea)* **sylvatica** (Draparnaud 1801)
Helix *(Cornu)* **aspersa** Müller 1774
Helix *(Helix)* **pomatia** Linné 1758

DESCRIPTIONS OF SPECIES

Subclass **PROSOBRANCHIA**

Order MESOGASTROPODA

Family **CYCLOPHORIDAE**

Members of this large family are nearly world-wide in warm climates. In the European genus *Cochlostoma* the shell is narrowly conical, usually finely ribbed, with a round mouth furnished with a deeply retractable horny operculum often formed of two layers. The head has a short proboscis and the eyes are set on slight protruberances at the base of the two conical tentacles. The sole is not longitudinally divided as in the Pomatiidae. The sexes are separate.

The genus *Cochlostoma* is circum-Mediterranean, with a large number of similar (and often poorly defined) species. They favour rocky habitats, usually on limestone, emerging in damp weather to crawl and feed on exposed surfaces.

COCHLOSTOMA SEPTEMSPIRALE (Razoumowsky 1789) **Pl.1**
Description. 7–8 × 3.8 mm. Outline straight-sided, with 8½ strongly rounded whorls separated by a deep suture. Mouth almost round; mouth-edge thick and white, strongly reflected (but not flat), usually double and consisting of an inner and outer part separated by a slight depression. Umbilicus small, partly hidden by expansion of columellar lip. Shell with regular, sharply-defined ribs, about 6–8 per mm; greyish-white to pale reddish-brown, with up to 3 rows of spirally arranged darker spots. Operculum membranous, deeply retractable within the shell.
Habitat. Rocks, screes, walls, woods, always on calcareous soils; common in both exposed and shaded places. Attaining over 2000 m in Switzerland.
Range. S. European.
Distribution. Map 1. The most common species of *Cochlostoma* in our area: S. and E. France, Switzerland, southernmost Germany (upper Rhine valley, calcareous Alps of S.E. Bavaria, Danube valley near Regensburg). Elsewhere an occasional adventive, as far as England and Belgium.

COCHLOSTOMA OBSCURUM (Draparnaud 1801) **Pl. 1**
Description. 10–14 × 4–5.5 mm. Shell relatively large, straight-sided, with 8½ rather *gently* rounded whorls, the last sometimes with a slight angulation below the periphery. Mouth slightly pear-shaped; mouth-edge moderately reflected, thick and white (but not double as in *C. septemspirale*). Umbilicus very small. Ribs rather regular, sharply-defined, about 8–9 per mm. Shell greyish- to reddish-brown, with 2 rows of obscure darker spots, most evident on the later whorls.
Habitat. Rocks, screes, woods, on calcareous soils.
Range. S. European.
Distribution. Map 2. C. and S. France: fairly widespread but more local than *C. septemspirale*.

COCHLOSTOMA CRASSILABRUM (Dupuy 1849)   Pl. 1
Syn. *C. obscurum* var. *crassilabra* Dupuy
Description. 10–14 × 4–6 mm. Shell closely similar to *C. obscurum*, but mouth-edge more strongly thickened, the outer and columellar lips forming a broad, nearly flat, white porcelain-like flange. Ribbing often finer and closer than in *C. obscurum*.
Habitat. Limestone rocks; montane.
Range. Pyrenean.
Distribution. Map 3. Northern slopes of the Pyrenees from Basses Pyrénées (Bayonne) to Ariège.

COCHLOSTOMA PARTIOTI (Saint-Simon 1848)   Pl. 1
Description. 9–10 × 3.5–4.5 mm. Shell with 8½ moderately tumid whorls, slightly less rounded than in *C. septemspirale*. Mouth slightly pointed at top; mouth-edge thickened, reflected rather more abruptly than in *C. septemspirale*. Ribbing *very fine* and somewhat irregular (13–17 ribs per mm), often hardly visible to the naked eye. Shell grey to brownish-violet, sometimes with 1 or 2 obscure darker bands.
Habitat. Rocks and screes; mainly montane.
Range. Pyrenean.
Distribution. Map 4. C. and W. Pyrenees (Basses Pyrénées, Hautes Pyrénées, Haute Garonne, Ariège).

COCHLOSTOMA NOULETI (Dupuy 1850)   Pl. 1
Description. 10–12 × 4–5 mm. Outline straight-sided, with 8 rather gently convex whorls, the last slightly flattened basally. Mouth-edge reflected, moderately thickened, flat, the outer edge often a little roughened and showing a finely layered structure. Ribs *prominent and widely-spaced* (only about 6 per mm). Colour dark greyish-brown, often with a spiral line of white spots close to the suture.
Habitat. Rocks and screes; montane.
Range. Pyrenean.
Distribution. Map 5. Rather rare: mainly C. Pyrenees (Basses Pyrénées, Hautes Pyrénées, Haute Garonne, Ariège).

COCHLOSTOMA APRICUM (Mousson 1847)   Pl. 1
Description. 7–10 × 3–4.5 mm. Shell similar to *C. obscurum*, with 8 feebly convex whorls separated by a rather shallow suture, the last whorl sometimes slightly angled below the periphery. Mouth pear-shaped; mouth-edge relatively thin and not strongly reflected or double. Ribs *fine and very regular*, about 9–10 per mm, often imparting a characteristic *silky or iridescent* appearance to the naked eye; occasionally almost smooth. Shell rather thin and slightly translucent, pale yellowish-brown, with numerous darker reddish-brown spots often coalescing to form 2 spiral bands on the last whorl.
Habitat. Rocks and screes, and in woods; mainly montane.
Range. Mediterranean and W. Alpine.
Distribution. Map 6. Locally common in S.E. France (Isère, Haute Savoie, Savoie).

COCHLOSTOMA PATULUM (Draparnaud 1801)   Pl. 1
Description. 5–8 × 2–3 mm. Shell small, often distinctly *concave-sided* in outline, with 7½–9 strongly convex whorls. Umbilicus *frequently closed* (cf. all other N.W.

European species). Mouth almost perfectly circular, mouth-edge strongly reflected, flat, usually double. Ribs 7–10 per mm, often weak and irregular on later whorls. Shell reddish-grey to whitish, without colour markings.
Habitat. Rocks, dry grassland, old walls.
Range. Mediterranean.
Distribution. Map 7. A common Mediterranean species, occasionally straying just within our area (Haute Garonne, Tarn).

Family **POMATIIDAE**

This family occurs in warmer latitudes in the Old World. The genus *Pomatias*, of which one species lives in our area, is principally Mediterranean. It has a thick, broadly conical shell, often with strong sculpture. There is a calcareous operculum. The animal has a long flexible proboscis, and the eyes are set at the base of the two cylindrical tentacles. The sole is divided longitudinally into halves which are moved independently in crawling. The sexes are separate and this is sometimes expressed in a slight dimorphism in the shell, that of the female being a little larger than that of the male.

POMATIAS ELEGANS (Müller 1774)   Pl. 1
Syn. *Cyclostoma elegans* (Müller)
Description. 13–16 × 9–11.5 mm. Shell conical, with 4½–5 strongly rounded whorls. Mouth nearly circular; mouth-edge simple, sometimes slightly thickened internally. Shell thick and solid, with a reticulate sculpture of fine spiral and transverse ribs, the former being the more pronounced, especially round the base of the shell; colour pale greyish-violet to yellowish, with a variable patterning of darker spots or interrupted spiral bands. Operculum a thick calcareous plate, closely fitting the mouth when the animal is retracted.
Habitat. Open woods, hedgebanks, screes; always on highly calcareous soils and requiring a loose friable substrate into which it can burrow.
Range. Mediterranean and W. European (see map, p. 35).
Distribution. Map 8. S. Britain, S. Ireland (Co. Clare), France, Switzerland (Geneva basin to Basel; Ticino), Belgium, S. Holland (Limburg), Germany (upper and middle Rhine valley, and several discontinuous areas in C. Germany as far east as Thuringia), Denmark (Seeland, Fünen).

Family **ACICULIDAE**

In this family the shell is small (2–4 mm) and glossy, and has the form of a narrow tapering cylinder with a blunt apex. The suture appears double (sometimes giving an illusion of channelling) owing to the inner surface of the shell showing through where it is attached to the preceding whorl. There is a very delicate horny operculum, deeply retractable. The animal has a rather long proboscis and the tentacles are long and slender, with the eyes set on small protruberances at their bases. The foot is very narrow and not longitudinally divided. The sexes are separate.

The Aciculidae occur in the western Palaearctic region. They are mainly woodland snails, characteristic of moist places under ground litter and in soil. Most of our N.W. European forms belong to the genus *Acicula*, which can be divided into two distinct groups of species: those with transverse (vertical) grooves on the shell (*A. fusca*, *A. lineata*, *A. lineolata*), and those without such grooves (*A. cryptomena*, *A. polita*, *A. gracilis*, *A. dupuyi*).

*ACICULA   FUSCA (Montagu 1803)

Syns. *Acme lineata* of British authors (*non* Draparnaud), *Acme inchoata* Ehrmann
Description. 2.2–2.5 × 0.8 mm. Outline almost straight-sided, with 5–5½ very gently convex whorls. Umbilicus minute. Mouth pear-shaped; columellar margin of mouth-edge reflected over umbilicus, elsewhere thin and simple. *No external rib.* Shell thin and translucent, pale golden-brown, very glossy, with widely and irregularly spaced, sharply incised transverse grooves.
Habitat. Damp places, especially ground litter in old deciduous woods or in moss by springs; more hygrophile than the next two species.
Range. W. European.
Distribution. Map 9. Fairly widespread in Ireland, very local in Britain, Belgium, N.W. Germany, France south to Dordogne and Basses Pyrénées.

ACICULA   LINEATA (Draparnaud 1801)

Syn. *Acme sublineata* Andreae
Description. 3–3.2 × 1.1 mm. Shell similar to *A. fusca*, but larger; parietal callus more obvious and mouth-edge *slightly thickened* internally; a barely perceptible transverse rib-like thickening also present externally a little way behind outer lip.
Habitat. Open woods, especially characteristic of screes.
Range. Alpine.
Distribution. Map 10. Somewhat uncertain owing to confusion with both *A. fusca* and *A. lineolata*; E. France (mainly in the Jura), frequent in Switzerland, and in the Bavarian Alps as far east as Berchtesgaden, scattered localities elsewhere in S. Germany.

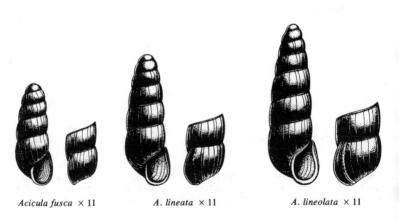

Acicula fusca × 11   *A. lineata* × 11   *A. lineolata* × 11

ACICULA LINEOLATA (Pini 1884)

Syn. *Acme lineata* of many authors (*non* Draparnaud)

Description. 3.3–3.7 × 1.2 mm. Shell very similar to *A. lineata* but *slightly larger*, with 6–6½ whorls; shape often tending towards conical rather than sub-cylindrical, with the later whorls less parallel-sided than in *A. lineata*; parietal callus distinct and mouth-edge *bluntly and distinctly thickened*; external transverse rib behind outer lip rather clearly developed.

Habitat. Open woods, rocks, screes.

Range. S. Alpine and S. European.

Distribution. Map 11. Somewhat uncertain owing to confusion with *A. lineata*; S. Switzerland, S. E. France, elsewhere doubtful.

ACICULA CRYPTOMENA (Folin & Bérillon 1877)

Syn. *Acme cryptomena* Folin & Bérillon

Description. 3 × 1 mm. Shell with 6 gently convex whorls; mouth pear-shaped; mouth-edge thickened internally. An *extremely broad and prominent* transverse rib present externally just behind outer lip, sharply delimited posteriorly. Shell reddish-yellow, very glossy and without transverse grooves.

Habitat. Ground litter in moist deciduous woodland.

Range. Pyrenean.

Distribution. Map 12. Rare: Basses Pyrénées only (Bayonne, La Preste).

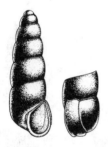

Acicula cryptomena × 11

A. polita × 11

ACICULA POLITA (Hartmann 1840)

Syn. *Acme polita* Hartmann

Description. 2.8–3 × 1.2 mm. Shell relatively broad, with 5½–6 gently convex whorls; outline almost straight-sided, apex bluntly rounded. Mouth pear-shaped; mouth-edge thickened internally, a *prominent* transverse rib present externally immediately behind outer lip, sharply delimited posteriorly. Shell reddish-brown, very glossy, without transverse grooves.

Habitat. Moderately damp places, such as deciduous woodland or on mossy screes.

Range. Alpine and C. European.

Distribution. Map 13. French and Swiss Jura and Alps; C. and S. Germany (mainly montane); also in scattered localities in N. German plain, Danish islands, southernmost Sweden (Skäne).

ACICULA   GRACILIS (Clessin 1877)

Syn. *Acme polita rothi* Clessin

Description. 2.5–2.7 × 0.8 mm. Shell closely resembling *A. polita*, but smaller and more slender, and often paler and more translucent. External transverse rib less well developed, frequently separated from the margin of the outer lip by a slight groove.

Habitat. Deciduous woodland and screes; calciphile.

Range. S.E. Alpine.

Distribution. Map 14. Calcareous Alps of S.E. Bavaria (Schellenberg, Berchtesgaden).

ACICULA   DUPUYI (Paladilhe 1868)

Syn. *Acme dupuyi* Paladilhe

Description. 3.2–3.4 × 1.1 mm. Shell somewhat resembling *A. polita*, but longer and relatively more slender, with 6–6½ whorls. External rib much less prominent than in *A. polita*, and not abruptly delimited posteriorly but fading away gradually into the thickness of the shell wall. Shell reddish-brown, very glossy and without transverse grooves.

Habitat. Deciduous woods and well-vegetated screes.

Range. W. European.

Distribution. Map 15. Poorly known owing to confusion with other species: Switzerland (Geneva basin), local in France but possibly widespread.

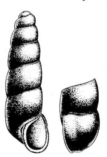

Acicula gracilis × 11   *A. dupuyi* × 11

RENEA   VENETA (Pirona 1865)

Renea veneta × 11

Syn. *Pleuracme veneta* (Pirona)

Description. 3.8–4.2 × 1.3 mm. Outline almost straight-sided, with 7 moderately convex whorls. Mouth-edge thickened internally; a deep sinus at the top of outer lip, with a small parietal tooth set very close to it. An external transverse rib present immediately behind outer lip. Shell brown, rather glossy, with sculpture of *prominent and extremely regular* ribs.

Habitat. Screes and woods on limestone; montane.

Range. S. Alpine.

Distribution. Map 16. Calcareous Alps of S.E. Bavaria (Schellenberg, Berchtesgaden).

Subclass **PULMONATA**

Order BASOMMATOPHORA

Family **ELLOBIIDAE**

The Ellobiidae are regarded as the most primitive members of the subclass Pulmonata. The shell is fusiform, with a pointed spire. The mouth has thickened lips and is provided with teeth, including spiral folds. The inner walls of the shell between the earlier-formed whorls are frequently partly resorbed in the adult. The animal has a single pair of short conical tentacles (as in the prosobranchs), with the eyes set near their bases and a little behind them.

The Ellobiidae are world-wide, mainly in warmer latitudes. They live principally in aquatic habitats in estuaries or on sea-coasts, but a few, like *Carychium*, live in moist places on land.

*CARYCHIUM MINIMUM Müller 1774

Description. 1.6–1.9 × 0.9 mm. Shell fusiform, relatively broad, with 4½ gently convex whorls. Mouth-edge thickened, slightly reflected. Outer lip with 1 central denticle; inner lip with 1 columellar and 1 parietal fold, the latter internally developed as a spiral lamella (often clearly visible through the shell to the left of the columella) having a *simple, smoothly-curving* profile (cf. *C. tridentatum*). Shell colourless, glossy, nearly transparent when fresh.

In this and the next species it is sometimes necessary to break away part of the shell wall with the point of a needle to see the internal lamella clearly.

Habitat. Wet places, such as marshes or very moist woods.
Range. European and Siberian.
Distribution. Map 17. Common nearly throughout, but mostly coastal beyond 60°N, and absent from northern Scandinavia and Iceland.

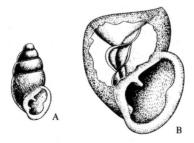

Carychium minimum   A, whole shell × 11   B, interior of last whorl, showing parietal and columellar folds × 27

*CARYCHIUM TRIDENTATUM (Risso 1826)
Syn. *C. minimum* var. *tridentata* Risso
Description. 1.8–2 × 0.8–0.9 mm. Shell relatively taller, narrower and more coni-cal than *C. minimum*, with 5 rather more tumid whorls; mouth-edge more thickened and teeth more prominent. The parietal fold has a different form: the expanded part is distinctly flared and in profile shows a characteristic *double flexure*. Shell colour-less, growth-lines stronger and more regular than in *C. minimum*, making fresh shells appear somewhat less glossy and translucent.
Habitat. Catholic: woods, damp grassland, well-vegetated places generally. Usu-ally in drier habitats than *C. minimum*, though frequently associated with it.
Range. European.
Distribution. Map 18. Similar to *C. minimum*.

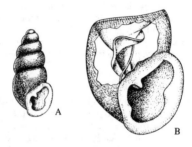

Carychium tridentatum　A, whole shell × 11　B, interior of last whorl, showing parietal and columellar folds × 27

Order STYLOMMATOPHORA

Family SUCCINEIDAE

In the Succineidae the body is relatively large and scarcely retractable within the shell. The anterior pair of tentacles (characteristic of the Stylommatophora) is vestigial. The shell is usually pale brown, thin, glossy and translucent, with a short spire and a relatively very large body whorl and mouth. There is no umbilicus. The mouth-edge is simple and delicate and the columellar margin is never strongly thickened or twisted (cf. shells of the freshwater family Lymnaeidae, sometimes found in the same habitats).

Succineids live in permanently wet places, such as marshes and the margins of lakes and rivers; many species are virtually amphibious. They have a nearly world-wide distribution. Their highly variable and somewhat rudimentary shells can often be difficult to name with certainty and dissection may sometimes be necessary for secure identification. In N.W. Europe the pairs of species most likely to be confused on external criteria are *Catinella arenaria* and *Succinea oblonga*; *S. putris* and *Oxyloma pfeifferi*; and *O. pfeifferi* and *O. sarsi*.

*CATINELLA   ARENARIA (Bouchard-Chantereaux 1837)   **Pl. 2**
Syn. *Succinea arenaria* Bouchard-Chantereaux

Description. 5–9 mm. Shell with about 3 extremely tumid whorls separated by a deep suture; mouth almost round, forming about ½ the total height. Shell rather thick and scarcely translucent, often reddish-amber, not glossy, growth-lines rather coarse, prominent and irregular.

The body is dark grey or black.

This species cannot reliably be separated from *Succinea oblonga* on external criteria alone.

Anatomy. Internally this species differs from *S. oblonga* in lacking a penial sheath and epiphallus, and in having a very short vagina and vas deferens. There is a characteristic dark arrow-shaped mark on the penis just below the insertion of the vas deferens.

Habitat. Damp sparsely-vegetated hollows in coastal sand dunes, and on bare mud in marshes.

Range. W. European.

Distribution. Map. 19. Rare: a few places on the coasts of France, Belgium, Holland, West Germany, Sweden (Öland, Gotland), England (N. Devon), Ireland (Co Mayo). Also C. Ireland, and mountains of C. Scandinavia and E. Switzerland.

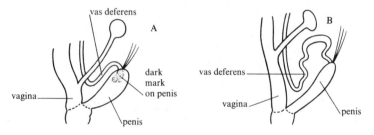

Distal genitalia of   A, *Catinella arenaria*   B, *Succinea oblonga*

*SUCCINEA   OBLONGA Draparnaud 1801   **Pl. 2**

Description. 6–8 mm. Shell closely resembling *Catinella arenaria*, but usually more elongate, with less tumid whorls and a correspondingly more oval mouth, slightly pointed at the top. Shell rather thick and opaque, not very glossy, pale amber to greenish-white, with somewhat coarse and irregular growth-lines; often encrusted with a muddy film.

The body is usually dark grey.

Anatomy. Internally *S. oblonga* differs sharply from *Catinella arenaria* in having an epiphallus partially enclosed within a penial sheath. The vas deferens is also longer and more convoluted, with a distinctive thickening in the middle.

Habitat. Damp sparsely-vegetated places: floodplains of rivers, marshes, among rocks; characteristically on dried-out bare muddy surfaces.

Range. European and W. Asiatic.

Distribution. Map 20. Very local in British Isles and S. Scandinavia to about 61°N, elsewhere moderately common.

*SUCCINEA PUTRIS (Linné 1758)   **Pl. 2**

Description. 10–17 mm (occasionally 24 mm). Shell with 3 very rapidly enlarging whorls, the last forming about two-thirds of the total height. Whorls gently rounded, suture rather shallow. Mouth broad and well rounded. Shell fragile and translucent, pale greenish-yellow to amber, glossy, growth-lines rather irregular and not very prominent.

The body is generally pale yellowish-brown, but dark grey forms also occur.

Anatomy. This species differs from *Oxyloma pfeifferi* (which externally it may closely resemble) in having a simple and freely exposed epiphallus, and lacking a penial appendix.

Habitat. Fens, marshes, water-meadows; often on flags at the margins of lakes and rivers.

Range. European and Siberian.

Distribution. Map 21. Widespread, becoming rare or absent in the highland zones of N. Britain and N. Scandinavia.

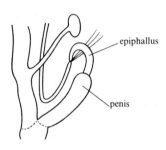

Distal genitalia of *Succinea putris*

*OXYLOMA PFEIFFERI (Rossmässler 1835)   **Pl. 2**

Syns. *Succinea pfeifferi* Rossmässler, *S. elegans* of many authors, *S. groenlandica* Mörch

Description. 9–12 mm (occasionally 20 mm). Shell with 3 rapidly expanding whorls, the last forming about two-thirds of the total height; shape rather variable but whorl-profile usually flatter than in *Succinea putris*, with mouth correspondingly narrower and more pear-shaped. Shell translucent, glossy, often rather bright amber colour, with numerous irregular growth-lines.

The body is generally darkly pigmented, but pale forms also occur.

This is a very variable species; on external criteria alone certain forms are scarcely separable from *Succinea putris*.

Anatomy. Internally the genus *Oxyloma* may be distinguished from *Succinea* by the presence of a closely-coiled epiphallus and of a penial appendix, both enclosed in the upper part of the penial sheath (but usually visible through the transparency).

Habitat. Fens, marshes, and similar permanently wet places; not in woods.

Range. Holarctic.

Distribution. Map 22. Widespread, becoming rare or absent in the highland zone of Scandinavia; Iceland.

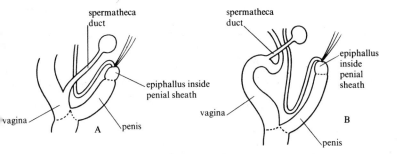

Distal genitalia of   A, *Oxyloma pfeifferi*   B, *O. sarsi*

*OXYLOMA SARSI (Esmark 1886) Pl. 2

Pl. 2

Syn. *Succinea elegans* of British authors after 1926

Description. 12–15 mm (occasionally 20 mm). Shell closely resembling *O. pfeifferi*, but larger and relatively narrower, with whorl-profile still flatter; lower margin of mouth characteristically rather straight, giving a somewhat triangular form to the mouth. Shell dark amber, rather strongly and irregularly striated.

The body is usually darkly pigmented.

On external criteria alone this species cannot reliably be separated from certain forms of *O. pfeifferi*.

Anatomy. Distinguishable from *O. pfeifferi* by the different proportions of the genitalia: penis and penial sheath longer and narrower; spermatheca duct shorter, and joining the longer, narrower vagina high up at the apex of a curve (in *O. pfeifferi* the long spermatheca duct joins the shorter, wider vagina in the middle of a straight portion).

Habitat. Richly vegetated fens and marshes, characteristically on *Glyceria* and floating water plants.

Range. N. European.

Distribution. Map 23. Local: incompletely known owing to confusion with *O. pfeifferi*; verified from S.E. England, Belgium, Holland, Germany, Denmark, E. Scandinavia.

Family **COCHLICOPIDAE**

In this family the shell is elongate-oval to fusiform, smooth and glossy, with rather flat whorls. There is no umbilicus. The mouth is obliquely pear-shaped, sometimes with teeth, and the mouth-edge is somewhat thickened and bluntly rounded, without a reflected lip.

The Cochlicopidae occur in North America and in the western Palaearctic region.

*AZECA   GOODALLI (Férussac 1821)   **Pl. 1**
Syns. *A. menkeana* (Pfeiffer), *A. tridens* (Pulteney)
Description. 5.3–6.8 × 2.4–2.7 mm. Shell rather fusiform, with 6½–7 flat-sided
whorls; suture almost flush, often presenting an illusory channelled appearance.
Mouth-edge prominently thickened, whitish, incurved at base. Last whorl with a
variable number of internal denticles and folds, of which at least 6 (1 palatal, 3
parietal, 2 columellar) are usually visible within the mouth. Shell a warm reddish-
brown, translucent and extremely glossy.
Habitat. Moss and ground litter in open woods, hedgerows and scrub, often in
rocky places.
Range. W. European.
Distribution. Map 24. Local in England and Wales, France, S. Belgium, C. Germany as far east as Thuringia; isolated in N. Germany (Schleswig-Holstein) and
Scotland (Perthshire).

*COCHLICOPA   LUBRICA (Müller 1774)   **Pl. 1**
Description. 5–7.5 × 2.4–2.9 mm. Shell elongate-oval tending towards conical,
with 5½ gently convex whorls and a rather blunt apex. Outer lip bluntly rounded,
slightly thickened internally to form a pale rib. Shell translucent, pale to dark brown
(sometimes white), very glossy.
Habitat. Catholic: moderately damp places of all kinds; marshes, grasslands,
woods.
Range. Holarctic.
Distribution. Map 25. Common throughout.

*COCHLICOPA   LUBRICELLA (Porro 1838)   **Pl. 1**
Syns. *C. lubrica* var. *lubricella* Porro, *C. minima* (Siemaschko)
Description. 4.5–6.8 × 2.1–2.5 mm. Shell similar to *C. lubrica*, but smaller and
relatively *more slender*, and *more cylindrical* in shape; whorls less swollen, with a
correspondingly shallower suture; apex appearing blunter; shell usually less glossy
and translucent, and paler in colour.
   It should be noted that individual shells may be very difficult to assign to either *C.
lubrica* or *C. lubricella* and some populations may show anomalous features. Some
authors recognize a further species within our area (*C. repentina* Hudec), with shell
characters intermediate between those of *C. lubrica* and *C. lubricella*.
Habitat. Catholic: characteristically in drier places than *C. lubrica* (limestone
grassland, calcareous sand dunes, screes) but the two species are often associated.
Range. Holarctic.
Distribution. Map 26. Common nearly throughout, but more local than *C. lubrica*,
and absent from N. Scandinavia.

COCHLICOPA   NITENS (Gallenstein 1848)   **Pl. 1**
Description. 6.2–7.5 × 2.8–3.2 mm. Shell similar to *C. lubrica*, but larger and relatively much broader; whorls markedly convex, separated by a pronounced suture;
apex appearing relatively more pointed. Outer lip only feebly thickened. Shell a
warm brown, very glossy and transparent.
Habitat. Calcareous fens and marshes; sometimes in very wet calcareous woodland.
Range. C. and E. European.

Distribution. Map 27. Rare: a few isolated colonies in S.E. Sweden, Denmark (Seeland), Germany, Switzerland.

Family **PYRAMIDULIDAE**

This family comprises only the genus *Pyramidula*, represented by several species living in the southern Palaearctic region from Spain to Japan. They are snails of dry rocky habitats, and are ovo-viviparous.

PYRAMIDULA RUPESTRIS (Draparnaud 1801)

Description. 1.5–2 × 2.5–3 mm. Shell top-shaped, with a low obtuse spire; 4½ rather convex whorls separated by a deep suture, the last bluntly keeled at the periphery. Umbilicus very broad and deep. Mouth rounded; mouth-edge simple, thin and brittle. Growth-ridges well defined, somewhat irregular, giving a silky appearance to the shell; apical whorls smooth. Shell dark reddish-brown, often bleaching to nearly white in old specimens.

Habitat. Dry limestone rocks and walls fully exposed to the sun, hiding in crevices and emerging in damp weather to feed on lichens.

Range. Mediterranean and W. European.

Distribution. Map 28. Common in most limestone areas of Britain, Ireland, France, Switzerland, S. Belgium, C. and S. Germany (not in East Germany).

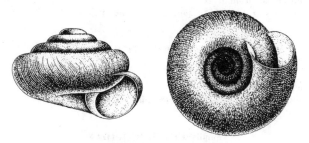

Pyramidula rupestris × 12

Family **VERTIGINIDAE**

In the Vertiginidae the shell is very small (usually about 2 mm), oval or sub-cylindrical, and the mouth often contains denticles. The mouth-edge may be slightly expanded, but is not strongly thickened or flange-like. The shell may be smooth, or finely ribbed or striated. In the animal the front pair of tentacles is absent. The penis is devoid of accessory organs (many species are commonly aphallic).

The Vertiginidae are world-wide. Their habitats are varied. *Truncatellina* species live in dry, exposed, calcareous places, especially grassy limestone screes.

Plate 1

Family CYCLOPHORIDAE
(×4)

1. **Cochlostoma septemspirale** The commonest *Cochlostoma*. Small, whorls strongly rounded.	51
2. **Cochlostoma obscurum** S. France. Large, whorls only gently rounded.	51
3. **Cochlostoma crassilabrum** Pyrenees only. Like *C. obscurum* but lip very thick.	52
4. **Cochlostoma partioti** Pyrenees only. Ribbing fine and delicate.	52
5. **Cochlostoma nouleti** Pyrenees only. Ribs coarse and prominent.	52
6. **Cochlostoma apricum** S. France. Thin and silky. Outer lip delicate, not strongly reflected.	52
7. **Cochlostoma patulum** Mediterranean. Small. Lip quite flat, indented below columella.	52

Family POMATIIDAE
(×4)

8. ***Pomatias elegans** W. Europe. Common on limestone soils.	53

Family COCHLICOPIDAE
(×7)

9. ***Azeca goodalli** Very glossy, furnished with teeth.	62
10. ***Cochlicopa lubricella** Local. Smaller and slenderer than *C. lubrica*.	62
11. ***Cochlicopa lubrica** The commonest *Cochlicopa*, nearly ubiquitous.	62
12. **Cochlicopa nitens** Rare, mainly C. Europe.	62

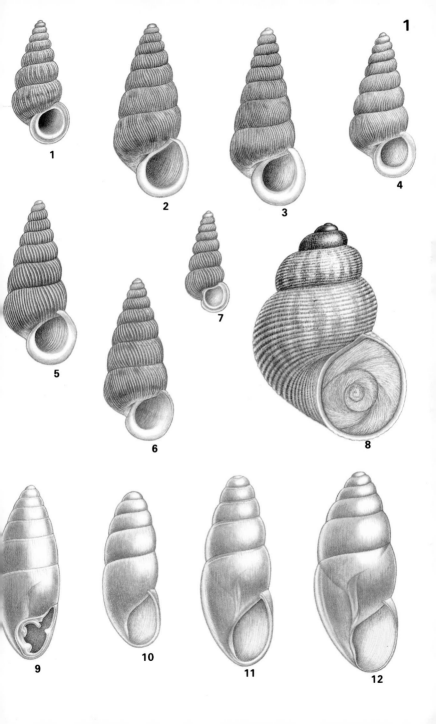

2

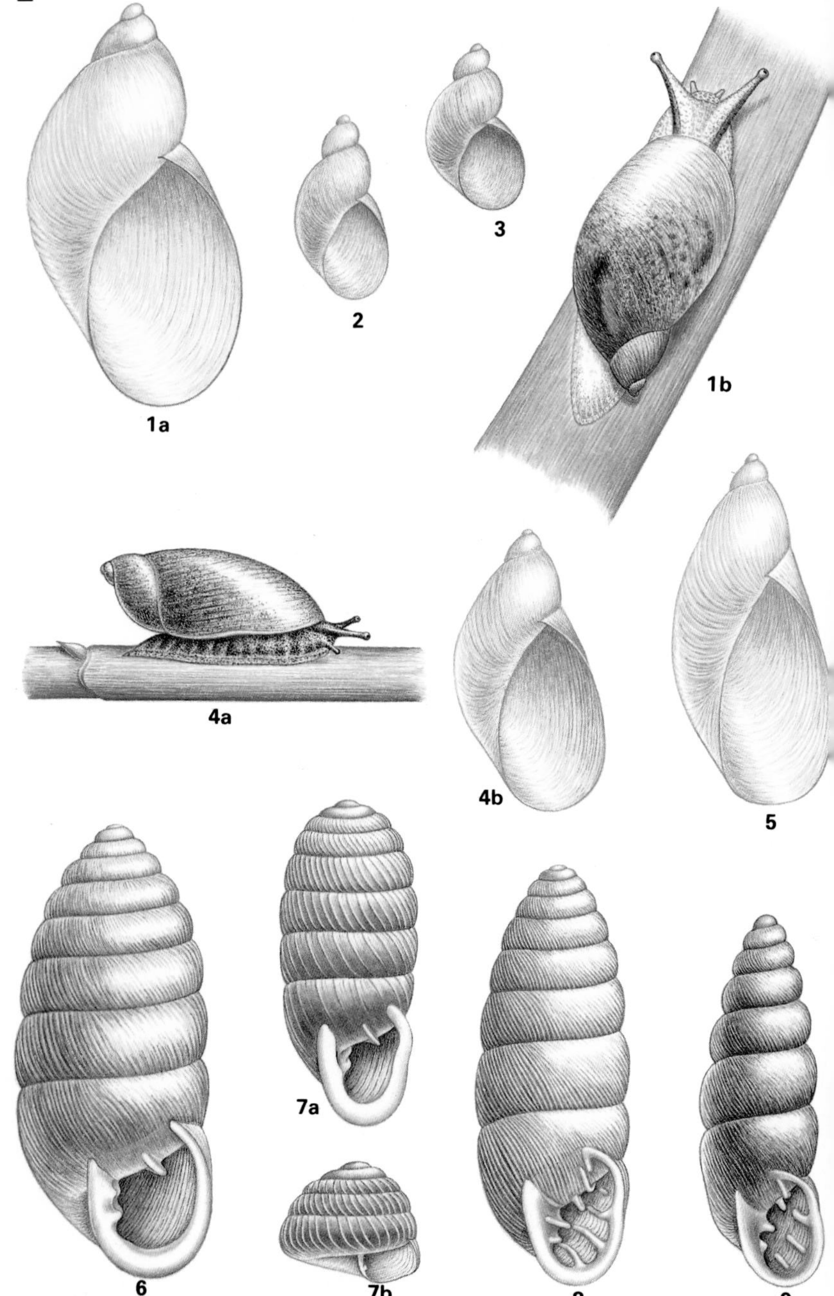

Family SUCCINEIDAE
(×3)

Plate 2

1. *Succinea putris   60
Common in marshes.
   1a. Shell: last whorl very large, broadly rounded.
   1b. Living animal: typically pale, but dark forms may occur.

2. *Succinea oblonga   59
Local. Small, with tall spire and deep suture. Shell often coated with mud.

3. *Catinella arenaria   59
Mainly maritime, very rare. Only reliably separable from *Succinea oblonga* by dissection.

4. *Oxyloma pfeifferi   60
Common in marshes.
   4a. Living animal: typically dark, but pale forms may occur.
   4b. Shell.

5. *Oxyloma sarsi   61
Local. Usually larger and narrower than *O. pfeifferi*, but reliably separable only by dissection.

Family ORCULIDAE
(×7)

6. Orcula dolium   76
Mainly C. Europe, in limestone woods.

7. Orcula doliolum   77
   7a. Adult: last 2-3 whorls narrowed. Sharp delicate ribbing.
   7b. Juvenile.

Family CHONDRINIDAE
(×7)

8. *Abida secale   84
The commonest *Abida*.

9. Chondrina avenacea   87
The commonest *Chondrina*. More conical than *Abida*, with rounder whorls and weaker teeth.

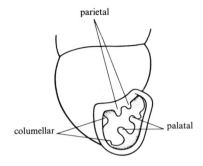

Nomenclature of teeth in Vertiginidae

Columella and *Vertigo* species favour moist places, especially marshes; many are consequently becoming rare in lowland Europe owing to the destruction of their habitats by man.

The N.W. European genera are assignable to two subfamilies:

Subfamily Truncatellininae (*Columella*, *Truncatellina*)

Shell relatively tall and nearly cylindrical, mouth without teeth or with 1–3 feeble teeth only.

Subfamily Vertigininae (*Vertigo*)

Shell rather oval and relatively squat, occasionally sinistral. Mouth usually with 4–6 teeth.

Subfamily **TRUNCATELLININAE**

COLUMELLA   EDENTULA (Draparnaud 1805)

Description. 2.5–3 × 1.3–1.5 mm. Shell sub-cylindrical, tapering to a bluntly domed apex, with 5½–6½ gently convex whorls separated by a moderately deep suture. Last whorl often distinctly broader than the middle cylindrical part of the spire. Mouth-edge simple and delicate, columellar lip reflected, nearly covering minute umbilical opening. Shell thin and translucent, pale yellowish-brown, rather shiny, with poorly defined irregular growth-lines only.

Habitat. Catholic: marshes, woods, grasslands; usually in moderately damp and calcareous places, and typically lowland.

Range. Palaearctic.

Distribution. Map 29. Probably throughout, but uncertain owing to confusion with *C. aspera*.

COLUMELLA   COLUMELLA (Martens 1830)

Syns. *C. edentula* var. *columella* Martens, *C. edentula* var. *gredleri* Clessin

Description. 2.7–3.3 × 1.3–1.5 mm. Similar to *C. edentula*, but taller (up to 7½ whorls) and more nearly cylindrical, the upper part of the spire being *less tapered* and the apex correspondingly *flatter*; suture deeper. Last whorl often markedly

Columella edentula   × 12   C. columella   × 12

expanded. Shell often pale greenish rather than brownish, delicate and translucent, shiny, with poorly defined irregular growth-lines only.

Habitat. Calcareous places; typically in marshy grassland or wet subarctic woodland, often favouring stony ground. Attaining 2900 m in the Alps (Graubünden).

Range. Arctic and Alpine.

Distribution. Map 30. Mountains of N. Scandinavia, mainly beyond the Arctic Circle; Swiss Alps; a few places in the Alps of S. Germany.

*COLUMELLA   ASPERA Waldén 1966

Description. 2–2.5 × 1.3–1.4 mm. Similar to *C. edentula*, but relatively shorter and broader; rarely with more than 6 whorls, the last never expanded; whorls more strongly convex and suture correspondingly deeper. Shell rather opaque, often darker than in *C. edentula*, and appearing less polished due to the presence of numerous *regular*, close-set growth-ridges, sometimes almost as clearly defined as in *Vertigo substriata* (p. 71).

Habitat. Coniferous and deciduous woodland, poor acid grassland; characteristically in drier, less calcareous habitats than *C. edentula*; often montane.

Range. Probably Palaearctic.

Distribution. Map 31. Widespread, but exact distribution uncertain owing to confusion with *C. edentula*. Absent from most of N. Scandinavia; Iceland.

Columella aspera   × 12

*TRUNCATELLINA   CYLINDRICA (Férussac 1807)

Syn. *T. minutissima* (Hartmann)

Description. 1.8–2 × 0.9 mm. Shell almost cylindrical, domed at apex, with 5½–6 moderately rounded whorls, the last two with a trace of flattening at the periphery giving a slightly shouldered appearance. Mouth a little elongated vertically, *without teeth*; mouth-edge slightly thickened, lips rather sharp and delicate, slightly reflected, especially basally and on columellar margin. Shell pale golden-brown, not glossy, with numerous fine and evenly spaced transverse ribs, giving a sparkling appearance at low magnifications.

Habitat. Very dry calcareous grassy places, characteristically among *Sedum* or *Artemisia*; screes, among rocks, occasionally on sand dunes.

Range. S. and W. European.

Distribution. Map 32. Widespread but always very local, north to coastal areas of S. Scandinavia (near Oslo, Danish islands, Bornholm, S. Sweden, Öland, Gotland).

Truncatellina cylindrica × 16

T. callicratis × 16

T. costulata × 16

*TRUNCATELLINA   CALLICRATIS (Scacchi 1833)

Syns. *T. strobeli* (Gredler), *T. rivierana* (Benson), *T. britannica* Pilsbry

Description. 1.8–2 (occasionally 2.2) × 0.9 mm. Shell similar to *T. cylindrica*, but outline even more perfectly cylindrical; whorls slightly more convex and suture correspondingly deeper. Three denticles characteristically present (parietal, columellar, palatal), deeply-set, but at least the palatal usually visible in frontal view (cf. *T. claustralis*). Ribbing often slightly weaker and less regular than in *T. cylindrica*; occasionally the shell is almost smooth.

This is a variable species; in some populations the teeth may be reduced or even absent, making the shell difficult to separate from *T. cylindrica*.

Habitat. Very dry calcareous grassy places; open rocky hillsides.

Range. Mainly Mediterranean and S. Alpine.

Distribution. Map 33. Common in the French and Swiss Jura; also Pyrenees, Dordogne, calcareous Alps of S.E. Bavaria, Belgium, S. coast of England from Devon to the Isle of Wight.

TRUNCATELLINA   COSTULATA (Nilsson 1823)

Description. 1.7–2 × 0.9 mm. Shell cylindrical, apex domed, 5½–6½ well-rounded whorls. Mouth-edge *white and prominent*, strongly thickened internally, sometimes appearing double-layered on outer lip; columellar lip reflected over umbilicus. Mouth with 3 denticles (parietal, columellar, palatal), the 2 latter deeply-set and only just visible in frontal view. Shell pale golden-brown, with distinctive sculpture of extremely regular, *strong*, sharply cut ribs, more *widely-spaced* than in *T. cylindrica* or *T. callicratis*.

Habitat. Dry calcareous grassland, coastal dunes, open woods; characteristic of less exposed places than *T. cylindrica* or *T. callicratis*.

Range. N.C. and E. European.

Distribution. Map 34. Principally around coasts of southern Baltic: Danish islands, S.E. Sweden, Öland, Gotland, Rugen, N.E. Germany; also isolated inland localities in Germany as far west as the R. Weser and south to the Thuringian Forest.

TRUNCATELLINA CLAUSTRALIS (Gredler 1856)

Description. 1.5–1.8 × 0.75 mm. Shell rather similar to *T. callicratis*, but smaller and relatively *narrower*, with 6 strongly rounded whorls, the last somewhat flattened at the periphery and appearing distinctly shouldered. Mouth-edge moderately thickened. Three denticles present (parietal, columellar, palatal), only the parietal and columellar visible in frontal view; palatal deeply-set and invisible from mouth but visible externally in rear view through the transparency of the shell as a *distinct white mark*. Shell with sculpture of fine regular ribs, imparting a silky lustre.

Habitat. Very dry limestone hillsides, among screes, characteristically with *Artemisia* and *Helianthemum*.

Range. Mediterranean and S. Alpine.

Distribution. Map 35. Very local: Switzerland (Geneva, Ticino), France (Ain, Haute Savoie, Dordogne).

Truncatellina claustralis × 16

T. monodon × 16

TRUNCATELLINA MONODON (Held 1837)

Description. 2.2–2.3 × 0.9 mm. Shell cylindrical, with 6 moderately (but not strongly) convex whorls. Mouth-edge rather thickened. Three denticles present (parietal, columellar, palatal), only the parietal normally visible in frontal view; columellar visible in oblique view; palatal large but deeply-set and invisible from mouth. Shell brown, *not ribbed*, with fine, close, irregular growth-lines only.

Habitat. Dry calcareous grassland and screes.

Range. E. Alpine.

Distribution. Map 36. Very local in the Alpine foreland region of S. Bavaria, and in easternmost Switzerland (Graubünden).

TRUNCATELLINA ARCYENSIS Klemm 1943

Description. 2.2–2.4 × 0.9 mm. Shell cylindrical, with about 7 rather feebly convex whorls separated by a shallow suture. Mouth *without teeth*; mouth-edge slightly thickened, outer and columellar lips a little reflected. Shell yellowish-brown, dull, *not ribbed*, with irregular growth-lines only.

Habitat. Dry calcareous grassland on stony slopes.

Range and distribution. Map 37. Apparently rare: known only from three localities on valley slopes between Auxerre and Avalon, Yonne, France (Arcy-sur-Cure, St Moré, Cravant-sur-Yonne).

Truncatellina arcyensis × 16

Subfamily VERTIGININAE

*VERTIGO PUSILLA Müller 1774

Description. 2 × 1.1 mm. Shell *sinistral* (like *V. augustior* only), with 5 moderately convex whorls, enlarging rapidly so as to produce a distinctly conical shape. Mouth-edge slightly thickened and reflected; mouth with at least 6 (sometimes 9) teeth (2 parietal, 2 columellar, 2 palatal). Shell pale yellowish-brown, glossy, with irregular poorly-defined growth-lines only (cf. *V. angustior*, p. 75).

Habitat. Rather dry places: rocks, stone walls, ground litter in open woodland, hedge-banks, occasionally in sand-dunes.

Range. European.

Distribution. Map 38. Widespread but local, becoming rare northwards (in Norway to 68° 30′ N).

*VERTIGO ANTIVERTIGO (Draparnaud 1801)

Description. 2–2.2 × 1.2 mm. Shell ovoid, with 5 feebly convex whorls separated by a shallow suture. Mouth-edge very slightly thickened, reflected; outer lip with a marked central indentation, behind which there is a strong but rather ill-defined transverse rib-like thickening. Mouth with 6–10 teeth (at least 2 parietal, 2 columellar, 2 palatal). Shell dark chestnut-brown, with a few feeble growth-lines only.

Habitat. Fens and marshes; often on the dead leaves of sedges and under flood rubbish at lake margins.

Range. Palaearctic.

Distribution. Map 39. Throughout, to about 63°N in Scandinavia.

Vertigo pusilla × 16

V. antivertigo × 16

VERTIGO SUBSTRIATA (Jeffreys 1833)

Description. 1.7 × 1.1 mm. Shell rather barrel-shaped, with 4½ strongly convex whorls separated by a deep suture. Mouth-edge thin, not strongly reflected; a slight transverse thickening present externally just behind lip. Mouth with 5–6 teeth (2 parietal, 1–2 columellar, 2 palatal). Shell pale brown, often appearing iridescent owing to a characteristic sculpture of *very fine and regular ribbing*, developed especially on the middle whorls.

Habitat. Damp places: woods, marshes, lake margins; in upland areas often in poor marshy grassland.

Range. C. and N. European.

Distribution. Map 40. British Isles (rare in S.E.); common throughout Scandinavia to about Arctic Circle; scattered localities in Germany, Holland, Belgium, E. France (Vosges), Switzerland.

Vertigo substriata × 16

V. pygmaea × 16

VERTIGO PYGMAEA (Draparnaud 1801)

Description. 1.7–2.2 × 1–1.2 mm. Shell ovoid (exact shape rather variable), with 5 gently convex whorls. Mouth-edge slightly thickened, moderately reflected; a *strong pale transverse rib* present externally a little way behind outer lip, separated from it by a depression. Mouth with 4–7 prominent white teeth (1 parietal only) usually linked by callus round their bases, especially in the palatal area where it may coalesce into a rib-like thickening. Shell pale to dark brown, usually somewhat dull, with obscure growth-lines only.

Habitat. Characteristic of dry calcareous grassy places; also sand-dunes; occasionally in marshes; not in woods.

Range. Holarctic.

Distribution. Map 41. The commonest *Vertigo* in most of lowland Europe, becoming rare in the highland zone to the north (to 64°N in Norway).

VERTIGO HELDI Clessin 1877

Syn. *V. pygmaea* var. *heldi* Clessin

Description. 2.5–2.7 × 1.2 mm. Shell similar to *V. pygmaea*, but taller, relatively narrower and more cylindrical, with up to 6¼ whorls; basal crest more distinct. Mouth-edge scarcely thickened, transverse rib behind lip feeble. Teeth very weak, sometimes entirely absent, internal callus very poorly developed. Shell shinier and more translucent when fresh than *V. pygmaea*.

This species can be difficult to distinguish from certain hypertrophied forms of the very variable *V. pygmaea*.

Habitat. Swampy meadows and damp grassy places; mainly montane.

Range. C. European.

Distribution. Map 42. Poorly known and apparently rare: scattered localities in Switzerland and in the Alpine foreland region of S. Germany; occasionally elsewhere in Germany.

Vertigo heldi × 16

V. moulinsiana × 16

*VERTIGO MOULINSIANA (Dupuy 1849)

Syn. *V. desmoulinsi* Germain

Description. 2.2–2.7 × 1.5 mm. Shell ovoid, with 5 rather tumid whorls, the last very large and accounting for nearly two-thirds of the total height. Mouth-edge rather delicate, slightly reflected; an irregular transverse thickening present behind the outer lip similar to that in *V. antivertigo*. Mouth somewhat triangular, narrowed towards the base, with 4–5 well-defined teeth (*I* parietal, 1 columellar, 2 palatal), the palatals arising from a pale rib-like callus, in front of which the lip presents a characteristic flange-like appearance. Shell pale yellowish- or reddish-brown, translucent, very glossy, growth-lines hardly visible.

Habitat. Calcareous fens and marshes; often on *Phragmites* at the edges of lowland lakes or rivers.

Range. European (probably Holarctic).

Distribution. Map 43. Very local: Ireland, England, France, Switzerland, Belgium, Germany, Denmark, southernmost Sweden. A declining species.

VERTIGO MODESTA (Say 1824)
Syn. *V. arctica* Wallenberg

Description. 2.2–2.7 × 1.4 mm. Shell ovoid, rather tapering towards apex, with 5 fairly well rounded whorls separated by a deep suture. Mouth-edge simple, scarcely thickened; no external rib or flexure behind outer lip and little development of internal callus. Mouth usually with 3–4 rather deeply-set small denticles: 1 parietal, 1 columellar, 1 lower palatal (the last sometimes absent, sometimes an additional upper palatal). Shell pale yellowish-brown, translucent, not glossy, usually with a silky sheen due to numerous regular fine growth-lines.

Habitat. Damp shaded places in calcareous mountain areas; in Scandinavia characteristically in subarctic woodland on valley slopes, under stones and ground litter. Mainly above 1700 m in the Alps.

Range. Circumpolar Holarctic (Arctic and Alpine in Europe).

Distribution. Map 44. Mountain valleys of N. Norway, Sweden and Finland; one site in S. Sweden (Schonen); Switzerland, S.W. Bavaria, Iceland.

Vertigo modesta × 16   *V. ronnebyensis* × 16

VERTIGO RONNEBYENSIS (Westerlund 1871)
Syn. *V. arctica* var. *ronnybyensis* Westerlund

Description. 2.2–2.4 × 1.2–1.4 mm. Shell closely resembling *V. modesta*, but usually smaller, more cylindrical and with a less tapered spire; whorls more weakly convex; last whorl more narrowed basally. Mouth and teeth as in *V. modesta*: 3 (occasionally 4) denticles: 1 parietal, 1 columellar, 1 lower palatal (occasionally a small upper palatal). Shell pale yellowish-brown, with distinct and rather regular growth-lines giving a characteristic silky sheen.

Habitat. Coniferous and deciduous woodland, under ground litter and moss; often among *Vaccinium* on poor non-calcareous soils. Less hygrophile than *V. modesta*.
Range. N. and E. European.
Distribution. Map 45. Common in the greater part of Scandinavia (though not in the most mountainous areas), becoming scarce towards the coast in Norway and in S.W. Sweden; also isolated localities around the southern Baltic (Denmark, Rugen) and in E. Germany (Erzgebirge).

*VERTIGO LILLJEBORGI (Westerlund 1871)

Description. 1.9–2.2 × 1.3 mm. Shell ovoid, with 5 strongly tumid whorls, the last relatively large and well rounded. Mouth-edge delicate, scarcely thickened, very slightly expanded; a slight transverse puckering present externally a little behind outer lip. Mouth usually with 4 well-defined narrow teeth (1 parietal, 1 columellar, 2 palatal), arising abruptly from the inner shell wall and with little or no callus surrounding their bases (cf. *V. pygmaea* and *V. moulinsiana*). Shell pale yellowish-brown, thin and translucent, rather glossy, with faint but regular growth-lines.
Habitat. Saturated decaying vegetation in marshes and alder fens at the margins of lakes and rivers, usually in places subject to flooding; only rarely associated with other species of *Vertigo*.
Range. N. European.
Distribution. Map 46. W. Ireland, N. Britain, Denmark (Jutland), the greater part of Scandinavia.

Vertigo lilljeborgi × 16

V. genesii × 16

VERTIGO GENESII (Gredler 1856)

Description. 1.7–2.1 × 1.2 mm. Shell ovoid, rather barrel-shaped, with 5 tumid whorls. Mouth-edge scarcely thickened, outer lip just perceptibly reflected; no external rib or flexure behind lip. Mouth rather rounded, *without teeth*, or occasionally a vestigial parietal denticle only. Shell pale reddish-brown, very smooth and glossy, growth-lines virtually imperceptible.
Habitat. Marshy ground: in Scandinavia characteristic of calcareous seepages on mountain hillsides. Attaining 2000 m in the Alps.
Range. Boreal and Alpine.
Distribution. Map 47. Fairly frequent in the mountains of C. Scandinavia (mainly Jämtland and S. Lappland); rare in S. Sweden (Westergötland), Finland and Switzerland.

*VERTIGO GEYERI Lindholm 1925
Syn. *V. genesii geyeri* Lindholm
Description. 1.7–1.9 × 1.2 mm. Shell similar to *V. genesii*, but slightly more conical, and with more strongly tumid whorls and a deeper suture. Mouth usually with 4
teeth (1 parietal, 1 columellar, 2 palatal) but sometimes fewer (3, 2 or 1), small and
peg-like, arising abruptly from the inner shell wall without surrounding callus. Shell
pale reddish-brown, glossy, with fine, rather regular growth-lines, especially on the
middle whorls.
Habitat. Marshes usually of upland type with a stable water level; calciphile.
Range. N. European and Alpine.
Distribution. Map 48. Mainly Sweden (to 68°20′ N), Finland (to 65°30′ N) and in the
Alps of Switzerland and S.W. Bavaria; also isolated sites in the lowlands of Ireland,
Denmark, the islands of the southern Baltic, and in N.E. and S.E. Germany.

*VERTIGO ALPESTRIS Alder 1838
Description. 1.8–2 × 1.1 mm. Shell rather cylindrical, with 5 moderately tumid
whorls, the last a little flattened laterally giving a gently shouldered appearance.
Mouth-edge a little thickened, scarcely reflected, and with no transverse rib behind
outer lip (cf. *V. pygmaea*). Mouth with 3–4 rather lamella-like teeth (1 parietal, 1
columellar, 1–2 palatal), rising abruptly from the shell wall and with little callus
around their bases. Shell pale yellowish-brown, translucent, glossy, very faintly
but regularly striated, especially on the middle whorls, giving a characteristic silky
lustre.
Habitat. Screes, rocks, old walls, rather dry open woodland. Attaining 2400 m in
the Swiss Alps.
Range. N. European and Alpine.
Distribution. Map 49. Frequent throughout Scandinavia and in Switzerland;
sporadic in Germany (mainly montane), E. France (Vosges) and N.W. England
(Lake District); single sites in Wales and Scotland; Iceland.

Vertigo geyeri × 16   *V. alpestris* × 16   *V. angustior* × 16

*VERTIGO ANGUSTIOR Jeffreys 1830
Description. 1.8 × 0.9 m. *Sinistral* (like *V. pusilla* only), with 5 rather strongly
convex whorls, the last flattened laterally and narrowed basally giving a somewhat
fusiform outline. Mouth-edge delicately thickened, sharply reflected; outer lip with
a deep central indentation, continued externally as a spiral groove and internally
corresponding with a long lamella-like upper palatal tooth; mouth with 5–6 teeth.

Shell pale yellowish-brown, rather glossy, with numerous close and regular *fine growth-ridges*, especially on the earlier whorls (cf. *V. pusilla*, p. 70).
Habitat. Very wet permanently marshy grassland; among moss in wet hollows in sand-dunes. More commonly found as dead shells in the flood rubbish of rivers.
Range. European.
Distribution. Map 50. Widespread but very local, reaching southernmost Norway, Sweden and Finland. A declining species.

Family **ORCULIDAE**

The shell is cylindrical, larger than in the Vertiginidae (3–10 mm) and composed of numerous rather low whorls. The mouth is rounded, with a reflected lip, and furnished with teeth, generally including a prominent narrow parietal fold and a columellar fold. There is no angular fold, unlike the Chondrinidae.

This is a small family, distributed through southern Europe and the Near East. The genus *Orcula* is represented by numerous species in the eastern Alps.

Orcula gularis × 6

ORCULA   DOLIUM (Draparnaud 1801)   **Pl. 2**
Description. 6.7–9 × 3–3.6 mm. Shell cylindrical, with a pointed conical apex; 8½–10 rather flat-sided whorls, the last ascending at the suture towards the top of the outer lip. Mouth-edge discontinuous in the parietal region, elsewhere thickened and sharply reflected; mouth with a prominent central parietal fold and 2 much weaker columellar folds, the lower larger than the upper. Shell yellowish or reddish-brown, slightly translucent, not very polished, with feebly developed, irregular growth-lines.

This is a highly variable species in which many geographical races have been distinguished, especially in central Europe.
Habitat. Ground litter and mossy rocks in woods, and among stone rubble on sheltered slopes; calciphile. Mainly montane, attaining 2000 m in Switzerland.
Range. Alpine and Carpathian.
Distribution. Map 51. S.E. France and Switzerland (Côte d'Or, Jura, calcareous Alps); S. Germany from the upper Rhine valley and S. Württemberg eastwards through the Bavarian Alps.

ORCULA GULARIS (Rossmässler 1837)

Description. 6.5–7 × 2.8 mm. Shell similar to *O. dolium*, but smaller and relatively narrower, and tapering more gradually towards apex; mouth furnished additionally with a *strong white palatal tooth*, set a little way in from the lip; upper columellar fold often weak or absent.

Habitat. Limestone rubble on cool moist slopes; montane.

Range. E. Alpine.

Distribution. Map 52. Calcareous Alps of S.E. Bavaria (near Berchtesgaden) only.

ORCULA DOLIOLUM (Bruguière 1792) Pl. 2

Description. 4.5–6 × 2.3–2.5 mm. Shell cylindrical, domed towards apex, with 7½–9 flattish whorls, the last 2–3 *narrowing distinctly*; last whorl ascending at the suture towards top of outer lip. Mouth-edge discontinuous in the parietal region, elsewhere strongly thickened, white, sharply reflected; mouth with a prominent central parietal fold and 2 indistinct columellar folds. Shell pale brown, slightly translucent, with a rather dull polish and with a characteristic sculpture of widely-spaced, very regular lamella-like ribs.

Habitat. Moist, shady places, under ground litter in woods and among rocks; at higher elevations tending towards more open habitats; calciphile. Attaining 1600 m in the Swiss Jura.

Range. S. and S.E. European.

Distribution. Map 53. Widespread but local in limestone areas in S. and E. France, Belgium, Holland (Limburg), Switzerland, C. and S. Germany.

PAGODULINA PAGODULA (Des Moulins 1830)

Description. 2.8–3.3 × 1.8–2 mm. Shell sub-cylindrical, with 7½–8 rather convex whorls, the last ¼ whorl ascending obliquely in a characteristic way, reaching almost to the preceding turn of the suture. Mouth-edge continuous, lips rather delicate, reflected. Mouth without visible teeth, but a columellar fold and a long lamella-like palatal fold present out-of-sight deep within the last whorl, the palatal externally marked by a spiral groove. Shell rather thin and translucent, pale yellowish-brown, with close and regular, sharply-defined lamella-like ribs, often giving a sparkling appearance to the naked eye.

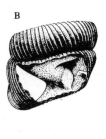

Pagodulina pagodula × 12 A, frontal view B, rear view of interior of last whorl, showing folds

Habitat. Moist shady places in woods and among rocks, in limestone country.
Range. C. and S.E. European.
Distribution. Map 54. Very local: a few localities in S. and E. France (Haute
Garonne, Dordogne, Puy de Dôme, Moselle, Haut Rhin, Savoie) and S. Germany
(calcareous Alps of S.E. Bavaria)

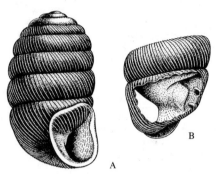

Pagodulina subdola × 12   A, frontal view   B, rear view of interior of last whorl, showing
folds

PAGODULINA SUBDOLA (Gredler 1856)

Description. 3–4 × 2 mm. Shell closely similar to *P. pagodula*, but taller, *more
nearly cylindrical*, and the upper part of the spire relatively broader. Internally
there is a variable number of extra teeth (2–5), only to be seen by breaking the shell;
in addition to the principal palatal fold there is always a lower, weaker palatal;
columellar fold stronger than in *P. pagodula*.
Habitat. Moist shady places in woods and among rocks, on limestone.
Range. S. Alpine and S.E. European.
Distribution. Map 55. S. Switzerland (Ticino) only.

Family **CHONDRINIDAE**

The Chondrinidae live in warm latitudes, principally in southern Europe, North
America and south-west Asia. In the European members (subfamily Chondrininae)
the shell is tall and narrow, medium-sized (about 5–10 mm), conical at first and
becoming more cylindrical in the later whorls. The mouth is rather elongate, with
reflected lips, and is furnished with complex ridge-like teeth, usually comprising an
angular, a spiral (a deeply-set tooth in line with the angular), a parietal *sensu stricto*,
1–2 columellar, and 2–4 palatal. The shell may be smooth or finely ribbed.

Most chondrinids live in dry open habitats, usually on limestone, and many are
exclusively montane. The genus *Chondrina* especially is characteristic of rocks,
often climbing high up on bare surfaces; other chondrinids may live in calcareous
grassland, on screes, or occasionally in open woods. Their shells tend to be very
variable, and geographical subspeciation is common.

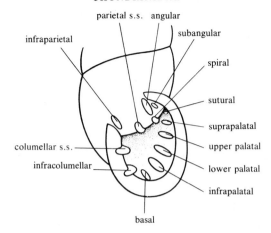

Nomenclature of teeth in Chondrinidae

The four N.W. European genera are unfortunately not sharply definable on shell characters alone. The following points are a rough guide:

Granopupa. One distinctive species only (*G. granum*), like a miniature *Granaria*.

Granaria. Shell rather pale, weakly-ribbed or smooth (especially on the later whorls). The shape tends to be more cylindrical than in *Abida* or *Chondrina*. The mouth-edge is strongly thickened, often rather bluntly swollen. The lower palatal tooth is always the most strongly developed palatal (cf. *Abida*).

Abida. Shell pale to dark brown, with relatively strong, sharply-defined ribbing on all the whorls (cf. *Granaria* and *Chondrina*). The shape is often rather gradually tapering, giving a bowed outline. The mouth-edge is strongly thickened. The lower and upper palatals are about equally developed.

Chondrina. Shell characteristically dark reddish-brown, often with a greyish-violet tinge, smooth, or with smoothed-out blunt ribbing or very fine ribbing only (cf. *Abida*). The shape is usually distinctly conical, and the individual whorls are rather tumid. The mouth-edge is weakly thickened. The teeth are usually short, weak, and sometimes greatly reduced.

GRANOPUPA GRANUM (Draparnaud 1801)
Description. 3.5–5.5 × 1.4–1.8 mm. Very *small* (the smallest chondrinid in N.W. Europe), with 6–8 moderately tumid whorls often a little flattened towards the periphery. Mouth-edge scarcely thickened, slightly reflected, discontinuous across the parietal region. Mouth with about 7 teeth: parietal prominent (angular *inconspicuous or absent*); 3–4 palatal, deeply-set within the mouth, not continuous with the outer lip. Shell pale reddish-brown, slightly translucent, with numerous fairly regular fine ribs.

Plate 3

Family ENIDAE
($\times 4$)

1. **Zebrina detrita**   101
   S. Europe, dry places. Creamy-white, with irregular reddish stripes.

2. ***Ena obscura**   100
   Shady places. Juveniles often covered with a crust of dirt.

3. **Chondrula tridens**   100
   S. Europe, dry places. Lip with three blunt teeth.

4. **Jaminia quadridens**   100
   S. Europe, dry places. Sinistral. Lip with four blunt teeth.

5. ***Ena montana**   100
   Mainly montane, in woods. Larger than *E. obscura*. Shell granular.
   5a. Adult.
   5b. Juvenile.

Family ENDODONTIDAE
($\times 4$)

6a-c. **Discus ruderatus**   102
   Mainly Scandinavia and the Alps. Uniformly greenish-brown. Keel
   blunt.

7a-c. ***Discus rotundatus**   102
   Nearly everywhere, except in Scandinavia. Regular reddish-brown
   stripes.

8a-c. **Discus perspectivus**   103
   S.E. Germany. Keel *very* sharp, outlined by groove. Umbilicus
   enormous.

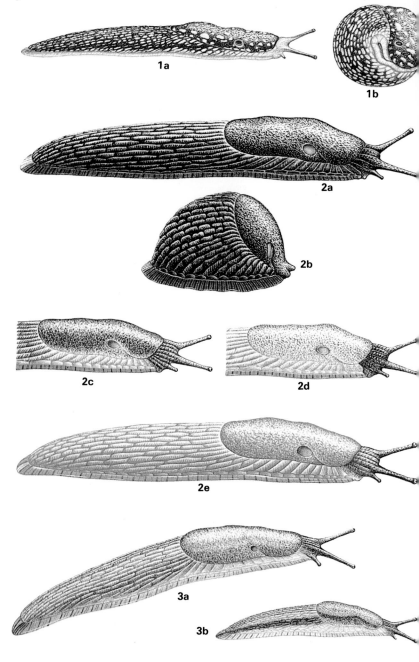

1a

1b

2a

2b

2c

2d

2e

3a

3b

Family ARIONIDAE
See also plate 5
(life size)

Plate 4

1. *Geomalacus maculosus   103

S.W. Ireland, on lichen-covered rocks. Spotted with green and white.
  1a. Extended.
  1b. Contracted into ball.

2. *Arion ater   104

Common, except in Scandinavia. The biggest *Arion*. Colour extremely
variable. Black forms (typical *ater*) are mostly montane and/or northern.
Brightly coloured forms (typical *rufus*) are commoner in the south, often
in cultivated places.
  2a. Black form extended (typical *A. ater ater*).
  2b. Black form contracted.
  2c. Brown form.
  2d. Grey-white form.
  2e. Red form (typical *A. ater rufus*)

3. *Arion lusitanicus   104

Local, mainly in the west. Difficult to distinguish from *A. ater* without
dissection.
  3a. Adult: often a dirty khaki-green.
  3b. Juvenile: lateral bands may persist in adult.

Habitat. Dry open calcareous places: grassland, rocks, screes. Attaining 1000 m in Switzerland.
Range. Mediterranean.
Distribution. Map 56. Frequent in S. France, S.W. Switzerland (Valais); occasionally elsewhere in France.

Granopupa granum × 6

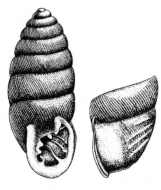

Granaria frumentum × 6

GRANARIA FRUMENTUM (Draparnaud 1801)
Syn. *Abida frumentum* (Draparnaud)
Description. 6.5–8 × 2.7–3 mm. Shell cylindrical, tapering rather suddenly to a conical apex; whorls 9–10, moderately convex, suture rather shallow. Mouth-edge broad and white, strongly reflected, discontinuous across the parietal area. A distinct *transverse white thickening* present a little behind the outer lip, followed by four white lines reflecting the palatal folds. Mouth with at least 8 teeth: angular prominent, continuous with the mouth-edge; parietal small; 2 columellar; 4 narrow prominent subparallel palatal, all *continuous with the outer lip* (cf. *G. variabilis*). Shell pale brown, slightly translucent, with close, fine and very regular growth-ridges.
Habitat. Dry open calcareous places: grassland, at the base of rocks, on screes, old walls. Rare above 1000 m.
Range. N. Alpine and C. European.
Distribution. Map 57. Widespread in limestone regions in E. and S.E. France, Switzerland, S. and C. Germany north to the Harz; occasional records, probably adventive, from N. France, Belgium, N.E. Germany.

GRANARIA ILLYRICA (Rossmässler 1837)
Syn. *Abida frumentum illyrica* (Rossmässler)
Description. 9–11.5 × 3.2–4 mm. Shell closely similar to *G. frumentum*, but larger, and with the transverse thickening behind the outer lip feebly developed or absent; also the fine ribbing becoming feeble or irregular on the last 2–3 whorls, which may be almost smooth.
Habitat. Dry open calcareous places.

Granaria illyrica × 6

G. variabilis × 6

Range. S. Alpine and S.E. European.
Distribution. Map 58. S. Switzerland (Ticino) only.

GRANARIA VARIABILIS (Draparnaud 1801)
Syn. *Abida variabilis* (Draparnaud)
Description. 7–10 (occasionally 15) × 3–4 mm. Shell cylindro-conical, tapering towards the apex more smoothly and gradually than in *G. frumentum*; whorls 8–12, at first feebly convex, later almost flat and separated by a very shallow suture. Mouth-edge broad and white, reflected to form a flat lip, discontinuous across the parietal region; no transverse thickening behind outer lip (cf. *G. frumentum*). Mouth with about 7 teeth: angular prominent, linked to the mouth-edge; 2 columellar; 3–4 palatal, the lower palatal narrow and *prominent, straight*, continuous with the outer lip, the upper palatal similar but feebler, the remaining palatals short, deeply-set and inconspicuous. Shell pale brown, slightly translucent, with faint growth-ridges, virtually smooth on later whorls.
    Very tall hypertrophied shells with up to 12 whorls are not uncommon in this species.
Habitat. Dry warm exposed places: calcareous grassland, rocks, screes. Mainly lowland, but attaining about 1600 m in the Alps.
Range. Mediterranean France and S.W. Alpine.
Distribution. Map 59. Common in France S. and E. of Lyons, extending eastwards along the Rhône into S.W. Switzerland (Lake Geneva basin and Valais).

GRANARIA STABILEI (Martens 1865)
Syn. *Abida stabilei* (Martens)
Description. 6–9 × 2–2.5 mm. Shell narrower than *G. variabilis*, with 7½–9 more strongly convex whorls. Mouth-edge rather delicate, white, sharply reflected, discontinuous across the parietal area. Mouth with about 7 teeth: angular *short*,

linked to the mouth-edge; 2 columellar; 3 palatal, the lower palatal narrow, prominent, *rather curved* (cf. *G. variabilis*), continuous with the outer lip, other palatals vestigial. Shell pale brown, with rather irregular growth-ridges, last whorl almost smooth.

Habitat. Dry exposed places among rocks and screes, mainly above 500 m; attaining 2700 m (Mt Cenis).

Range. S.W. Alpine.

Distribution. Map 60. Mountains of S.E. France (Savoie and Hautes Alpes) only.

Granaria stabilei × 6   *G. braunii* × 6   *Abida secale* × 6

GRANARIA BRAUNII (Rossmässler 1842)

Syn. *Abida braunii* (Rossmässler)

Description. 6–8 × 2.2–2.6 mm. Shell cylindro-conical, with 8–9 rather feebly convex whorls. Mouth-edge *very thick* and white, strongly reflected, with a marked swelling in the middle of the outer lip; columellar and outer lips linked by a distinct parietal callus. Mouth with about 6 teeth: angular prominent; *1 obvious columellar only* (infracolumellar weak and scarcely visible in frontal view); 2 subparallel palatal joining outer lip. Shell pale brown, growth-lines feeble and indistinct.

Habitat. Exposed places among rocks and screes; montane, attaining 1600 m. Not known to occur in association with other species of *Granaria*.

Range. S. Pyrenean.

Distribution. Map 61. Hautes Pyrénées only (but common on the Spanish side of the watershed)

*ABIDA SECALE (Draparnaud 1801)   Pl. 2

Description. 6–8.5 (occasionally 11 or more) × 2.3–2.8 mm. Shell cylindro-conical, with 8½–10 rather feebly convex whorls. Mouth-edge moderately thickened and reflected, usually discontinuous across the parietal region where there is only a thin callus. Mouth usually with about 9 teeth: angular prominent and lamella-like, with a small subangular close to it; a deeply-set spiral; 2 columellar; 3 subparallel palatal often running out to join outer lip, with a vestigial suprapalatal.

Shell brown, with very regular fine ribbing, often becoming less distinct on the last 2 whorls.

This is a highly variable species in which many geographical races have been distinguished and named, especially in the Pyrenees. These may differ from the type in being much taller or broader, in the degree of thickening of the mouth-edge, in having a simpler or more complex dentition, and in possessing weaker or stronger sculpture (the more extreme forms occur mostly outside our area).

Habitat. Rocks and screes, dry grassland, open woods; always on limestone. Attaining 2700 m in Switzerland.

Range. W. European and Alpine.

Distribution. Map 62. Widespread but local in France, England (north to Cumbria), S. Belgium, Switzerland, S. and C. Germany as far east as Thuringia.

ABIDA PYRENAEARIA (Michaud 1831)

Description. 6–8 × 2.2–2.5 mm. Shell similar to *A. secale*, but relatively narrower and more cylindrical, and with the mouth-edge continuous across the parietal area. Teeth like *A. secale*, but *subangular absent*, and suprapalatal only very rarely developed. Shell brown, with very regular fine ribbing.

Habitat. Calcareous rocks and screes; montane, mainly above 1000 m.

Range. N.-C. Pyrenean.

Distribution. Map 63. Common locally in Basses Pyrénées, Hautes Pyrénées, Haute Garonne, Ariège.

Abida pyrenaearia × 6   *A. occidentalis* × 6

ABIDA OCCIDENTALIS (Fagot 1888)

Description. 6–8 × 2.1–2.3 mm. Shell similar to *A. pyrenaearia*, but less cylindrical and more tapering towards apex. Mouth-edge continuous across parietal region, usually distinctly detached and projecting beyond shell wall. Teeth as in *A. pyrenaearia*, but infracolumellar weak or absent; palatals weaker, reaching *less far inside mouth* (inner ends usually visible) and more widely spaced. Shell brown, with very regular ribbing.

Habitat. Calcareous rocks and screes; montane, attaining 1400 m.

Range. N.C. Pyrenean.

Distribution. Map 64. Rare: Hautes Pyrénées, Haute Garonne, Ariège.

ABIDA PARTIOTI (Saint-Simon 1848)

Description. 7–8 × 2.3–2.6 mm. Shell cylindro-conical, with 9–10 very gently rounded whorls, the last with a sharp basal crest. Mouth-edge rather thick, reflected to form a flat white lip, discontinuous across the parietal region where there is only a thin callus. Mouth with 9 or more teeth: angular narrow and prominent; infracolumellar forming a *spiral fold downwardly twisted* within the mouth in a characteristic way; 3 strong palatal reaching the outer lip. Shell brown, with very fine regular ribbing.

Habitat. Calcareous rocks and screes; montane.

Range. S.C. Pyrenean.

Distribution. Map 65. A few places in Basses and Hautes Pyrénées close to the Spanish frontier only.

A. bigerrensis × 6

Abida partioti × 6

A. polyodon × 6

ABIDA BIGERRENSIS (Moquin-Tandon 1856)

Description. 5.5–6.5 × 2.3–2.6 mm. Shell cylindro-conical to fusiform, with 8–9 strongly convex whorls; outline usually broadest a little below the middle, the last whorl narrowing distinctly and somewhat shouldered towards the suture. Mouth-edge rather thick and reflected. Mouth with 9 or more teeth: a distinct infraparietal; 2 columellar; 3 very strong palatal, continuous with the outer lip, also a small deeply-set suprapalatal. Shell brown, with rather strong and regular ribbing.

Habitat. Calcareous rocks and screes up to about 1400 m; usually found in much smaller numbers than other associated species of *Abida* (*A. secale*, *A. occidentalis*, *A. pyrenaearia*).

Range. W. Pyrenean.

Distribution. Map 66. Fairly widespread in the Pyrenees from Ariège as far as the Atlantic.

ABIDA POLYODON (Draparnaud 1801)

Description. 7–9 (occasionally 12 or more) × 3–4 mm. Outline rather broad and fusiform, with maximum breadth about the middle; 8–10 feebly convex whorls. Mouth-edge strongly reflected, white and prominent; only a thin callus across the parietal area. Teeth strong, with numerous small extra intervening folds, giving a diagnostic *puckered or crenulated* appearance to the lip. Ribbing rather fine and very regular.

Habitat. Mainly in dry calcareous grassland or scrub; less frequent in rocky habitats. Mainly in lowlands, but attaining 1300 m.

Range. W. Mediterranean.

Distribution. Map 67. A common Mediterranean species, locally straying northwards into France (Isère, Haute Garonne).

CHONDRINA AVENACEA (Bruguière 1792)   Pl. 2

Description. 6–8 × 2.3–2.5 mm. Shell cylindro-conical, with 7–8 rather strongly convex whorls. Mouth-edge reflected, rather thin and delicate, white, discontinuous across the parietal region. Teeth: angular prominent; parietal deeply-set and less conspicuous; 3 distinctly developed short palatals (suprapalatal vestigial or absent), only the upper palatal reaching the outer lip; palatal teeth placed opposite to the columellar and parietal teeth (cf. *C. clienta*). Shell dark greyish- or reddish-brown, not glossy, almost smooth, with faint irregular growth-lines only.

Habitat. Dry open calcareous places; especially characteristic of rock faces and walls. Attaining over 2000 m in the Swiss Alps.

Range. W. European and Alpine.

Distribution. Map 68. Widespread but local: S. and E. France, S. Belgium, Luxemburg, Switzerland, S. and C. Germany as far east as Thuringia (Hörselberg); occasionally recorded as an adventive elsewhere.

Chondrina avenacea × 6

C. megacheilos × 6

CHRONDRINA MEGACHEILOS (Cristofori & Jan 1832)

Description. 6–12 × 2.5–4 mm. Shell resembling *C. avenacea* but frequently much larger, with a more strongly conical outline; mouth-edge thicker and more strongly reflected. Mouth usually with *4* palatal teeth, not generally reaching the outer lip, the infrapalatal about as strong as the suprapalatal but weaker than in *C. avenacea*; often a basal tooth.

Habitat. Dry open calcareous places, among rocks; mainly above 1000 m.
Range. S. Alpine.
Distribution. Map 69. S. Switzerland (Ticino) only.

CHONDRINA BIGORRIENSIS (Des Moulins 1835)

Description. 7–9 × 2.5–2.8 mm. Shell cylindro-conical, with about 8 well-rounded whorls, the last sometimes becoming somewhat flattened and shouldered. Mouth often rather pointed below; mouth-edge moderately thickened and reflected, but not flat (cf. *C. tenuimarginata*), discontinuous across the parietal region. Mouth with about 8 teeth: 3 rather short, strong palatals *reaching to the outer lip*; also usually a small and deeply-set suprapalatal. Shell reddish-brown, with very fine regular ribbing, sometimes becoming feebler and less regular on the last whorl.
Habitat. Open rocky places; mainly montane, extending up to 2000 m.
Range. N. Pyrenean.
Distribution. Map 70. Fairly common in the French Pyrenees from Ariège to the Atlantic.

Chondrina bigorriensis × 6

C. tenuimarginata × 6

CHONDRINA TENUIMARGINATA (Des Moulins 1835)

Syn. *C. bigorriensis* var. *tenuimarginata* Des Moulins

Description. 8–14 × 3–4 mm. Shell similar to *C. bigorriensis*, but larger and more conical, with a rather narrower spire and sharper apex; mouth-edge thicker, and reflected sharply to form a *flat* white lip, discontinuous in the parietal region. Teeth similar to *C. bigorriensis*, but with an additional *small deeply-set sutural tooth* (usually only visible in oblique view); colour of shell usually paler.
Habitat. Open rocky places; mainly montane, extending up to 1700 m.
Range. S. Pyrenean.
Distribution. Map 71. Very rare in the French Pyrenees (common on the Spanish side): a few spots in Basses Pyrénées (St Jean-de-Luz) and Hautes Pyrénées only.

CHONDRINA CLIENTA (Westerlund 1883)

Description. 5.5–6.5 × 2.5 m. Shell rather similar to *C. avenacea*, but smaller and more conical, with about 7 moderately convex whorls. Mouth-edge reflected, rather delicate, white, discontinuous across the parietal area. Teeth broadly as in *C. avenacea*, but only 2 *distinctly developed palatals* present (upper and lower palatal), placed *opposite to the interspaces* between the columellar and parietal teeth; remaining palatals vestigial. Shell dark greyish- or reddish-brown, not glossy, with strong, rather irregular growth-ridges.

Habitat. Dry open places on calcareous rocks and screes; mainly montane.

Range. E. Alpine and S.E. European.

Distribution. Map 72. Easternmost Switzerland; S. Germany (S. Bavaria from the Allgäuer Alps to Berchtesgaden, and in the Franconian Jura); S. Sweden (mainly on Öland and Gotland).

Chondrina clienta × 6

C. centralis × 6

C. ascendens × 6

CHONDRINA ASCENDENS (Westerlund 1878)

Description. 6.5–8.5 × 2.5–3 mm. Shell conical, with 7–8 moderately convex whorls. Mouth well rounded below; mouth-edge rather thick, white, sharply reflected, discontinuous across the parietal area. Teeth *very reduced*: usually a feeble angular and a columellar, sometimes traces of other teeth. Shell brown, rather glossy and translucent, almost smooth, with fine, somewhat irregular growth-lines.

Habitat. Open rocky places; montane.

Range. Pyrenean.

Distribution. Map 73. Local in Basses Pyrénées, Hautes Pyrénées, Haute Garonne, Ariège.

CHONDRINA CENTRALIS (Fagot 1891)

Description. 5.5–6.5 × 2.5–2.7 mm. Shell conical, with about 7 strongly rounded whorls. Mouth-edge rather thickened but not markedly reflected. Mouth with about 6 teeth: angular, continuous internally with a distinct spiral; parietal; 2 columellar; 2

palatal (often also a vestigial suprapalatal). Shell pale brown, rather translucent, with diagnostic sculpture of *strong, blunt, widely-spaced* ribs.

Habitat. Open rocky places; between 1000 and 1700 m.

Range. W.C. Pyrenean.

Distribution. Map 74. Very rare: a few spots in Hautes and Basses Pyrénées only.

Family **PUPILLIDAE**

In this family the shell is generally oval or sub-cylindrical, similar to the Vertiginidae but larger (commonly 2.5–5 mm). The mouth-edge is often thickened or reflected, and the mouth may be furnished with teeth (an angular is often found), although in many species these are reduced or even absent. The animal has a pair of short anterior tentacles (unlike the Vertiginidae) and the penis is characterized by complex accessory organs.

The Pupillidae are world-wide. Many species are ovo-viviparous.

*PUPILLA MUSCORUM (Linné 1758)

Syn. *Pupa marginata* Draparnaud

Description. 3–4 × 1.7 mm. Shell cylindrical tending towards ovoid, with 6–7 feebly convex whorls, the last often a little narrower than the penultimate. Mouth rounded; mouth-edge thickened internally, discontinuous across the parietal area, hardly reflected; a very distinct white rib present externally just behind outer lip. Mouth sometimes without teeth, but usually furnished with a small white parietal denticle. Shell brown, not glossy, slightly translucent, almost smooth, with fine growth-lines only.

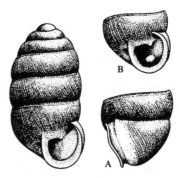

Pupilla muscorum × 11   A, typical form   B, form *bigranata*

This is a variable species: frequently an additional palatal denticle is present (form *bigranata* Rossmässler) and sometimes also a columellar denticle. The form *bigranata*, which usually has a smaller and thicker shell, is regarded by some authors as a distinct species.

Habitat. Dry exposed calcareous places: screes, stone walls, short-turfed grass-land; characteristic of coastal dunes. Attaining 1500 m in the Alps.
Range. Holarctic.
Distribution. Map 75. Common throughout in suitable habitats, becoming local and mainly coastal in Scandinavia, N. Britain and Ireland, Iceland.

PUPILLA ALPICOLA (Charpentier 1837)
Syn. *P. madida* (Gredler)
Description. 2.8–3.3 × 1.8 mm. Shell closely similar to *P. muscorum*, but outline relatively broader and more nearly cylindrical, with a flatter apex; whorls more strongly convex. Mouth without teeth or with a small parietal denticle only. Mouth-edge rather delicate, slightly reflected; external rib behind outer lip very weakly developed or absent. Shell thinner and more translucent than *P. muscorum*, with rather more obvious growth-lines.
Habitat. Marshes and boggy places in mountains, sometimes associated with *Vertigo genesii*. Mainly above 1000 m, attaining 2700 m (Valais).
Range. Alpine.
Distribution. Map 76. French and Swiss high Alps, and a few localities in the calcareous Alps of S. Bavaria.

Pupilla alpicola × 11   *P. triplicata* × 11

PUPILLA TRIPLICATA (Studer 1820)
Description. 2.2–2.8 (occasionally 4) × 1.4 mm. Shell cylindrical, with 6–7 strongly convex whorls. A distinct white rib present a little behind the outer lip, separated from the slightly expanded lip margin by a deep groove. Mouth usually with 3 teeth (parietal, columellar, palatal), *more lamella-like* than in any form of *P. muscorum*; palatal tooth usually visible through the translucency of the shell as a white *line*. Shell pale reddish-brown, very closely and finely striated, giving it a characteristic silky appearance.
Habitat. Very dry exposed calcareous places; often abundant on limestone screes with xerophilic vegetation. Mainly montane, between 300 and 1000 m.
Range. Alpine and E. European.
Distribution. Map 77. Pyrenees; French and Swiss calcareous Alps and Jura; a few isolated sites further north in France (S. Alsace; lower Meuse valley) and Germany (S. Franconian Jura).

PUPILLA STERRI (Voith 1838)

Description. 2.8–3.5 × 1.6 mm. Shell cylindrical, larger and relatively broader than *P. triplicata*, with 6–7 very strongly convex whorls, the last usually a little wider than the penultimate. A moderately strong white rib present a little behind the outer lip. Mouth usually with 2 teeth: 1 parietal, 1 palatal, less lamella-like than in *P. triplicata*. Shell with distinctive sculpture of relatively coarse growth-ridges, giving a well-marked striated appearance; a brown periostracum is often rather evident.

Habitat. Very dry exposed calcareous places, among rocks, screes, short-turfed grassland. Mainly montane, attaining 2800 m (Valais).

Range. C. and E. European.

Distribution. Map 78. French and Swiss calcareous Alps and Jura; Alpine fore-land of S. Bavaria; Belgium (Meuse valley); scattered localities in mountains of C. Germany, as far east as Thuringia and the Franconian Jura.

Pupilla sterri × 11   *Leiostyla anglica* × 11

*LEIOSTYLA ANGLICA (Wood 1828)

Syns. *Lauria anglica* (Wood), *Pupa ringens* Jeffreys

Description. 3–3.7 × 1.9 mm. Shell ovoid, rather conical, with 6 very feebly convex whorls. Mouth narrowed below; mouth-edge white and strongly thickened, especially in the middle of the outer lip where there is a marked inward swelling. Mouth with up to about 6 lamella-like teeth: a prominent angular, continuous with the top of the outer lip; 1 parietal, 1 columellar, 1 palatal, the last showing externally as a white line near the base of the last whorl. Shell dark reddish-brown, not glossy, with feeble growth-lines only.

Habitat. Damp places in woods, and in marshes.

Range. W. European Atlantic (mainly British Isles)

Distribution. Maps 79. Common in Ireland; local in N. and W. Britain, the Channel Islands, and W. France (Île de Ré).

*LAURIA CYLINDRACEA (da Costa 1778)

Syns. *Pupa umbilicata* Draparnaud, *P. anconostoma* Lowe

Description. 3–4.4 × 1.8 mm. Shell ovoid, with 6–7 moderately convex whorls, the last with a strong basal crest. Mouth-edge a little thickened, sharply reflected at right angles to form a *flat white lip*. An angular tooth is normally present, linked to the top of the outer lip and continued internally as a fine spiral lamella. In juveniles there is also a columellar lamella, and a series of very delicate transverse palatal ridges, showing as radial white lines through the base of the shell; these are resorbed in the adult. Shell pale brown, translucent, rather glossy, with feeble growth-lines only.

This is a variable species: the angular tooth may be absent, the reflected lip may be poorly developed, and the shape may vary from tall cylindrical to stumpy conical.

Habitat. Woods, rocks, grassland; not usually in very wet places. Often abundant under ivy on stone walls.

Range. W. European and Mediterranean.

Distribution. Map 80. Commonest near the Atlantic: British Isles, France, Belgium; coasts of Holland, N. Germany, Denmark, Sweden, Norway to 64°N (isolated in Lofoten Islands); also in W. Switzerland and a few places along the middle Rhine valley.

Lauria sempronii × 11

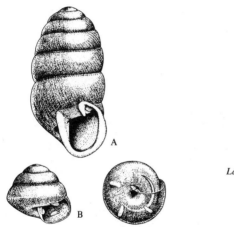

L. cylindracea × 11 A, adult B, juvenile, frontal and basal views

LAURIA SEMPRONII (Charpentier 1837)

Description. 3–3.2 × 1.5 mm. Shell similar to *L. cylindracea*, but smaller and narrower; whorls fewer (5–6) and more rounded so that the basal crest is absent or feebly developed. Mouth-edge reflected as in *L. cylindracea* but lip narrower and more delicate. Angular tooth either very small and denticle-like, or completely absent, never linked to outer lip. Shell pale reddish-brown, delicate and translucent, more glossy than in *L. cylindracea*.

Habitat. Woods, rocks, old walls; mainly montane, but rare above 1000 m.

Range. Alpine and S. European.

Distribution. Map 81. S. and E. France (mainly Pyrenees and Alps); S. Switzerland (Valais, Ticino); one locality in S. England (Gloucestershire, possibly extinct).

ARGNA FERRARII (Porro 1838)

Syn. *Agardhia ferrarii* (Porro)

Description. 4–5 × 1.8 mm. Shell almost perfectly cylindrical, with a low domed apex and 9–10 very flat-sided whorls; a strong basal crest present, surrounding a deep open umbilicus. Mouth narrow, rather pointed above and below; mouth-edge white, thickened and sharply reflected, with a strong denticle-like swelling on the inside of the outer lip. Mouth with 4 principal teeth; 1 parietal, 1 columellar, 2 palatal, all set well back from the mouth-edge. Shell pale golden-brown, slightly translucent, with very distinct regular ribbing, characteristic of this species.

Note that other species of *Argna* live in Mediterranean France and in the eastern Alps, and might be found just within our area.

Habitat. Moist places in woods and among rocks.

Range. S. Alpine.

Distribution. Map 82. S. Switzerland (Ticino) only.

Argna ferrarii × 11

Family **VALLONIIDAE**

The members of this world-wide family are very diverse in shell form, which allows of no simple characterization; they are united only by certain peculiarities of the genital anatomy. The N.W. European species fall into two groups:

Subfamily Valloniinae (*Vallonia*)

Shell small (2–3 mm), whitish, discoidal, with a rounded periphery and a large open umbilicus. Mouth round; mouth-edge more or less strongly expanded to form a flat lip.

These are snails of open grassy habitats; their shells often occur in large numbers in the flood rubbish of rivers.

Subfamily Acanthinulinae (*Acanthinula, Spermodea, Planogyra, Zoogenetes*)

Shell small (2–4 mm), brown, usually top-shaped or squatly conical and with a narrow umbilicus. Mouth-edge scarcely thickened or expanded. There is a distinctive sculpture of widely-spaced sharp narrow ribs, developed largely in the periostracum only.

These are mainly snails of moist woodland habitats.

Subfamily VALLONIINAE

*VALLONIA COSTATA (Müller 1774)

Syns. *V. helvetica* Sterki, *V. jurassica* Geyer

Description. br. 2.2–2.7 mm. Shell discoidal, with a nearly flat spire; 3¼ whorls, often slightly shouldered; umbilicus very broad. Mouth almost circular, oblique; mouth-edge sharply reflected to form a strong, pure-white flange-like lip. Shell greyish-white, slightly translucent, with a sculpture of rather regularly-spaced sharp ribs, often giving a characteristic sparkle to fresh shells (the ribs are partly in the periostracum, and are less easily seen in weathered shells).

Habitat. Dry open calcareous places: screes, stone walls, short-turfed grassland, sand-dunes; occasionally in dry open woods; rarely in marshes.

Range. Holarctic.

Distribution. Map 83. Widespread, becoming rare and largely coastal in N. Britain and Scandinavia (to 70°N in Norway)

Vallonia costata × 9

VALLONIA SUEVICA Geyer 1908

Description. br. 2.2–2.5 mm. Shell closely similar to *V. costata* in shape and size, but *without ribs*; whorls less shouldered, and the last ¼ whorl a little more expanded towards the lip. Shell very finely and closely striated, giving a silky or waxy appearance.

Habitat. Dry grassland; found more commonly in the flood rubbish of rivers.

Range and distribution. Map 84. Apparently endemic in S.W. Germany (Württemberg): rare, living mainly in a few places in the valley of the Neckar; also recorded from the Ammer, Kocher, Tauber, Nagold and upper Danube valleys.

Vallonia suevica × 9

*VALLONIA PULCHELLA (Müller 1774)

Description. br. 2–2.5 mm. Shell discoidal, with 3¼ well-rounded (not shouldered) whorls, enlarging in an even and regular spiral, giving a rather circular outline to the shell. Mouth-edge abruptly reflected to form a white flange-like lip, weaker and more delicate than in *V. costata*. Shell pale, translucent, rather glossy, with only faint and irregular growth-lines.

Habitat. Open calcareous habitats, usually in wetter places than *V. costata* or *V. excentrica*: moist meadows, marshes, sand-dunes; occasionally in dry grassland or on screes; not in woods.

Range. Holarctic.

Distribution. Map 85. Widespread, becoming rare in N. Britain and Scandinavia (to 71°N in Norway); Iceland (probably introduced).

Vallonia pulchella × 9

VALLONIA ENNIENSIS (Gredler 1856)

Syns. *V. pulchella* var. *enniensis* Gredler, *V. costellata* Sandberger

Description. br. 2.2–2.5 mm. Shell almost exactly similar to *V. pulchella* in shape and size, but with sculpture of closely-spaced, *very regular fine ribs*, about 50–60 on the last whorl (much closer than in any form of *V. costata*).

Habitat. Exclusively in wet places, mainly in calcareous marshes.

Range. C. and S. European.

Distribution. Map 86. Rare: a few spots in S. and E. Germany, S. Sweden, Switzerland (Geneva basin).

Vallonia enniensis × 9

*VALLONIA EXCENTRICA Sterki 1892

Syn. *V. pulchella* var. *excentrica* Sterki

Description. br. 2–2.2 mm. Shell rather similar to *V. pulchella*, but usually smaller (about 3 whorls) and with the last ¼-whorl expanding noticeably, producing a distinctly *elliptical* outline; profile of the last whorl as viewed from above running *smoothly into the mouth-edge* (i.e., lip not reflected sharply almost through a right

Vallonia excentrica × 9

angle as in *V. pulchella*). Shell pale and translucent, glossy, with faint growth-lines only.

Habitat. Open, usually dry calcareous places: short-turfed grassland, screes, sand-dunes; not normally in woods or marshes.

Range. Holarctic.

Distribution. Map 87. Widespread, but rare in northern Britain and scarcely beyond 60°N in Scandinavia.

VALLONIA DECLIVIS Sterki 1892

Syn. *V. adela* of many authors, *non* Westerlund

Description. br. 2.6–3 mm. Shell larger than other N.W. European species, with 3¾ well-rounded whorls, increasing in a very even and regular spiral. Mouth-edge only slightly thickened and reflected, *without a strong flat lip*. Shell pale and translucent, rather silky in appearance, growth-lines moderately pronounced.

Habitat. Moist open grassland; found more commonly as dead shells in the flood rubbish of rivers.

Range. C. European.

Distribution. Map 88. Germany: living in a few places in the river valleys of S. Swabia; elsewhere known mainly as dead shells in scattered localities in C. and S. Germany and in the Swiss Jura.

Vallonia declivis × 9

Subfamily ACANTHINULINAE

*ACANTHINULA ACULEATA (Müller 1774)

Description. 2 × 2 mm. Shell conical, with 4 well-rounded whorls, umbilicus narrow but deep. Mouth almost round; mouth-edge slightly thickened, hardly expanded. In fresh shells there is a thick brown periostracum, raised into regular, sharp lamella-like ribs bearing a row of flexible *spines* a little above the periphery of

the whorls (in weathered shells the spines are lost, but faint traces of the ribs can usually be seen).
Habitat. Woods, hedgerows, scrub; in leaf litter and under fallen timber; occasionally in more open habitats. Attaining about 1500 m in the Alps.
Range. W. Palaearctic.
Distribution. Map 89. Widespread, but scarcely beyond about 62°N in Scandinavia.

Acanthinula aculeata × 11   *Spermodea lamellata* × 11

*SPERMODEA LAMELLATA (Jeffreys 1830)

Syn. *Acanthinula lamellata* (Jeffreys)
Description. 2 × 2 mm. Shell beehive-shaped, domed above and rather flattened below, with 5½–6 well-rounded whorls, a little shouldered towards the suture. Umbilicus distinct but very narrow. Mouth-edge delicate and unthickened. Shell pale golden-brown, slightly translucent, with a characteristic sculpture of exceedingly regularly-spaced sharp periostracal ribs, giving an iridescent appearance to the naked eye.
Habitat. Old native deciduous woods, in leaf litter and under fallen timber.
Range. N.W. European Atlantic.
Distribution. Map 90. Widespread but very local in Ireland and N. Britain; Norway (to 64°N, mainly coastal), southernmost Sweden, Denmark, near North Sea and Baltic coasts of Germany; relic outposts in Holland (probably extinct) and S.E. England.

PLANOGYRA SORORCULA (Benoit 1857)

Syn. *Spelaeodiscus astoma* (Boettger)
Description. br. 2.3–2.6 mm. Shell discoidal, spire slightly raised, with 4 well-rounded whorls. Umbilicus broad and deep. Mouth almost circular; mouth-edge simple, thin and brittle. Shell pale yellow, slightly translucent, with delicate and rather regularly-spaced ribs separated by an *extremely regular fine striation*; also a hint of spiral striation under high magnifications.

Planogyra sororcula × 9

This species somewhat resembles an immature *Vallonia costata*, but the fine sculpture is diagnostically different.

Habitat. Rocks and screes, mainly montane.

Range. S.E. European.

Distribution. Map 91. Apparently rare: known at present only from a few places above 1000 m in the mountains of Isère, E. of Clelles, France.

Microsculpture of shell of *Planogyra sororcula*

Zoogenetes harpa × 11

ZOOGENETES HARPA (Say 1824)

Syn. *Acanthinula harpa* (Say)

Description. 3–4 × 2.4–3 mm. Shell conical, with 3½–4 moderately rounded whorls, often a little flattened at the sides. Mouth almost round; mouth-edge delicate and unthickened, not expanded. Shell poorly calcified, pale brown, the periostracum raised into fine lamella-like ridges (weaker and less regularly-spaced than in *Acanthinula aculeata*), giving a rather waxy iridescence to the naked eye.

Habitat. Coniferous woods, often on non-calcareous soils with *Vaccinium*. Attaining 2100 m in the Alps.

Range. Circumpolar Holarctic, and high Alpine.

Distribution. Map 92. Common throughout most of Scandinavia (absent from coastal regions of the W. and S.); Öland and Gotland; very rare in Switzerland (Riffelalp and near Sion, Valais).

Family ENIDAE

In the Enidae the shell is of moderate size (commonly 8–20 mm), elongate, generally conical or sub-cylindrical, with numerous rather flat-sided whorls, and is usually brown and rather smooth. The mouth-edge is expanded and often thickened, and the mouth may contain teeth, which are characteristically developed as blunt swellings on the lip.

This large family is mostly Palaearctic.

CHONDRULA TRIDENS (Müller 1774)   **Pl. 3**
Description. 9–12 (occasionally 14) × 4–4.5 mm. Shell cylindro-conical, with 7–8
feebly convex whorls. Mouth-edge strongly thickened, reflected to form a flat white
lip, with only a thin callus across the parietal area. Mouth with 3 principal teeth: 1
parietal, 1 columellar, 1 outer, the last formed as a strong denticle-like thickening on
the lip; frequently there is also a small angular denticle. Shell rather thick and
opaque, pale reddish-brown, not glossy, with weak irregular growth-lines only.
Habitat. Dry open calcareous places, especially in short-turfed grassland; less
commonly in rocky habitats. Rare above 700 m.
Range. C. and E. European.
Distribution. Map 93. S. and E. France, Luxemburg, Switzerland, C. and S.W.
Germany.

JAMINIA QUADRIDENS (Müller 1774)   **Pl. 3**
Syn. *Chondrula quadridens* (Müller)
Description. 7–12 (occasionally 15) × 3.5–4 mm. Shell cylindro-conical, *sinistral*,
with 7–9 whorls, the later whorls virtually flat-sided. Mouth-edge thickened, white,
moderately reflected. Mouth with 4 teeth: 1 parietal, 2 columellar, 1 outer. Shell
rather thick and opaque, pale brown, not very glossy, with faint growth-lines only.
Habitat. Very dry exposed places, especially among calcareous rocks and screes,
less commonly in grassland. Attaining over 2000 m in the Alps.
Range. Mediterranean and W. European.
Distribution. Map 94. France (mainly S. and S.E.), Luxemburg, Switzerland, West
Germany (local in the upper and middle Rhine valley).

*ENA MONTANA (Draparnaud 1801)   **Pl. 3**
Description. 14–17 × 6–7 mm. Shell ovoid-conical, with 7–8 rather flat whorls.
Mouth-edge pinkish-white, slightly thickened and reflected, lip replaced by a thin
callus in the parietal area. Shell brown, not very glossy, with the growth-ridges
crossed by fine irregular spiral striae, producing a granular or shagreened texture.
Habitat. Old woodland, under ground litter or among rocks; in wet weather climb-
ing tree trunks (especially beech); less commonly in hedgerows or old scrub.
Mainly montane, attaining over 2000 m in the Alps.
Range. C. European and Alpine.
Distribution. Map 95. Widespread in the Pyrenees, Alps, Jura, Vosges, mountains
of C. and S. Germany; rare and local further north: S. England, Belgium, N.E.
Germany, S. Sweden (Jönköping).

*ENA OBSCURA (Müller 1774)   **Pl. 3**
Description. 8.5–9 × 3.7 mm. Shell similar to *E. montana*, but much smaller, with
6½–7 whorls. Mouth-edge pure white, reflected, lip discontinuous in the parietal
area. Shell brown, not very glossy, with fine, rather irregular growth-lines. The
shell, especially when juvenile, may be covered with a crust of soil hardened by
mucus, making it difficult to see.
Habitat. Woods, hedgerows, walls, shaded rocky places; climbing bare surfaces in
wet weather. Attaining over 2000 m in the Alps.
Range. European.
Distribution. Map 96. Widespread, becoming local in Scotland and Ireland and
generally scarce across the N. European plain; in Scandinavia hardly beyond 60°N;
Åland Islands in Finland.

ZEBRINA   DETRITA (Müller 1774)   **Pl. 3**
Syn. *Ena detrita* (Müller)
Description. 12–25 × 8–12 mm. Shell ovoid-conical, with 6½–7 feebly convex
whorls. Mouth-edge white, a little thickened and reflected, lip usually discontinuous in the parietal area. Shell solid and rather shiny, greyish-white or cream, with a
highly variable and irregular patterning of *transverse reddish stripes*, often more
translucent than the paler areas between them. Growth-lines rather coarse and
irregular, crossed by very fine spiral striations on the early whorls.
Habitat. Dry exposed places, mainly on calcareous soils: screes, open grasslands,
vineyards. Attaining about 1600 m in the Alps.
Range. S. European.
Distribution. Map 97. S. and S.E. France; Switzerland; S.W. and C. Germany as
far north as Düsseldorf, the Harz, and Thuringia (also formerly near Berlin);
occasionally as an adventive elsewhere (Belgium, England).

Family **ENDODONTIDAE**

This is a very large and ancient family, occurring in all parts of the world. The
anatomy shows several primitive features, notably a jaw made of separate plates
(sometimes incompletely fused together, as in *Discus*) and simple genitalia without
accessory organs. The shell is minute to medium-sized (rarely more than 10 mm),
generally discoidal with a large shallow umbilicus, and usually brown and with
well-marked transverse striation or ribbing. The mouth-edge is neither thickened
nor expanded, and the mouth generally lacks teeth.
    Endodontids are characteristic of moist, shaded habitats.

*PUNCTUM   PYGMAEUM (Draparnaud 1801)
Description. br. 1.2–1.5 mm. Shell minute, discoidal, with 3½ moderately convex
whorls; suture deep, somewhat channelled. Umbilicus large and open. Mouth
rounded, mouth-edge thin and brittle, not reflected. Shell golden-brown, with
numerous extremely fine regular growth-ridges, giving a characteristic sheen.
Habitat. A wide variety of moderately moist and well vegetated places, especially
common in leaf litter in deciduous woods; also in marshes.
Range. Holarctic.
Distribution. Map 98. Common nearly throughout.

Punctum pygmaeum × 11

*HELICODISCUS   SINGLEYANUS (Pilsbry 1890)
Description. br. 1.8–2.5 mm. Shell discoidal, spire nearly flat; with 3½–4 well-
rounded whorls, slowly and regularly increasing. Suture rather deep, slightly

Helicodiscus singleyanus × 9

channelled. Umbilicus very broad and open. Mouth-edge simple, unthickened. Shell pale yellowish-brown, thin, translucent, rather glossy, with faint irregular growth-lines and sometimes a hint of spiral striation under high magnification.

Most European finds have been referred to the N. American subspecies *H. singleyanus inermis* Baker, distinguished from the type by its smaller size and virtual absence of spiral striae.

Habitat. Little known: found in a variety of lowland habitats from damp to dry, usually as dead shells; probably subterranean.

Range. N. American and European.

Distribution. Map 99. Rare: a very few localities in S. Britain, the Channel Islands, Holland, Belgium, Switzerland, East Germany; also occasionally in greenhouses.

DISCUS RUDERATUS (Férussac 1821)   Pl. 3
Syn. *Goniodiscus ruderatus* (Férussac)

Description. br. 5.5–7 mm. Shell discoidal, spire slightly raised; with 4–4½ moderately convex whorls, only very faintly keeled at the periphery; suture rather shallow. Umbilicus wide and deep. Mouth rounded; mouth-edge delicate, unthickened, not reflected. Shell a uniform yellowish or greenish-brown, not glossy, with numerous strong regularly-spaced ribs.

Habitat. Woods (mainly coniferous), especially under logs and bark; also marshes and moist grassland. In the Alps mainly between 1000 and 2500 m.

Range. Holarctic (in Europe Boreal and Alpine)

Distribution. Map 100. Common throughout Norway, Sweden, Finland; also in the Pyrenees (rare), Alps and Jura, and in scattered localities in the mountains of S. and C. Germany; very occasionally in the N. German plain.

*DISCUS ROTUNDATUS (Müller 1774)   Pl. 3
Syn. *Goniodiscus rotundatus* (Müller)

Description. br. 5.5–7 mm. Shell somewhat similar to *D. ruderatus*, but distinctly keeled at the periphery and usually flatter, with 5½–6 narrower and more tightly coiled whorls. Ribbing a little coarser than in *D. ruderatus*. Shell pale yellowish-brown, with *reddish-brown transverse stripes* at regular intervals.

Habitat. Moist sheltered places of all kinds: woods, under ground litter and stones, in damp herbage; often among rubbish in gardens. Attaining 2700 m in Switzerland (Graubünden).

Range. W. and C. European.

Distribution. Map 101. Common throughout, as far as southernmost Scandinavia, where it has been spread by man (in Finland in gardens and greenhouses only).

DISCUS PERSPECTIVUS (Mühlfeldt 1816) **Pl. 3**
Syn. *Goniodiscus perspectivus* (Mühlfeldt)
Description. br. 5.5–6.5 mm. Shell extremely flat and compressed, with 5½–6 virtually flush whorls; keel very sharp and prominent, outlined on the under surface by a *shallow groove* running parallel to it. Mouth rhomboidal. Umbilicus much wider than in *D. ruderatus* or *D. rotundatus*. Shell a uniform pale yellowish or greenishbrown, not glossy, with numerous regularly-spaced ribs.
Habitat. Ground litter in calcareous woodland; montane.
Range. E. Alpine, Carpathian and Balkan.
Distribution. Map 102. S.E. Bavaria (calcareous Alps and Bavarian Forest); a few isolated sites west to S. Swabia and north to the Franconian Jura.

Family **ARIONIDAE**

Slugs with an internal shell which is usually degenerate (a few calcareous granules in some). None have a keel, and all have a caudal mucus gland just above the tip of the tail. The mantle is shagreened but not grooved. The respiratory pore is in front of the mid-point of the mantle.

Distribution Holarctic, but typical members of the family (subfamily Arioninae) are virtually confined to Europe. All but one of our species belong to the genus *Arion*. They are generally herbivorous, although not averse to rubbish and carrion, and some, e.g. *Arion hortensis* (Plate 5) are pests. Amongst the species in this genus is the ubiquitous big black slug *Arion ater* (Plate 4) which is, in fact, one of the most variable of all slugs in colour.

Most species of *Arion* in our area are identifiable on external characters, but new work by specialists is showing that many so-called species are aggregates of several closely related species. We have only given details of these where the characters separating the new forms are clear, and where the nomenclature is generally agreed. Internal characters of use in confirming the trickier determinations are given on p. 106.

One species is in a separate genus: *Geomalacus maculosus* (Plate 4). Unlike all the *Arion* species, it is spotted. It is found only in S.W. Ireland (and again in N. Spain and Portugal), but there are old records from Brittany. It is a classic example of a species with an extreme Atlantic or 'Lusitanian' distribution.

*GEOMALACUS MACULOSUS Allman 1843 **Pl. 4**
Description. Medium to large slug, extended length 6–9 cm. Body dark greenishgrey, paling towards the foot-fringe, and spotted with white or yellow, tubercles small and elongated. There are two slightly darker lateral bands on each side, most conspicuous in juveniles, and which are less spotted with white. Mantle likewise marbled with white spots, posterior tentacles short and grey. Sole creamy-white, mucus colourless to milky. Some paler varieties occur. Noticeably flattened above when at rest, and often rolls into a ball when molested, unlike other Arionidae.
Habitat. Lichen-covered rocks in open country and on moss and lichen encrusted trees in woods. Very hard to find in dry weather.
Range. Lusitanian.
Distribution. Map 103. Locally common in extreme S.W. Ireland. Also recorded in Brittany (last record 1868).

*ARION   ATER (Linné 1758)   **Pl. 4**
Syns. *A. rufus* (Linné), *A. empiricorum* Férussac
Description. Very large slug, extended length 10–15 (rarely 20) cm. Very variable in
colour, completely black specimens being commonest in north of range, but also
brick-red, orange, and grey. The foot-fringe is often paler and redder than body.
Dark lateral bands are usually present only in small juveniles, but occasionally
persist in adults. Tubercles large and elongate. When contracted and irritated,
may rock from side to side for some time.
    There is also considerable variation in internal anatomy, and two subspecies
Arion ater ater and *Arion ater rufus* may be distinguished. They are regarded by
some as separate species. Neither colour nor locality are reliable guides as to which
is present – internal characters of both are shown on p. 107.
Similar species. *A. lusitanicus* is usually smaller (up to *c*. 10 cm) but has a similar
range of colour variants (never black). It is often banded. See also internal features
p. 107.
Habitat. Very catholic – grassland, moors, hedges, woods and gardens, even on
the most acid terrain. Up to *c*. 1800 m in Alps and Pyrenees.
Range. W. and C. European.
Distribution. Map 104. Common, except in Scandinavia; mainly coastal in Norway, in Sweden to about 61°N., not in Finland (*A. ater rufus* in greenhouses). *A.
ater rufus* tends to be more southerly in distribution than *A. ater ater*.

*ARION   LUSITANICUS Mabille 1868   **Pl. 4**
Description. Medium to large slug, extended length 7–10 cm. Variable in colour:
often dirty grey-green, but often one dark lateral band on each side of the body,
forming a lyre shape on the mantle; sole whitish, mucus colourless. Common
variants are grey or brown in colour, and bands are not always present in the adult.
For internal characters see p. 107.
Similar species. *A. ater*; *A. subfuscus* is smaller (up to 7 cm), has finer tubercles and
yellow or orange body-mucus.
Habitats. Not clearly defined – often in cultivated and waste ground. Generally
very localized north of its original range.
Range. W. and S.W. European.
Distribution. Map 105. Ireland, England, France, Switzerland, S.W. Germany
(Baden-Württemburg). Locally frequent in natural habitats near western coasts,
elsewhere sporadic and mainly spread by man.

*ARION   SUBFUSCUS (Draparnaud 1805)   **Pl. 5**
Description. Medium slug, extended length 5–7 cm. Usually dark brown, with a
single darker longitudinal band on each side, which passes above and below the
respiratory pore, and with small, elongate tubercles. Mantle usually slightly paler
than rest of body. Sole yellowish, body mucus bright yellow (often orange), sole
mucus colourless. This species cannot contract into as hemispherical a shape as
other *Arion* spp. Colour is somewhat variable, with reddish and grey variants quite
common.
    This species, like *A. ater*, shows considerable variation in internal anatomy, and
may possibly include more than one species.
Similar species. *A. lusitanicus*. Unbanded and unicolorous variants may be confused with small *A. ater*, the fine tubercles, and coloured body mucus distinguish

them, as do the poor powers of contraction and absence of the rocking movement when irritated.

Habitats. Very catholic – woods, pastures, gardens, hedges and dunes, up to 2500 m in the Alps.

Range. European.

Distribution. Map 106. Common nearly throughout N.W. Europe.

*ARION FASCIATUS (Nilsson 1823)   Pl. 5

Description. Medium slug, extended length 4–5 cm. Greyish above, becoming paler at the sides, all with a yellow flush most clearly visible just below the dark lateral bands, the right one of which passes above the respiratory pore. Whitish near the foot-fringe. Sole greyish-white, mucus colourless. This species, and the two following have a very slight keel, and are bell shaped in transverse section when contracted.

Similar species. *A. circumscriptus* and *A. silvaticus* (until recently, not always distinguished from *A. fasciatus*) lack the yellow background colour, are usually slightly smaller (to 4 cm) and are also distinguished internally (p. 107). Pale *A. subfuscus* (p. 104) have yellow body slime and a spherical spermatheca.

Habitat. Very catholic, more often associated with gardens and waste ground than *A. circumscriptus* and *A. silvaticus*.

Range. N.W. European.

Distribution. Map 107. Limits uncertain because of confusion with other species (old records not reliable). Most common in the north.

*ARION CIRCUMSCRIPTUS Johnston 1828   Pl. 5

Syn. *A. fasciatus* of many authors (*non* Nilsson)

Description. Small to medium slug, extended length 3–4 cm. Dark grey or occasionally brown, *mantle lightly speckled with black*, lighter towards the foot fringe, with one, thin dark longitudinal band on each side. Sole whitish, mucus colourless.

Similar species. *A. fasciatus*; *A. silvaticus* is paler, has thicker lateral bands, and differs internally (p. 107).

Habitat. Catholic.

Range. European.

Distribution. Map 108. Poorly known, especially due to confusion with *A. silvaticus*. Common in N.W. Europe but absent from C. and N. Scandinavia.

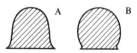

Cross section of   A, *Arion circumscriptus*   B, *A. hortensis*

*ARION SILVATICUS Lohmander 1937   Pl. 5

Syn. *A. fasciatus* of many authors (*non* Nilsson)

Description. Small to medium slug, extended length 3–4 cm. Pale grey above, fading to whitish at the sides, with one broad dark and conspicuous longitudinal band on each side. Sole whitish, mucus colourless.

Similar species. *A. fasciatus* (p. 105). *A. circumscriptus* (p. 105).
Habitat. Catholic.
Range. European.
Distribution. Map 109. As for *A. circumscriptus* above.

*ARION   HORTENSIS Férussac 1819   Pl. 5

Description. At least three distinct forms of this slug are known, and it is clear that
these are different species. All are small, extended length 2.5–3 (rarely 4) cm. Form
'A' is grey to blue-black above, with a single rather indistinct dark band on each
side, bluish tentacles and a blue-black tip to the tail when extended. Sole usually
bright orange. Form 'R' is similar, but more strikingly marked, with mantle-bands
higher, with reddish tentacles and an orange tip to the tail. Form 'B' is usually
brownish rather than blue-black, also with reddish tentacles, coarser tubercles
and a striped tip to the tail. Sole yellow. All forms have yellow-orange body mucus.
Body semicircular in transverse section when contracted.
Habitat. Catholic – gardens, woods, agricultural land (a major pest), with a slight
preference for calcareous or neutral soils. To 2000 m in the Alps.
Range. W. and S. European.
Distribution. Map 110. Widespread, becoming rarer and more restricted to
humanly disturbed sites in the north and east, reaching Iceland and S. Scandinavia
(to 63°N. in Norway). Form 'B' is as yet known only from scattered localities in
Britain and Ireland.

*ARION   INTERMEDIUS Normand 1852   Pl. 5
Syn. *A. minimus* Simroth

Description. Very small slug, extended length *c*.2 cm. Greyish-yellow to white,
with darker head and tentacles, sometimes with faint darker longitudinal bands on
each side. Sole yellowish, mucus yellow. Has a characteristically prickly appearance when contracted due to soft spikes on tubercles. There are a number of
colour variants from white to brown and dark grey.
Habitat. Catholic, in woods, hedges, gardens and pastures, especially on poor
soils.
Range. W. European.
Distribution. Map 111. British Isles, Iceland, W. and C. France, Belgium, Netherlands, N.W. Germany and Denmark – rare in Scandinavia (Norway on coast to
65°N., southernmost Sweden, absent from Finland).

INTERNAL DIAGNOSTIC CHARACTERS OF SOME *ARION* SPECIES

Many species of *Arion* can be identified on external appearance, but internal
features are of use in checking the distinctions between *Arion ater* and *A.
lusitanicus* and between *A. circumscriptus*, *A. fasciatus* and *A. silvaticus*. *Arion* as
a whole is unusual in that the penis is absent, but a stimulating organ or *ligula* is
sometimes present in the atrium. *Arion lusitanicus* differs from *Arion ater* in having
a smaller atrium and a large, swollen oviduct. Typical *A. ater ater* has a smaller
and more symmetrical atrium than *A. ater rufus*. *A. subfuscus*, which may also be
confused with *A. ater,* has an oviduct similar to that of *A. lusitanicus*.

With practice, well-grown *A. circumscriptus, A. fasciatus* and *A. silvaticus* can
be distinguished on external characters, at least in an area one has worked over for

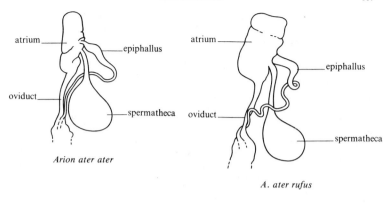

Arion ater ater

A. ater rufus

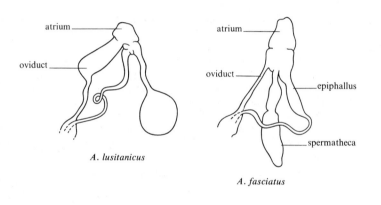

A. lusitanicus

A. fasciatus

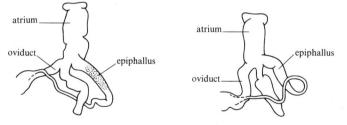

A. circumscriptus

A. silvaticus

Distal genitalia of Arionidae

some time. Internally, *A. fasciatus* has a much narrower oviduct than the other two. *A. circumscriptus* has a heavily pigmented epiphallus, while that of *A. silvaticus* is un- or very slightly pigmented.

Family **VITRINIDAE**

In this family the shell is very thin, glossy, pale and translucent, and consists of a few rapidly expanding whorls. The mouth is relatively extremely large and highly oblique, and the mouth-edge is simple and delicate. There is usually no umbilicus. Frequently there is a membranous uncalcified strip along the lower edge of the mouth. Under high magnification, the apical whorl of the shell may show minute, very regular spirally-arranged pittings.

The body is very large compared to the shell, and is generally not fully retractable. The mantle projects in front of the shell, and also backwards on the right side as a more or less well-developed thin mobile flap (here called the *mantle lobe*), sometimes covering the apex. The anterior tentacles are small and inconspicuous.

The Vitrinidae are Holarctic, and are mostly snails of cool, moist habitats. Some species cannot be named with certainty on external characters alone and dissection may be needed. In spite of the similarity of their shells, their genital anatomy shows strong divergencies. A peculiarity of the species of *Vitrinobrachium* and *Semilimax* is the presence of a blind sac of uncertain function (here called the *penial appendage*) opening into the genitalia at the same level as the penis.

The following table presents a guide to the N.W. European genera:

	Shell shape	Mouth-membrane	Mantle lobe	Penial appendage	Other anatomical peculiarity
Vitrina	rather globular	absent	very small	absent	penis, oviduct and spermatheca duct join at common point (i.e., no vagina)
Vitrino-brachium	strongly ear-like	narrow	very large	present	penis, oviduct and spermatheca duct join at common point (i.e., no vagina)
Semilimax	extremely ear-like	broad	very large	present	penis joins vagina below point of entry of spermatheca duct.
Eucobresia	moderately ear-like	broad or narrow	large	absent	penis joins vagina below point of entry of spermatheca duct; upper part of vagina not strongly swollen.
Phenaco-limax	globular to moderately ear-like	very narrow	small to very large	absent	penis joins vagina below point of entry of spermatheca duct; upper part of vagina strongly swollen

In the following descriptions, figures for breadth refer in all cases to maximum measurable breadth, not to true breadth as normally measured at right angles to the shell axis (cf. figure p. 14).

*VITRINA PELLUCIDA (Müller 1774)   Pl. 6

Syns. *Helicolimax pellucidus* (Müller), *Phenacolimax pellucidus* (Müller)

Description. br. 4.5–6 mm. Shell rather globular, with 2½–3 whorls, the last forming distinctly less than half the total breadth as viewed from above, well-rounded at the periphery. Mouth with no membraneous margin (or with a mere trace only). Umbilicus open, but extremely small. Shell smooth and glossy, very thin and translucent, usually pale greenish.

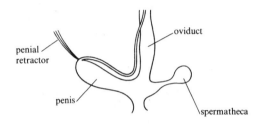

Distal genitalia of *Vitrina pellucida*

Body usually pale grey, with darker head and tentacles; when fully extended, mantle lobe scarcely encroaching over upper surface of shell.

Anatomy. The spermatheca duct, the penis and the oviduct come together virtually at a common point above the atrium. There is no penial appendage.

Habitat. Common in a wide variety of moderately humid places: woods, grassland, among rocks; often abundant in the grassy hollows of coastal sand-dunes.

Range. Holarctic.

Distribution. Map 112. Throughout.

VITRINOBRACHIUM BREVE (Férussac 1821)   Pl. 6

Syn. *Semilimax brevis* (Férussac)

Description. br. 5–5.5 mm. Shell compressed, ear-like, with about 1¾ whorls, the last forming about two-thirds of the total maximum breadth as viewed from above. Mouth-membrane fairly narrow but distinct, extending back less than half a whorl to the base of the columella. Shell glossy, sometimes with faint ripple-like growth-ridges, very translucent, pale greenish.

Body large (10–12 mm) and not retractable, very dark grey or black. Mantle very voluminous, reaching well forward over the neck; mantle lobe reaching back to cover the apex of the shell.

Anatomy. The spermatheca duct, the penis and the oviduct all come together at a common point, and are joined by a large and characteristic penial appendage.

Habitat. Moist open woods, especially on the floodplains of rivers; rare above 1000 m.

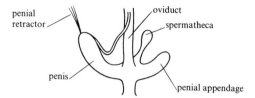

Distal genitalia of *Vitrinobrachium breve*

Range. W.C. European and S. Alpine.

Distribution. Map 113. Local in S.W. Germany from S. Bavaria (Isar valley) to the lower Rhine, extending just into Holland (Gelderland); also in S. Switzerland (Ticino).

SEMILIMAX SEMILIMAX (Férussac 1802)   Pl. 6
Syn. *Vitrinopugio elongatus* (Draparnaud)

Description. br. 4–5 mm. Shell with about 1¾ whorls, the last *extremely* expanded and forming nearly three-quarters of the total maximum breadth as viewed from above, giving a highly elongate appearance. Spire a little raised. Mouth-membrane broad, encroaching considerably on the base of the shell and extending back about two-thirds of a whorl to the columella. Shell glossy, very thin and translucent, pale greenish; growth-lines faint; the spirally arranged pittings on the apical whorl unusually distinct under high magnification.

Body relatively large (12–15 mm), dark grey above, paler below; mantle very voluminous; mantle lobe rather narrow, reaching back to cover apex of shell.

Anatomy. Penis short and sac-like, without a retractor muscle, joining the vagina at a common point with a penial appendage.

Habitat. Mainly woods, in moist shady places under stones and ground litter; principally montane.

Range. Alpine and C. European.

Distribution. Map 114. Pyrenees, Alps and Jura (but scarce in Switzerland); widespread but local in the mountains of S. and C. Germany, as far north as the Harz.

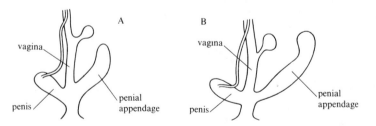

Distal genitalia of   A, *Semilimax semilimax*   B, *S. pyrenaicus*

SEMILIMAX   KOTULAE (Westerlund 1883)   **Pl. 6**
Syn. *S. goeotiformis* (Pollonera)
Description. br. 4.3–6 mm. Shell similar to *S. semilimax* when viewed from above, though with a flatter spire; when viewed from below the mouth-membrane is seen to be considerably broader, extending in a *spiral* much further back, virtually eliminating the columella and allowing the earlier whorls to become *fully visible* almost to the apex. Shell very thin and translucent, even smoother and glossier than *S. semilimax*.
   Body similar to *S. semilimax*.
Anatomy. Penis rather elongate, with a retractor muscle, joining the vagina at a common point with a large complex penial appendage, divided into upper and lower portions.
Habitat. Mainly woods, in cool moist shady places under stones and litter; exclusively montane, attaining 2200 m in Switzerland (Valais).
Range. Alpine and Carpathian.
Distribution. Map 115. Mountains of S. and S.E. Germany (Allgäuer Alps, Bavarian Alps, Bavarian Forest, Fichtelgebirge, Erzgebirge); S. Switzerland (Vaud, Valais).

*SEMILIMAX   PYRENAICUS (Férussac 1821)   **Pl. 6**
Syns. *Vitrina pyrenaica* (Férussac), *Vitrinopugio pyrenaicus* (Férussac), *Vitrina hibernica* Taylor.
Description. 5–6 mm. Shell similar to *S. semilimax*, but spire almost completely flat, with a virtually flush suture; last whorl expanding less strongly, forming no more than about three-fifths of the total breadth as viewed from above. Mouth-membrane shorter than in *S. semilimax*, encroaching less on the base of the shell.
   Body relatively very large and not retractable, pale grey; mantle voluminous, with blackish pigment spots; mantle lobe entirely covering apex of shell.
Anatomy. Broadly similar to *S. semilimax*: penis short, without retractor muscle, joining the vagina at a common point with a glandular, very prominent penial appendage, *much larger* than in *S. semilimax*.
Habitat. Moist shaded places in woods and among rocks.
Range. Pyrenean and Irish.
Distribution. Map 116. French Pyrenees from Ariège to the Atlantic; scattered localities in Ireland from Kerry to Antrim.

EUCOBRESIA   DIAPHANA (Draparnaud 1805)   **Pl. 7**
Syns. *Helicolimax diaphanus* (Draparnaud), *Phenacolimax diaphanus* (Draparnaud)
Description. 6–6.5 mm. Shell with about 2¼ whorls, the last forming rather over half the total maximum breadth as viewed from above, expanding relatively less than in *Semilimax*; spire almost *completely flat*, with a virtually flush suture. Mouth-membrane broad, about a third to half the visible width of the base, extending back about 1 whorl towards the apex; columellar edge of mouth somewhat cut-away so that part of the preceding whorl can be seen. Shell very thin and glossy, growth-lines rather regular and often visible as fine whitish lines.
   Body relatively very large and not retractable; mantle voluminous, dark grey; mantle lobe broad and entirely covering spire.
Anatomy. Penis large, with a retractor muscle, joining the short vagina close to the external pore (i.e., atrium very short); no penial appendage.

Plate 5   **Family ARIONIDAE**
                              See also plate 4
                                (life size)

1. *Arion subfuscus   104
    1a. Typical form, extended: mucus orange, staining the fingers.
    1b. Contracted.
    1c. Grey form, extended.

2. *Arion fasciatus   105
This and the next two species (*A. circumscriptus, A. silvaticus*) have
opaque white soles and are bell-shaped in cross-section (see Fig., p. 105).
    2a. Extended: orange pigment, especially below lateral bands.
    2b. Contracted.

3. *Arion circumscriptus   105
    3a. Extended: grey, mantle finely speckled with black.
    3b. Contracted.
    3c. Sole.

4. *Arion silvaticus   105
    4a. Extended: pale silvery grey, flanks markedly paler than back.
    4b. Contracted.

5. *Arion hortensis *sensu stricto* (form R)   106
The *A. hortensis* species have yellow or orange soles and are semicircular in cross-section (see Fig., p.105).
    5a. Extended.
    5b. Contracted.
    5c. Sole.

6. *Arion hortensis form A   106

7. *Arion hortensis form B   106
    7a. Extended.
    7b. Sole.

8. *Arion intermedius   106
    8a. Extended: small.
    8b. Contracted: prickly appearance.
    8c. Sole: pale greenish-yellow.

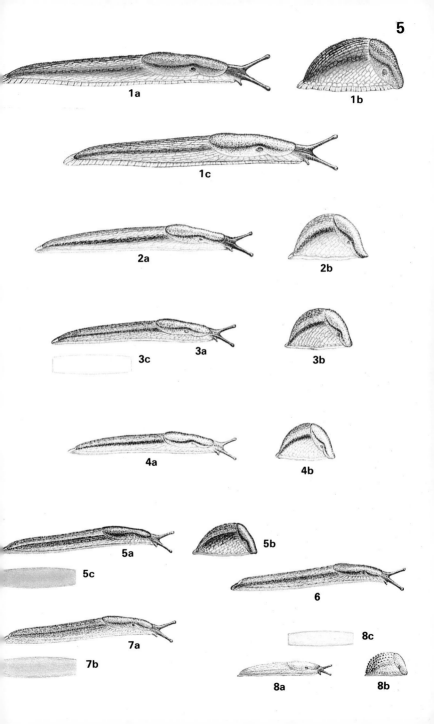

1a 1b 1c 2a 2b 3c 3a 3b 4a 4b 5a 5b 5c 6 7a 7b 8c 8a 8b

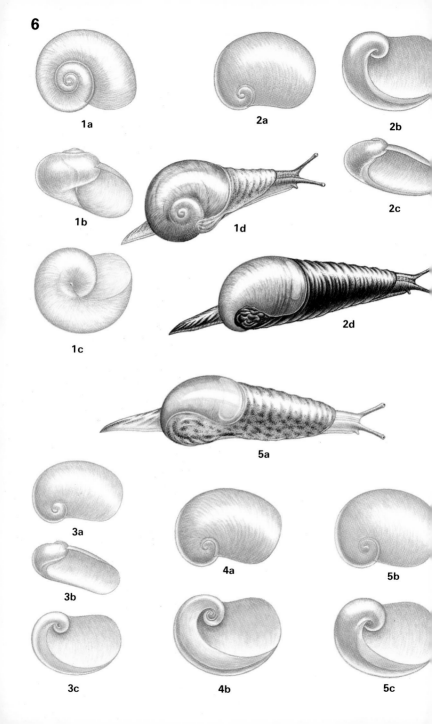

6

1a

2a

2b

1b

1d

2c

1c

2d

5a

3a

4a

5b

3b

3c

4b

5c

Family VITRINIDAE

See also plate 7

($\times 5$)

Plate 6

1.   ***Vitrina pellucida**   109

The commonest vitrinid, nearly ubiquitous.

    1a-c. Shell: relatively globular. Mouth-membrane vestigial or absent.

    1d. Living animal: usually pale.

2.   **Vitrinobrachium breve**   109

Mainly in the Rhine valley.

    2a-c. Shell: very ear-like.

    2d. Living animal: mantle voluminous, jet-black.

3a-c.   **Semilimax semilimax**   110

Mainly S. Germany, montane. The commonest *Semilimax*. Shell small, extremely ear-like.

4a-b.   **Semilimax kotulae**   111

S. Germany, montane. Mouth-membrane very broad, running in a spiral to the apex.

5.   ***Semilimax pyrenaicus**   111

Pyrenees and Ireland only.

    5a. Living animal: mantle voluminous, spotted with black.

    5b-c. Shell.

Habitat. Moderately moist places: woods, herbage, among rocks; principally montane, attaining 2800 m in Switzerland (Valais).
Range. Alpine and C. European.
Distribution. Map 117. Widespread in the Alps, Jura, Vosges and Ardennes, and in S. and C. Germany; S. Holland (Limburg); a few localities in the N. German plain.

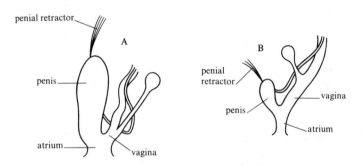

Distal genitalia of   A, *Eucobresia diaphana*   B, *E. pegorarii*

EUCOBRESIA   NIVALIS (Dumont & Mortillet 1852)   Pl. 7

Syns. Semilimax nivalis (Dumont & Mortillet), *Vitrinopugio nivalis* (Dumont & Mortillet), *Vitrina kochi* of some authors, *non* Andreae
Description. br. 5.5–6 mm. Shell with 2¼–2½ whorls, enlarging more slowly than in *E. diaphana* and giving the shell a more globular, compact appearance; spire distinctly raised, with slightly convex whorls. Mouth relatively a little higher than in *E. diaphana*; mouth-membrane much narrower (less than a quarter the visible width of the base) and extending less far back, so that little can be seen of the preceding whorl. Shell very thin and glossy.
  Body similar to *E. diaphana*, but mantle lobe smaller and hiding less of upper surface of shell.
Anatomy. Similar to *E. diaphana*, but atrium longer, and penis much shorter and stockier.
Habitat. Moist screes and grassy places above the tree-line, often at the edges of snow-fields; occasionally in damp mountain woods. Almost exclusively high montane, attaining 3100 m in the Alps (Valais).
Range. Alpine and Carpathian.
Distribution. Map 118. Fairly widespread in the French and Swiss Alps; a few places in the Alps of S. Germany, and in East Germany in the mountains of Saxony and Thuringia.

EUCOBRESIA   PEGORARII (Pollonera 1884)   Pl. 7

Description. br. 6 mm. Last whorl more expanded than in *E. nivalis* and total shape of shell distinctly more compressed; spire almost flat, with a flush suture. Mouth-membrane relatively narrow, rather short. Shell extremely glossy, very thin and delicate, often flexible due to imperfect calcification.

The shell of *E. pegorarii* is virtually indistinguishable from that of *Phenacolimax glacialis*, although as viewed from above the mouth-edge tends to show a slightly concave rather than convex profile close to the point of attachment with the preceding whorl.

Body similar to *E. diaphana* and *E. nivalis*, but distinguished by the presence of a small backwardly-pointing finger-like projection of the mantle immediately above the breathing-hole (also a point of distinction from *Phenacolimax glacialis*).

Anatomy. Similar to *E. diaphana*, but penis relatively much smaller, and atrium longer. Distinguished from *E. glacialis* by the more slender penis, rounded at the upper end.

Habitat. Moist grassy places and under stones, mainly above the tree-line; exclusively high Alpine (2000–3000 m in Switzerland)

Range. Alpine.

Distribution. Map 119. Swiss Alps, rather rare.

*PHENACOLIMAX MAJOR (Férussac 1807)   Pl. 7

Syn. *Vitrina major* (Férussac)

Description. br. 5–6 (occasionally 7) mm. Shell with 2½–3 whorls, the last forming about half the total maximum breadth as viewed from above. Spire almost flat, suture very shallow. Mouth more oval and compressed than in *Vitrina pellucida*, with a short and very narrow mouth-membrane, not cutting into the base of the columella. Shell pale greenish, delicate and translucent, very glossy, apical whorls often dull due to the presence of microscopic spiral pittings.

Body mid to dark grey, relatively larger than in *V. pellucida*, with the mantle lobe more obvious and often extending back as far as the apex.

Anatomy. No penial appendage; spermatheca duct joining oviduct about 2–3 mm above junction with penis. The most distinctive feature is the presence on the oviduct of a firm, glistening, globular swelling, the function of which is obscure.

Habitat. Moist sheltered places in woods, grasslands, among rocks. Rare above 1000 m, though recorded to 1700 m in Switzerland (Valais).

Range. W. European.

Distribution. Map 120. France, W. Switzerland, W. Germany, Luxemburg, Belgium; very local in Holland (Limburg) and in southern Britain.

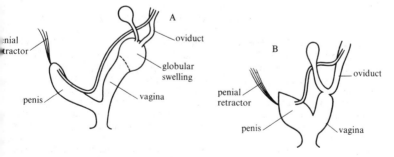

Distal genitalia of   A, *Phenacolimax major*   B, *P. glacialis*

PHENACOLIMAX ANNULARIS (Studer 1820) Pl. 7

Syns. *Helicolimax annularis* (Studer), *Oligolimax annularis* (Studer)

Description. br. 4–5 mm. Shell rather globular, with 3 relatively tightly-coiled whorls, the last forming only about two-fifths of the total breadth as viewed from above. Spire distinctly raised, whorls well-rounded, suture deep; a minute umbilical opening often present. Mouth-membrane absent or very feebly developed. Shell pale greenish, with a diagnostic sculpture of *clearly-defined, rather coarse growth-ridges*.

Body dark grey; mantle lobe virtually lacking.

Habitat. Moderately moist to fairly dry places, among stones and in grassland. Almost exclusively high Alpine, attaining 2600 m in Switzerland (Graubünden).

Range. Alpine.

Distribution. Map 121. C. Pyrenees; French and Swiss Alps; Allgäuer Alps of S.W. Bavaria.

PHENACOLIMAX GLACIALIS (Forbes 1837) Pl. 7

Syns. *P. diaphanus* var. *glacialis* Forbes, *Insulivitrina glacialis* (Forbes)

Description. br. 4.5–6 mm. Shell very closely resembling *Eucobresia pegorarii*, although as viewed from above the upper margin of the mouth tends to show a slightly convex rather than concave profile towards the point of attachment of the preceding whorl.

The mantle is relatively larger than in any other N.W. European vitrinid, the anterior border reaching almost to the base of the tentacles, and the nearly black mantle lobe entirely covering the spire of the shell. Distinguished from *E. pegorarii* by the absence of the finger-like projection above the breathing-hole, which is simple and slit-like.

Anatomy. Distinguished from *E. pegorarii* by penis being much broader and conically pointed, and the upper part of the vagina being rather swollen.

Habitat. Moderately moist places, among rocks and herbage. Almost exclusively high Alpine, attaining 2900 m in Switzerland (Valais).

Range. Alpine.

Distribution. Map 122. Alps of France, Switzerland, and S. Germany (Allgäuer and Berchtesgaden Alps).

Family ZONITIDAE

In the Zonitidae the shell is generally thin, glossy and translucent, discoidal, and with a rounded periphery. The suture is usually very shallow, though the translucency of the shell often gives it an illusory channelled appearance. The mouth-edge is delicate, simple and unreflected. After death the shell quickly becomes dull, white and opaque.

This is a large family, occurring throughout the northern Hemisphere. Zonitids favour damp habitats, such as under stones and among ground litter in woods. Some species are subterranean, and many are partly carnivorous; the genus *Daudebardia* is exclusively so.

Zonitids are notoriously troublesome for the beginner to name. In a few cases dissection may be necessary to discriminate between closely allied species (e.g., in

Aegopinella), though with practice and some field experience most of our N.W. European forms can be identified from external characters alone. It is particularly important in this group for the beginner to restrict himself to fresh, well-grown specimens, and avoid juveniles or bleached dead shells. The appearance of the living animal can also be helpful for identification.

The N.W. European species belong to three distinct subfamilies:

Subfamily Zonitinae (all genera except *Daudebardia* and *Zonitoides*).

Typical zonitids, with discoidal shells, minute to very large (2.5–30 mm). There is no dart-sac (cf. the Gastrodontinae). The genera occurring within our area may be characterized as follows:

Vitrea. Small (2.5–4 mm), with numerous very tightly-coiled whorls, not flaring towards the mouth; shell colourless, glassy and transparent.

Aegopis. Extremely large (>25 mm): one distinctive species only (see *A. verticillus*, p. 119).

Nesovitrea. Small (3.5–5 mm), with rather rapidly enlarging whorls crossed by distinct regularly-spaced transverse striations; shell colourless or brown.

Aegopinella. Small to medium-sized (3.5–12 mm), the spire often slightly raised, and the last quarter whorl flaring more or less distinctly towards the mouth. Shell normally pale brown, waxy (not glossy), with extremely fine spiral striations.

Retinella. Similar to *Aegopinella*, but larger (10–20 mm) and usually glossier (no spiral striations)

Oxychilus. Medium-sized (commonly 5–15 mm) and very flat, the whorls increasing in a regular and even spiral, the last not flaring towards the mouth. Shell glossy and translucent, usually without any distinct microsculpture.

Subfamily Daudebardiinae (*Daudebardia*)

Slug-like: body much larger than shell and not retractable. Shell very flat and ear-like, composed of only 2–3 rapidly enlarging whorls.

Subfamily Gastrodontinae (*Zonitoides*)

Shell as in the Zonitinae, but the genitalia are equipped with a dart-sac, as in the Helicidae but unlike all other zonitids.

Subfamily ZONITINAE

VITREA DIAPHANA (Studer 1820)
Description. br. 3.7–4.2 mm. Shell with 5½ closely-coiled whorls, very gradually and regularly increasing in breadth; spire almost flat. Mouth-edge sometimes slightly thickened internally. Umbilicus *entirely closed*, often covered by a distinct callus plug. Shell thin, shiny, almost colourless, glassy and transparent when fresh.
Habitat. Moderately moist places, characteristically among rocks and screes on wooded slopes; mainly montane.

Range. Alpine and S. European.
Distribution. Map 123. Fairly widespread in S. and C. Germany; distribution in France and Switzerland uncertain owing to confusion with *V. subrimata*.

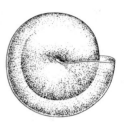

Vitrea diaphana × 7

*VITREA SUBRIMATA (Reinhardt 1871)
Syn. *V. diaphana* var. *subrimata* Reinhardt
Description. br. 2.5–3 (occasionally 3.5) mm. Shell closely similar to *V. diaphana*, but smaller, with 4½–5 whorls, and with a *minute* umbilical opening. No perceptible thickening to mouth-edge.
Habitat. Mainly rocks and screes, often in woodland. Mainly montane, attaining 2400 m in Switzerland (Bernese Alps).
Range. Alpine and S. European.
Distribution. Map 124. Common in the Pyrenees, Jura and Alps; scattered localities in the mountains of S. and C. Germany as far north as the Harz, the Thuringian Forest and the Erzgebirge; England (N. Pennines).

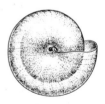

Vitrea subrimata × 7

*VITREA CRYSTALLINA (Müller 1774)   **Pl. 8**
Description. br. 3–4 mm. Shell with 4½–5 whorls, slightly convex below; umbilicus rather narrow, a little eccentric in last whorl. In mature specimens there is usually a distinct internal whitish thickening or rib set back a little way from the mouth. Shell glassy and transparent, colourless, or sometimes tinged with green.
Habitat. Catholic, but commonest in damp places, such as marshes and moist grassland.
Range. European.
Distribution. Map 125. Widespread, but absent from most of Scandinavia (Norway to 65°N, Sweden to 61°N); Iceland.

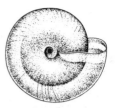

Vitrea crystallina × 7

VITREA CONTRACTA (Westerlund 1871)

Syn. *V. crystallina* var. *contracta* Westerlund

Description. br. 2.5 mm. Shell similar to *V. crystallina*, but smaller, more compressed, and more tightly-coiled, the last whorl *distinctly narrower* and its underside flatter. Umbilicus deep, relatively broader than in *V. crystallina*, not eccentric. Mouth without internal thickening. Shell usually glassy and transparent, but frequently rather clouded with white, even when fresh.

Habitat. Catholic, but favouring drier and more calcareous habitats than *V. crystallina*, though the two species are often associated. Common among rocks and screes; also in caves.

Range. C. and N.W. European.

Distribution. Map 126. Widespread, but more local than *V. crystallina*, and absent from much of C. and N. Scandinavia; Iceland.

Vitrea contracta × 7

AEGOPIS VERTICILLUS (Férussac 1822)

Description. br. 26–30 mm. Shell *very large*, with about 6 regularly increasing whorls, the last well-rounded at the periphery (juveniles show a sharp keel). Mouth-edge simple, sometimes with a slight internal white callus. Shell pale

Aegopis verticillus × 1⅓

greenish-yellow, opaque and rather thick. The sculpture is diagnostic: upper surface with a clear trellis pattern formed by transverse growth-ridges intersected by finer spiral striae, lower surface smooth and glossy, the change occurring abruptly on the periphery.

Habitat. Moist shaded woodland, under ground litter and especially among rocks; montane.

Range. E. Alpine and Balkan.

Distribution. Map 127. Calcareous Alps of S.E. Bavaria (near Schellenberg) and in the S. Bavarian Forest; occasionally introduced elsewhere (gardens at Landsberg a. Lech).

*NESOVITREA HAMMONIS (Ström 1765) Pl. 8
Syn. *Retinella radiatula* (Alder)

Description. br. 3.5–4.2 mm. Shell with 3½ rather flat whorls separated by a very shallow suture, the last very well-rounded at the periphery. Umbilicus moderately wide, slightly eccentric in the last whorl. Mouth-edge delicate, very slightly thickened internally. Shell translucent, usually pale brown (sometimes colourless or greenish), rather glossy, with a characteristic sculpture of strong *regular transverse striations*.

Habitat. Catholic: damp to moderately dry places of all kinds: marshes, coniferous and deciduous woods, grassland; often in poor acidic places.

Range. Holarctic.

Distribution. Map 128. Throughout, though often somewhat local in drier lowland areas.

NESOVITREA PETRONELLA (Pfeiffer 1853) Pl. 8
Syn. *Retinella radiatula* var. *petronella* Pfeiffer

Description. br. 4.2–5 mm. Shell closely similar to *N. hammonis*, but larger; the last whorl relatively a little narrower; spire often more raised. Shell *always colourless or pale greenish* (never brown). Sculpture similar to *N. hammonis*, but striae usually more irregular and less well-defined, especially on the last half whorl.

Habitat. Similar to *N. hammonis*, though somewhat less catholic; most commonly in woods, especially montane. Attaining 2500 m in Switzerland (Graubünden).

Range. Boreal and Alpine.

Distribution. Map 129. Common in Scandinavia and in the Swiss and French Alps; local in mountains of S. and C. Germany as far north as the Harz; very occasionally in the N. German plain.

*AEGOPINELLA PURA (Alder 1830) Pl. 8
Syn. *Retinella pura* (Alder)

Description. br. 3.5–4.2 mm. Shell with 3½ gently convex whorls, somewhat compressed and with a hint of keeling at the periphery; last quarter whorl widening rather noticeably. Spire a little raised. Umbilicus wide, slightly eccentric. Shell translucent, usually colourless (though often pale brown), not very glossy, with faint irregular growth-lines crossed by delicate interrupted spiral striations, visible under high magnification.

A. pura may be distinguished from juveniles of larger species of *Aegopinella* by the tighter coiling of the initial whorls and by the more distinct microsculpture.

Habitat. Moderately moist places; characteristic of ground litter in deciduous woods.

Microsculpture of shell of *Aegopinella pura*

Range. European.
Distribution. Map 130. Widespread, becoming mainly coastal in Scandinavia; Iceland.

The following four species of *Aegopinella* (*A. nitidula*, *A. nitens*, *A. minor*, *A. epipedostoma*) have very similar shells, and dissection may be required to be certain of the identification.

*AEGOPINELLA NITIDULA (Drapamaud 1805)   Pl. 8
Syn. *Retinella nitidula* (Draparnaud)
Description. br. 8–10mm. Shell with 4½ moderately convex whorls, the last quarter whorl expanding perceptibly (though *not strongly*) towards the mouth; suture well-defined. Umbilicus widely open, slightly eccentric. Shell pale yellowish-brown (occasionally white), clouded with white around umbilicus, waxy rather than glossy, with faint growth-lines crossed by exceedingly delicate spiral striations, less distinct than in *A. pura*.
Anatomy. Distinguished from related large species of *Aegopinella* by the relatively small penis, which is not clearly divided into upper and lower parts (cf. *A. nitens*); penial retractor muscle attached close to the upper (distal) end.
Habitat. Common in a variety of moderately moist places: woods, hedgerows, herbage, among rocks; often in humanly disturbed habitats.
Range. N.W. European.
Distribution. Map 131. British Isles, N. and W. France, Belgium, Holland, N. Germany; in S. Scandinavia mainly coastal or synanthropic (Norway to 65°N).

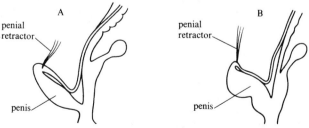

Distal genitalia of   A, *Aegopinella nitidula*   B, *A. nitens*

AEGOPINELLA NITENS (Michaud 1831) **Pl. 8**

Syn. *Retinella nitens* (Michaud)

Description. br. 8–11 mm. Shell similar to *A. nitidula*, but the last quarter whorl flatter and *expanding more strongly* towards the mouth, sometimes slightly down-turned. Umbilicus markedly eccentric. Colour often darker than in *A. nitidula*, characteristically with a greenish-brown tinge.

Anatomy. Distinguished from related species of *Aegopinella* by the large broad penis, divided by a constriction into two parts; upper (distal) end narrowing abruptly where the retractor muscle is inserted.

Habitat. Moderately moist places: woods, among rocks. Principally montane, attaining 2500 m in the Alps (Valais).

Range. Alpine and C. European.

Distribution. Map 132. Mountains of E. France; Switzerland; S. and C. Germany as far north as the Harz; isolated sites in Belgium and S. Holland.

AEGOPINELLA MINOR (Stabile 1864) **Pl. 8**

Description. br. 6–9 mm. Shell similar to *A. nitens*, but slightly smaller, with narrower whorls, and with the last quarter whorl not expanding so strongly. Shell rather compressed, often giving a hint of keeling to the periphery. Colour pale yellowish-brown (usually paler than *A. nitens*).

Anatomy. Sharply distinct from *A. nitidula* and *A. nitens* in the presence of a very long narrow epiphallus, intervening between the upper end of the penis and the point of insertion of the retractor muscle.

Habitat. Usually in dry places: grassland and scrub on open hillsides; less commonly in woods.

Range. C. and S.E. European.

Distribution. Map 133. Poorly known, possibly very local: a few places in France (Savoie, Hautes Alpes), W. Germany (Württemberg, Franconia, Bavarian Forest), E. Germany (Thuringia, S. Saxony).

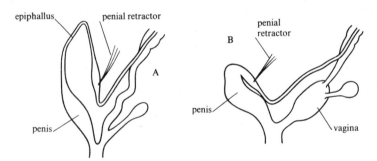

Distal genitalia of   A, *Aegopinella minor*   B, *A. epipedostoma*

AEGOPINELLA EPIPEDOSTOMA (Fagot 1879)

Description. br. 8–11 mm. Shell virtually identical with *A. nitens*, from which it can only be distinguished with certainty by the anatomy. Last whorl close to the mouth sometimes downturned a little more strongly than in *A. nitens*, and growth-lines may be a little more pronounced.

Anatomy. Distinguished from *A. nitens* by having a large ovoid swelling on the upper part of the vagina, into which the very short spermatheca duct is inserted.

Habitat. Woods and among rocks; montane.

Range. C. and E. European.

Distribution. Map 134. Poorly known, possibly rare: fairly common in the central Pyrenees (Hautes Pyrénées, Haute Garonne, Ariège); E. Taunus mountains (Hesse, W. Germany)

AEGOPINELLA RESSMANNI (Westerlund 1883)   Pl. 9

Syn. *Retinella hiulca* of many authors (*non* Albers)

Description. br. 10–12 mm. Shell larger than other N.W. European *Aegopinella*; upper surface often markedly convex, with a raised spire; last quarter whorl expanding strongly, both outwardly and especially *basally*, giving the mouth a relatively tall shape with the width little greater than the height.

The shell closely resembles that of *Retinella hiulca*, but has a duller, more waxy appearance due to the presence of distinct spiral striations crossing the growth-lines.

Anatomy. Spermatheca duct very short, joining oviduct some distance above penis (cf. *Retinella hiulca*).

Habitat. Moist woodland, under ground litter; montane.

Range. S.E. European.

Distribution. Map 135. S.E. Bavaria (near Burgkirchen a. Alz) only.

RETINELLA HIULCA (Albers 1850)   Pl. 9

Description. br. 10–14 mm. Shell closely resembling *Aegopinella ressmanni*, but usually a little larger, and glossy rather than waxy, with no distinct spiral striations.

Anatomy. Spermatheca duct very long, joining oviduct near common point with penis (i.e., no vagina) (cf. *A. ressmanni*).

Habitat. Moderately moist places: woods, among rocks; not above 1000 m.

Range. S. Alpine.

Distribution. Map 136. S. Switzerland (S. Ticino) only.

RETINELLA INCERTA (Draparnaud 1805)   Pl. 9

Description. br. 15–20 mm. Shell *very large*; general shape much less compressed than in any other N.W. European zonitid, with about 5 rather convex whorls, the last not flared, well-rounded at the periphery. Height of mouth approximately equal to the breadth. Umbilicus deep, symmetrical. Shell very glossy, pale brownish above, clouded with white below.

Habitat. Moist to moderately dry places: herbage, scrub, woods.

Range. Pyrenean.

Distribution. Map 137. S.W. France from Ariège to the Atlantic, as far north as the valley of the Garonne.

*OXYCHILUS DRAPARNAUDI (Beck 1837)   Pl. 9

Syns. *O. draparnaldi* (Beck), *O. lucidus* (Draparnaud)

Description. br. 11–16 mm. Shell discoidal, with 5½–6 whorls, the last widening rather rapidly, *distinctly broader than in O. cellarius*; last quarter whorl sometimes slightly downturned and compressed. Umbilicus moderately deep and open. Shell not usually very glossy, pale brownish-yellow, rather opaque, the growth-lines often rather well-defined and giving a slightly wrinkled appearance, especially at the suture.

Body dark cobalt blue, with grey mantle.

Habitat. Moist sheltered places: woods, among rocks; characteristic of gardens and greenhouses. Markedly carnivorous.

Range. W. Mediterranean and W. European.

Distribution. Map 138. Common in natural habitats in south-western areas (France, Switzerland, S. Ireland, S.W. England), but becoming largely synanthropic to the east and north-east; rare beyond the Rhine valley; in Scandinavia virtually only in gardens and greenhouses.

*OXYCHILUS CELLARIUS (Müller 1774)   Pl. 9

Description. br. 9–12 (occasionally 14) mm. Shell with 5½–6 whorls, gradually and regularly increasing in breadth; last whorl relatively narrower than in *O. draparnaudi*. Umbilicus symmetrical, moderately deep and open. Shell shiny, pale and translucent, growth-lines scarcely visible. Suture virtually flush, but often presenting an illusory channelled appearance.

Body usually pale bluish-grey, but darkly pigmented forms are also known.

Habitat. Moist, shaded places of all kinds: woods, rocks, gardens, under rubbish; frequently in caves.

Range. W. European.

Distribution. Map 139. Throughout, to southernmost Scandinavia, there becoming mainly coastal and synanthropic (Norway to 63°N, Sweden to 61°N, southernmost Finland); introduced in Faroes.

OXYCHILUS MORTILLETI (Pfeiffer 1859)   Pl. 10
Syn. *O. villae* (Strobel)

Description. br. 12–14 (occasionally 17 mm in the S. Alps). Shell closely similar to *O. cellarius*, and distinguishable with certainty only by the anatomy; larger, with 6–6½ whorls, the last relatively somewhat broader and with the mouth taller and more rounded at the periphery; spire often virtually flat. Colour of shell darker than in *O. cellarius*, varying from yellowish to pale-brown.

Anatomy. Penis, vas deferens and spermatheca duct longer and relatively narrower than in *O. cellarius* and *O. draparnaudi*.

Habitat. Moist shaded places: woods, mossy rocks, screes. Mainly montane, attaining 1600 m in Switzerland (Valais).

Range. Mainly S. Alpine.

Distribution. Map 140. S. Switzerland (Valais, Ticino); S. Germany (Allgäuer and Berchtesgaden Alps, and a few scattered localities in S. Bavaria as far north as the Altmühl valley).

OXYCHILUS HYDATINUS (Rossmässler 1838)   Pl. 10
Syn. *Vitrea pseudohydatina* (Bourguignat)

Description. br. 5–6.2 mm. Shell small, with 4½–5½ closely-coiled narrow whorls, well-rounded at the periphery; spire often a little raised. Umbilicus deep and *very narrow*. Shell thin and shiny, colourless to pale greenish, glassy and translucent when fresh.

This species somewhat resembles a very large *Vitrea crystallina*, but may be distinguished by the lack of any internal rib within the mouth.
Habitat. Rather dry places: among rocks and in waste ground (within our area mostly collected from the flood rubbish of rivers).
Range. Mediterranean.
Distribution. Map 141. S. France (Haute Garonne, Isère, Ain).

*OXYCHILUS ALLIARIUS (Miller 1822)   **Pl. 10**
Description. br. 5.5–7 mm. Shell with 4–4½ very gently convex whorls, more closely-coiled than *O. cellarius* and suture a little deeper; spire a little raised; last quarter whorl sometimes slightly compressed and downturned. Umbilicus rather broad, eccentric. Shell shiny, translucent, pale yellowish-brown or greenish, often whiter below.
Body dark bluish-grey, *smelling strongly of garlic* if disturbed or fingered.
Habitat. Catholic: woods, fields, rocks, occasionally in gardens and greenhouses. Tolerant of poor acidic places, such as conifer plantations.
Range. W. European.
Distribution. Map 142. Common in the west as far as Iceland, increasingly local to the east; very rare in Switzerland, and in S.E. and E. Germany; Norway (to Lofoten Islands), S. Sweden, southernmost Finland; elsewhere in Scandinavia only in greenhouses.

*OXYCHILUS HELVETICUS (Blum 1881)   **Pl. 10**
Syn. *O. rogersi* (Woodward)
Description. br. 8–10 mm. Shell with 5 scarcely convex whorls, very regularly enlarging; spire a little raised; periphery very slightly but perceptibly keeled. Umbilicus *narrow* (narrower than in *O. cellarius*). Shell extremely glossy, warm brownish-yellow, translucent, clouded with white immediately around umbilicus.
Body bluish-grey, often with faint oblique darker stripes on flanks. Mantle-edge *jet black*, when retracted visible through the shell as a *black band*. This species may emit a garlic-like smell if disturbed, but less strongly than *O. alliarius*.
Habitat. Moist shaded places: woods, hedgerows, among rocks. In Switzerland mainly montane, commonest above 700 m, extending to 2400 m (Valais); elsewhere locally common in lowland habitats.
Range. N.W. European.
Distribution. Map 143. Switzerland, Belgium, Britain (mainly S.), Ireland (Co Limerick), N.E. France, W. Pyrenees; distribution elsewhere in France uncertain owing to confusion with other species.

OXYCHILUS CLARUS (Held 1837)   **Pl. 10**
Syn. *Retinella clara* (Held)
Description. br. 4–4.2 mm. Shell small, general shape not unlike *Nesovitrea hammonis*, with 3½–4 rather rapidly expanding whorls, the last well-rounded at the periphery; spire a little raised. Umbilicus rather broad, slightly eccentric. Shell shiny, colourless and translucent when fresh, with a *very fine spiral microsculpture* similar to that of *Aegopinella*.
Habitat. Poorly known; montane (within our area found mainly in flood rubbish).
Range. Alpine.
Distribution. Map 144. Very rare: dead shells recorded from a few places in S.

Bavaria, from the Isar valley south of Munich; probably also present in N.E. Switzerland.

OXYCHILUS GLABER (Rossmässler 1835)   Pl. 10

Description. br. 11–14 mm. Shell with 5–5½ slightly convex whorls, very regularly enlarging; spire distinctly raised; whorls slightly angled at the periphery giving a gently *keeled* appearance. Umbilicus deep, symmetrical, *very narrow*. Shell extremely glossy, translucent, brownish-yellow above, clouded with white below.

Body very dark bluish-grey.

Habitat. Woods and moist shaded places, but also among rocks and screes on open hillsides, especially at higher altitudes. Mainly montane, attaining 1850 m in Switzerland (Valais).

Range. Alpine and Carpathian.

Distribution. Map 145. Frequent in the Alps and in the French and Swiss Jura; Pyrenees; several discontinuous areas in S. Germany (upper Rhine valley, Berchtesgaden Alps, Franconian Jura, Thuringian Forest, S. Saxony); Isle of Gotland.

OXYCHILUS DEPRESSUS (Sterki 1880)   Pl. 11

Description. br. 7–8.5 mm. Shell very flat above, with 4½–5 scarcely convex whorls, enlarging gradually and regularly; periphery well-rounded. Umbilicus deep and *extremely narrow* (narrower than in any other N.W. European *Oxychilus*). Shell shiny, almost colourless, very translucent when fresh.

Habitat. Moist places in woods and among rocks; also in caves. Montane, attaining 2600 m in Switzerland (Engadine).

Range. Carpathian and Alpine.

Distribution. Map 146. Rare: France (Haute Savoie), Switzerland, S. Germany (isolated occurrences in the Allgäuer Alps, S. Black Forest, Franconian Jura, Bavarian Forest, Thuringian Forest, Erzgebirge).

Subfamily DAUDEBARDIINAE

DAUDEBARDIA RUFA (Draparnaud 1805)   Pl. 11

Description. br. 4–5.3 mm. Shell with 2½ very flattened whorls, the last flaring strongly into an ear-like extension, the periphery becoming nearly straight (occasionally slightly concave) as viewed from above. Mouth extremely oblique, lower and upper margins sub-parallel, giving a rather oblong outline to the shell. Umbilicus small and shallow. Shell yellowish, moderately glossy, rather delicate, last part sometimes not fully calcified.

Body bluish-grey, *much larger than shell* (17–20 mm) and not retractable.

Habitat. Leaf litter and under stones in moist woods; montane. Carnivorous and largely subterranean.

Range. C. and S. European.

Distribution. Map 147. Local but widespread in mountain areas of S.W. and C. Germany north to the Harz and east to S. Saxony; N. Switzerland (Basel to L. Constance); Alsace.

DAUDEBARDIA BREVIPES (Draparnaud 1805)   **Pl. 11**
Description. br. 4–4.5 mm. Shell similar to *D. rufa*, but slightly smaller; apical whorls more closely coiled; shape *oval* (not oblong), with periphery of last quarter whorl markedly convex (not straight) as viewed from above. Upper edge of mouth downturned more strongly than in *D. rufa*.
    Body similar to *D. rufa*.
Habitat. Leaf litter and under stones in moist woods; montane. Carnivorous and largely subterranean.
Range. C. and S. European.
Distribution. Map 148. Local in mountain areas of S.W. Germany, N. Switzerland, Alsace (distribution closely similar to that of *D. rufa*, though not extending so far east in Germany).

Subfamily **GASTRODONTINAE**

*ZONITOIDES EXCAVATUS (Alder 1830)   **Pl. 11**
Description. br. 5.3–6 mm. Shell with 4½ regularly enlarging whorls, rather narrow and tightly coiled; umbilicus *extremely broad and open* (resembling that of *Discus rotundatus*). Shell pale brown (animal dark), occasionally colourless or pale greenish, shiny, feebly translucent, with rather strongly-marked growth-ridges.
Habitat. Ground litter in woods; occasionally in marshes. Restricted to non-calcareous soils.
Range. N.W. European Atlantic (mainly British Isles)
Distribution. Map 149. Fairly widespread in non-calcareous areas of the British Isles; local in Belgium, Holland, N.W. Germany (Oldenberg to Schleswig-Holstein), Denmark (S. Jutland).

*ZONITOIDES NITIDUS (Müller 1774)   **Pl. 11**
Description. br. 6–7 mm. Shell with 4½ moderately convex whorls, less tightly coiled than in *Z. excavatus*; periphery well-rounded; umbilicus rather broad. Shell pale brown, glossy and translucent, growth-lines rather irregular and pronounced.
    When alive, the shell appears almost black owing to the very dark body showing through. There is a characteristic dull orange spot on the mantle, usually visible just above the periphery of the shell.
Habitat. Very moist places: fens and marshes, especially at the margins of lakes and rivers in places liable to flooding.
Range. Holarctic.
Distribution. Map 150. Widespread, but absent from large areas of western Scandinavia; Iceland (possibly introduced).

Family **MILACIDAE**

Slugs with a symmetrical internal shell, keeled from tail to mantle, with an anterior, shagreened mantle which is characteristically grooved (Plate 12). The respiratory pore is on the right, behind the mid-point of the mantle. The muscles of the mid-part of the sole have a characteristic chevron pattern.

Plate 7   Family **VITRINIDAE**
See also plate 6
(×5)

1.   **Eucobresia diaphana**   111
C. Europe, common in montane habitats.
1a-c. Shell: very flattened. Mouth-membrane broad.
1d. Living animal: mantle dark and voluminous.

2a-b. **Eucobresia nivalis**   114
Mainly high Alpine. Mouth-membrane much narrower than in
E. diaphana.

3a-b. **Eucobresia pegorarii**   114
High Alpine, rare. Very like *Phenacolimax glacialis*; not distinguishable with certainty by shell.

4.   ***Phenacolimax major**   115
Mainly lowland France, widespread.
4a-c. Shell: larger and more flattened than *Vitrina pellucida* (see
plate 6).
4d. Living animal: mantle more voluminous than in *V. pellucida*,
usually darker.

5a-b. **Phenacolimax glacialis**   116
High Alpine. Very like *Eucobresia pegorarii*; not distinguishable with
certainty by shell.

6a-c. **Phenacolimax annularis**   116
High Alpine. Globular, with coarse growth-ridges.

7

1a

1b

1c

1d

2a

2b

3a

3b

4a

4b

4c

4d

5a

5b

6a

6b

6c

Family ZONITIDAE

See also plates 9-11

(1-4, ×5; 5-7, ×4)

Plate 8

1a-b. ***Vitrea crystallina** 118

A typical *Vitrea* (see p. 117): small, glassy, tightly-coiled.

2. ***Aegopinella pura** 120

Flattened, very slightly keeled. Spiral striations crossing growth-lines (see Fig., p. 121).

    2a-c. Typical pale form.

    2d. Brown form.

3a-c. ***Nesovitrea hammonis** 120

Distinct regular transverse striations. Usually brown but sometimes colourless.

4a-c. **Nesovitrea petronella** 120

Mainly Scandinavia and the Alps. Like *N. hammonis*, but always colourless or greenish (never brown).

5a-c. ***Aegopinella nitidula** 121

Common in north-western areas. Last whorl not strongly flared towards mouth.

6a-c. **Aegopinella nitens** 122

Common in C. Europe, mainly montane. Last whorl strongly flared. Often darker than *A. nitidula*.

7a-c. **Aegopinella minor** 122

Rather rare, mainly C. Europe. Like a small *A. nitens* but genitalia distinct (see Fig., p. 122).

The family is primarily southern European, but several species have been widely dispersed by man. The Milacidae are closely related to the Limacidae (p. 135) but not to other European slugs. All but one of our species belong to the genus *Milax*. They can usually be identified on external characters, but variation in colour sometimes makes this difficult, so the most useful internal characters are shown together on p. 134. *Milax* species tend to be partly subterranean, and are very extensible. They are herbivorous, and *M. budapestensis* and *M. sowerbyi* are often pests.

The exceptional species, *Boettgerilla pallens*, is a very narrow, wormlike slug. It is probably a new arrival to N.W. Europe, having spread from the Caucasus in the last 20 years, undoubtedly assisted accidentally by man.

Internal shell ('slug plate') of *Milax* × 3½

*MILAX GAGATES (Draparnaud 1801)   Pl. 12
Description. Medium slug, extended length 5–6 cm. Body black or dark grey becoming paler towards the foot-fringe, rather smooth, and with about 14 longitudinal grooves on each side which are paler. No bands. Respiratory pore lacks pale rim. Keel prominent, truncated at tail, usually same colour as body but sometimes lighter. Sole whitish, mucus white or colourless. Some paler and browner variants occur. For internal features see p. 134.
Habitat. Gardens and agricultural land, occasionally a pest, also in woods and hedges, and often in grassy places near the sea.
Range. W. European and Mediterranean.
Distribution. Map 151. Frequent in W. coastal regions of France, Ireland and Britain, elsewhere mostly in gardens, as far east as Netherlands (Limburg) and the Rhine valley.

MILAX NIGRICANS (Philippi 1836)   Pl. 12
Syn. *M. insularis* (Lessona & Pollonera)
Description. Medium slug, extended length 5–6 cm. Intensely black above, often paler on the sides, roughly tuberculate, and without bands or a pale rim to the respiratory pore. Keel black and prominent, truncated at the tail. Sole brownish, often dark; mucus white or colourless. For internal features see p. 134.
Habitat. Probably only in gardens and other cultivated ground.
Range. Mediterranean.
Distribution. No map. A Mediterranean species, once recorded from a garden in S.E. England (Bexhill, Sussex) but probably also occurs within our area in S. France.

*MILAX SOWERBYI (Férussac 1823)   Pl. 12
Description. Medium to large slug, extended length 6–7.5 cm. Body pale brownish-grey speckled with black, with grooves between tubercles also pig-

mented. Respiratory pore with pale orange rim. Keel lighter than body, usually
yellow or orange, crinkled when animal contracted, not truncate. Sole whitish,
mucus thick, yellowish and sticky. Some colour variants occur, and the keel is
occasionally the same colour as the body. For internal characters see p. 134.

Habitat. Gardens, hedges and agricultural land. Rather subterranean, and a notable pest.

Range. W. European and Mediterranean.

Distribution. Map 152. Britain and Ireland, W. and N. France, Netherlands,
mostly spread by man.

MILAX RUSTICUS (Millet 1843)   Pl. 12

Syn. *M. marginatus* (Draparnaud)

Description. Large slug, extended length 8–10 cm. Reddish or yellowish-grey,
paler towards the foot-fringe, and very distinctly spotted with black, especially in
the grooves between tubercles. Respiratory pore with pale rim, mantle with two
thin, dark lateral bands, keel usually paler than dorsal part of body. Sole yellowish-
white, mucus white or colourless. For internal features see p. 134.

Habitat. In woods and waste ground, not usually in cultivated places, especially in
mountainous areas and on calcareous soils.

Range. C. and S. European.

Distribution. Map 153. France (mostly in E.), Belgium, S. Netherlands, Switzerland and Germany (not in N. German plain).

*MILAX BUDAPESTENSIS (Hazay 1881)   Pl. 12

Syn. *M. gracilis* (Leydig)

Description. Medium slug, extended length 5–6 cm. Variable in colour from
yellowish-grey through browns to dark grey, with a reticulation of black spots.
Very slender when fully extended. Respiratory pore rimmed with black. Keel clear
yellow or orange. Sole yellowish-white, usually with a darker central strip, but
sometimes darker at the sides. Mucus colourless. For internal features see p. 134.

Habitat. Mostly in parks, gardens and crops, in association with man. A notable
pest.

Range. European (originally E. European only).

Distribution. Map 154. Common in Britain and Ireland, also sporadically in Belgium, S. Germany and Switzerland; greenhouses only in Iceland. Probably entirely
spread by man.

*BOETTGERILLA PALLENS Simroth 1912   Pl. 12

Syn. *B. vermiformis* Wiktor

Description. Small to medium slug, extended length 3–4 cm. Pale translucent
greyish-yellow, with keel, back and head darker bluish-grey. Very narrow, almost
worm-like, when fully extended. Sole pale yellow, mucus colourless. For internal
features see p. 134.

Habitat. Mostly in gardens and parks, probably recently introduced in the west,
more widespread and in woods in E. Europe.

Range. S.E. European but recently spread rapidly in N.W. Europe.

Distribution. Map 155. Local, but still apparently spreading rapidly. Now recorded
from most countries, north to Finland (greenhouses) and S. Sweden, west to
Channel Islands and N. Ireland.

Plate 9   **Family ZONITIDAE**

See also plates 8, 10, 11

(×2)

1a-c.   **Aegopinella ressmanni**   123
S.E. Bavaria. Last whorl expanding very quickly, mouth large and rounded. Clear spiral striations.

2a-c.   **Retinella hiulca**   123
S. Switzerland. Like *Aegopinella ressmanni* but glossier (no spiral striations).

3a-c.   **Retinella incerta**   123
Pyrenees and S.W. France. Large, reddish-brown, very glossy.

4.   ***Oxychilus draparnaudi**   123
W. Europe, common in gardens and greenhouses.
    4a-c. Shell: last whorl broad (compare with *O. cellarius*).
    4d. Living animal: dark cobalt blue.

5.   ***Oxychilus cellarius**   124
Common, except in Scandinavia.
    5a-c. Shell: last whorl relatively narrow (compare with *O. draparnaudi*).
    5d. Living animal: usually pale bluish-grey, but dark forms also occur.

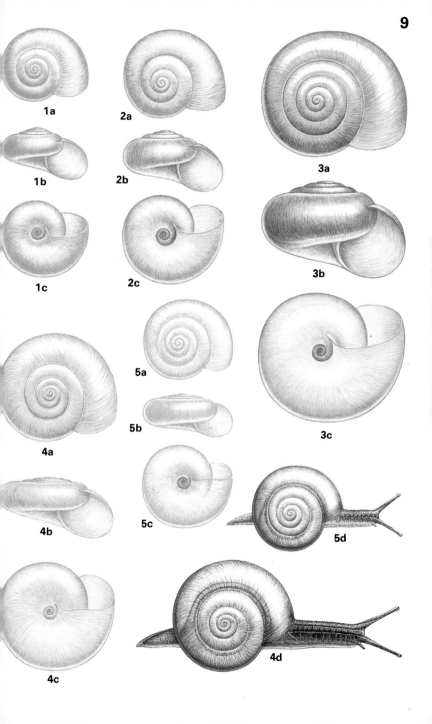

1a

1b

1c

2a

2b

2c

3a

3b

3c

4a

4b

4c

4d

5a

5b

5c

5d

10

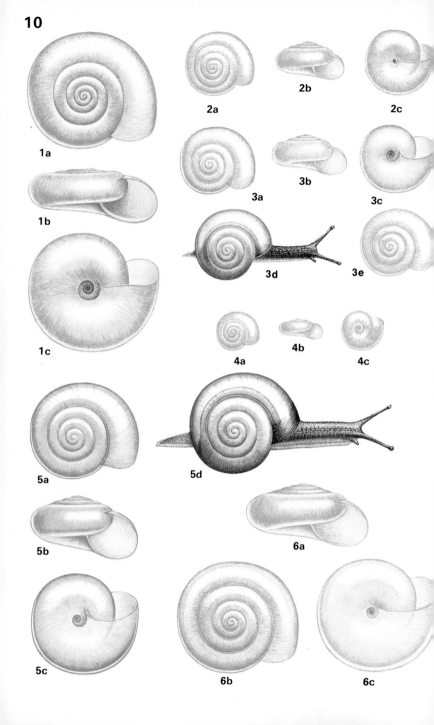

1a

1b

1c

2a

2b

2c

3a

3b

3c

3d

3e

4a

4b

4c

5a

5b

5c

5d

6a

6b

6c

Family ZONITIDAE

Plate 10

See also plates 8, 9, 11

(×3)

1a-c. **Oxychilus mortilleti**   124
Switzerland and S. Germany, mainly montane. Like a big *O. cellarius* (see plate 9).

2a-c. **Oxychilus hydatinus**   124
S. France. Umbilicus very narrow. Like a big *Vitrea crystallina* (see plate 8) but mouth lacks internal rib.

3. ***Oxychilus alliarius**   125
W. Europe, common.
    3a-c. Typical form.
    3d. Living animal: emits a strong smell of garlic if fingered.
    3e. White form.

4a-c. **Oxychilus clarus**   125
Bavarian Alps, very rare. Delicate spiral striations.

5. ***Oxychilus helveticus**   125
    5a-c. Shell: very glossy. Umbilicus narrower than in *O. cellarius* (see plate 9).
    5d. Living animal: edge of mantle black.

6a-c. **Oxychilus glaber**   126
Mainly C. Europe, montane. Large, very glossy, umbilicus very narrow.

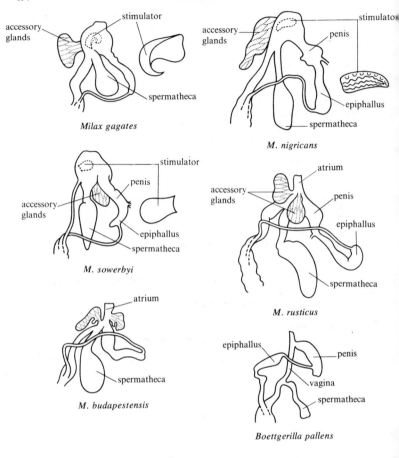

INTERNAL DIAGNOSTIC CHARACTERS OF
MILAX AND *BOETTGERILLA* SPECIES

The most important diagnostic features of this group are the shape and size of the spermatheca and epiphallus, and the presence or absence and shape of the stimulator or sarcobelum in the atrium. See p. 19 for the general account of reproductive organs of slugs and snails.

Milax All *Milax* species in N.W. Europe have accessory glands opening into the atrium, unlike other slugs.

Milax rusticus and *M. budapestensis* do not have a stimulator, and the atrium is rather small in these two species. They are very dissimilar in external appearance.

M. sowerbyi, *M. gagates* and *M. nigricans* all have a stimulator.

M. sowerbyi has a thick, blunt stimulator, an elongate spermatheca tapering to its apex and an epiphallus widest distally.

M. gagates has a smooth, curved and pointed stimulator and a rather rounded spermatheca.

M. nigricans has a rather blunt stimulator with four rows of large papillae, and an epiphallus with a proximal swelling.

Boettgerilla pallens has a very long vagina, and a swollen epiphallus separated from the penis by a narrow duct. There are no accessory glands.

Family **LIMACIDAE**

Slugs with a small asymmetrical internal shell, keeled, but not right up to the mantle. The mantle is anterior and covered with fine concentric folds rather like a finger-print. The respiratory pore is behind the mid-point of the mantle on the right side. These slugs cannot contract up into a hemispherical shape like the *Arion* slugs.

The Limacidae occur in Europe, N. Africa and N. America. The family is closely related to the Milacidae (p. 127), also slugs, which have a grooved and granular mantle, and a keel stretching from tail to mantle. *Testacella* (p. 173) and *Arion* (p. 103) slugs are not closely related, and are very different externally and internally.

Internal shell ('slug plate') of Limacidae (*Limax*) × 3½

There are two genera of Limacidae in N.W. Europe:

Limax species are generally large (more than 5 cm), and the keel slopes gently down the tail. The pattern of concentric rings on the mantle is centred on the mid-line. Internally there is no stimulating organ.

Deroceras species are smaller (usually less than 5 cm), and the keel is truncated, turning down sharply at the tail tip. The pattern of concentric rings on the mantle is centred to the right of the mid-line, just above the respiratory pore. Internally, there may be both a stimulator (a penial sarcobelum) and a flagellum or multiple appendices on the penis.

Limax species are found in woodland, feeding on fungi, algae or dead material rather than green plants. They include the largest of European slugs, *Limax cinereoniger*, which may be up to 30 cm. long when fully extended. In most cases, identification in the field is straight-forward, but the diagnostic internal features of each species are shown together on p. 139.

Deroceras species are found in many habitats, and tend to feed on living green plants: *D. reticulatum* is a serious agricultural pest. Some species can be difficult to identify on external characters alone, and the diagnostic internal features are shown on p. 147. Many species have recently been described from E. Europe, and some of these may well occur in S.E. Germany.

*LIMAX   MAXIMUS Linné 1758   **Pl. 13**
Description. Very large slug, extended length 10–20 cm. Usually pale brown to grey, with two or three darker longitudinal bands on each side – sometimes broken up into spots. Tubercles rather small. Mantle well anterior, raised as flap over head when animal retracted, spotted or marbled, but *not* banded, with darker pigment. Tentacles uniform reddish-brown. Keel short, about one-third distance from tail to mantle. Sole uniform whitish, body and foot slime colourless and sticky. There are a number of colour varieties. For internal features see p. 138.
Similar species. *L. cinereoniger* has tentacles spotted with black, a longer keel, and usually a tripartite sole with dark outer portions. *L. marginatus* (p. 138) has copious watery mucus, is smaller, and has lyre-shaped bands on the mantle.
Habitat. Widespread – in woods, hedgerows and gardens.
Range. S. and W. European.
Distribution. Map 156. Common in west, becoming scarcer and increasingly synanthropic in north-east. Rare in Scandinavia beyond 60°N, only in greenhouses in Finland.

*LIMAX   CINEREONIGER Wolf 1803   **Pl. 13**
Description. Very large slug – extended length 10–20 (rarely 30) cm, usually ashy-black with two faint darker longitudinal bands on each side, and with large tubercles. Tentacles spotted with black, keel long and pale, extending about two-thirds distance from tail to mantle. Sole whitish centrally, but in adult usually with grey to black stripes on either side. Body and foot-slime colourless. There are a number of colour varieties. For internal features see p. 138.
Similar species. *Limax maximus.*
Habitat. Woodlands. often under logs. Much less common than *L. maximus*, and intolerant of human disturbance.
Range. European.
Distribution. Map 157. Widespread but local. Absent from N. Scandinavia and Iceland.

*LIMAX   TENELLUS Müller 1774   **Pl. 13**
Description. Small slug, extended length 2.5–4.0 cm. Usually yellow with very faint darker lateral bands. The tubercles are small, and the body has a gelatinous and translucent appearance. Head and tentacles much darker than rest of body. Keel short, sole yellowish-white, body slime yellow to orange, copious when handled, foot slime colourless. There are some minor colour variants. For internal features see p. 142.
Habitat. Usually very local, in old woodland, both deciduous and coniferous.

Range. N. and C. European.
Distribution. Map 158. Widespread but local. Absent from Ireland, Iceland, and N. Scandinavia.

*LIMAX   FLAVUS Linné 1758   Pl. 13
Syn. *Lehmannia flava* (Linné)
Description. Medium to large slug – extended length 7.5–10 cm. Body usually yellow overlaid with pale greyish mottling, and without longitudinal bands. Tentacles pale blue. Mantle coloured as body. Keel short, sole unicolourous yellowish-white, body slime yellow, foot slime colourless. There is some variation in colour, and juveniles have a greenish tinge. For internal features see p. 142.
Similar species. *L. pseudoflavus* is greyer, has much darker mottling, larger tubercles, grey tentacles, and less obviously yellow body slime.
Habitat. Usually strongly associated with man – in gardens, outhouses, damp cellars and kitchens.
Range. S. and W. European, possibly Mediterranean in origin.
Distribution. Map 159. Local, nearly always synanthropic, north to Denmark and southernmost Sweden. Some confusion may have occurred with *L. pseudoflavus* (below).

*LIMAX PSEUDOFLAVUS Evans 1978   Pl. 13
Syn. *L. grossui* of British authors, *non* Lupu.
Description. Medium to large slug, extended length 7–13 cm. Body pale greenish-grey overlaid with very dark mottling, and without lateral bands. Mantle coloured as body, tentacles grey. Keel short, sole yellowish-white. Body slime faintly yellow or colourless, foot slime colourless. For internal features see p. 142.
Similar species. *L. flavus; L. pseudoflavus* is a recently described species, at present known with certainty only from the British Isles. It is likely to be found elsewhere in W. Europe, and has probably been identified as *L. flavus*.
Habitat. Wild places – woods and under stones in open ground. Not clearly associated with man.
Range. W. European – limits uncertain.
Distribution. Map 160. Scarcely known, as confused with *L. flavus*. Common in Ireland, rare in W. Britain.

LIMAX   NYCTELIUS Bourguignat 1861
Syn. *Lehmannia nyctelia* (Bourguignat)
Description. Medium slug, extended length *c*.5 cm. Body pale greyish-yellow, translucent, with a pair of dark lateral bands high up near the mid-line. One pair of dark bands on mantle forming a lyre shape. Respiratory pore with a pale border. Keel short. Sole greyish-white, mucus colourless. For internal characters see p. 142. Not reliably distinguished from *L. marginatus* on external characters alone.
Similar species. All the smaller *Limax* species. Specimens from greenhouses need dissection to confirm identity.
Habitat. Woodland (but more usually in greenhouses).
Range. N. African and S.E. European.
Distribution. Map 161. One open site near Obernburg, S. Germany (possibly more widespread in this area), and in greenhouses in Scotland (Edinburgh, Glasgow).

*LIMAX MARGINATUS Müller 1774   Pl. 13

Syns. *Lehmannia marginata* (Müller), *Limax arborum* Bouchard-Chantereaux

Description. Medium to large slug, extended length 7–8 cm. Usually greyish and gelatinous and translucent in wet weather, and with two darker lateral bands on each side of the mid-line behind the mantle, and with a pair of bands on the mantle forming a lyre shape. Keel short, usually paler than body. Sole greyish-white, mucus colourless. There are a number of body colour variants and the dark bands may be broken up into rows of spots. For internal features see below. Often exudes masses of watery mucus when disturbed.

Similar species. Young *L. maximus* (p. 136) are never *banded* on the mantle, and lack the gelatinous appearance and watery mucus. *L. valentianus* differs internally (p. 139) and is usually paler with a yellowish tinge, and with the lateral bands higher – nearer the mid-line. See also *L. nyctelius* (p. 137) and *L. macroflagellatus*.

Note. Two other *Limax*, *L. rupicola* (Lessona & Pollonera) and *L. janetscheki* (Forcart) occur in the Alps, and have been recorded in the Bavarian Alps. They are very similar to *L. marginatus*, and can be distinguished only on small differences in internal anatomy. A similar form, *L. islandicus*, is found in Iceland. Further work is needed to clarify the status of these forms.

Habitat. In woodlands – especially under bark of dead timber, and climbs readily; also in open habitats – rocky ground and stone walls especially in areas of heavy rainfall.

Range. European.

Distribution. Map 162. Throughout, except northernmost Sweden, and not beyond 62°N in Finland.

LIMAX MACROFLAGELLATUS (Grossu & Lupu 1962)

Syn. *Lehmannia macroflagellata* Grossu & Lupu

Description. Small to medium slug, extended length 4–5 cm. Slim, very variable in colour, usually a light cream covered with darker flecks, which may be arranged to form bands. Mantle has two lateral bands joining posteriorly. Keel pale, and central paler band extends from keel to mantle, flanked by dark bands, giving the body a stripy appearance. Sole and foot fringe pale, mucus watery and colourless. For internal characters see p. 142. Not reliably separated from *L. marginatus* on external characters alone.

Similar species. *L. marginatus, L. nyctelius* (p. 137).

Habitat. Montane woodland (usually above 900 m) and also above tree line under rocks and boulders. Sometimes found with *L. marginatus*.

Range. Carpathian.

Distribution. Map 163. East Germany near Polish frontier (near Görlitz) only.

INTERNAL DIAGNOSTIC CHARACTERS OF *LIMAX* SPECIES

The important diagnostic features in these species are concerned with the length and shape of the penis, and with the presence, size and shape of the penial appendix (or flagellum).

Limax maximus Penis long and coiled in *situ*, thickening proximally, and not as long as in *L. cinereoniger*.

L. cinereoniger Penis very long and coiled in *situ*, and of roughly uniform thickness throughout.

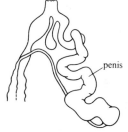

Limax maximus

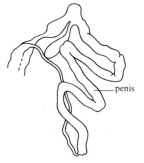

L. cinereoniger

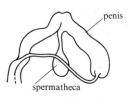

L. tenellus

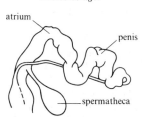

L. flavus

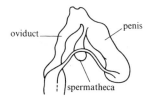

L. pseudoflavus

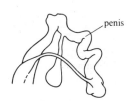

L. nyctelius

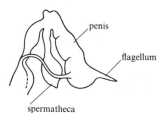

L. marginatus

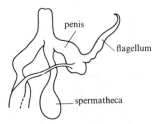

L. macroflagellatus

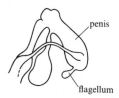

L. valentianus

Distal genitalia of *Limax*

Plate 11

Family ZONITIDAE
See also plates 8-10
(×3)

1a-c. **Oxychilus depressus**   126
Mainly in the Alps and S. Germany, rare. Colourless and glassy.
Umbilicus minute.

2. **Daudebardia rufa**   126
    2a-b. Shell: oblong, upper margin nearly straight.
    2c. Living animal.

3a-b. **Daudebardia brevipes**   127
Shell smaller than *D. rufa*: oval, upper margin strongly convex.

4a-c. ***Zonitoides nitidus**   127
Common in marshes. Warm glossy brown (nearly black when alive).

5a-c. ***Zonitoides excavatus**   127
Mainly British Isles, in acid woodland. Umbilicus extremely large,
like that of *Discus rotundatus* (see plate 3).

Family CLAUSILIIDAE
(×4)

6. ***Cochlodina laminata**   155
The commonest *Cochlodina*.

7. **Macrogastra ventricosa**   162
C. Europe. The largest *Macrogastra*.

Family SUBULINIDAE
(×3)

8. **Rumina decollata**   151
Mediterranean, dry places.
    8a. Top view of adult shell.
    8b. Juvenile shell, before truncation.
    8c. Adult shell, after truncation.

1a
1b
1c

2a
2b
2c

3a
3b
3c

4a
4b
4c

5a
5b
5c

6

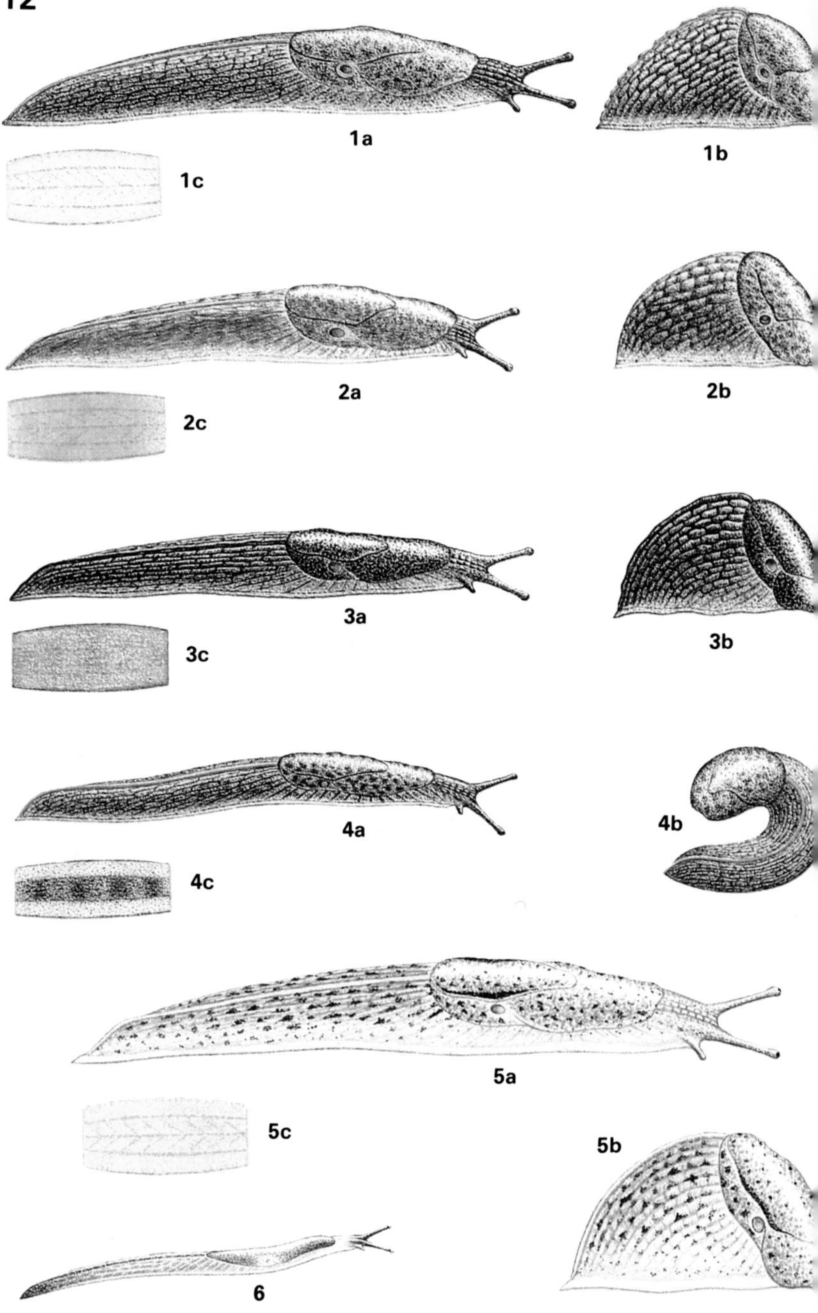

Family MILACIDAE
(life size)

Plate 12

1. *Milax sowerbyi   130
Mainly in cultivated places.
  1a. Extended: usually brown, often a pale tan colour. Mucus yellowish. Rim of respiratory pore pale.
  1b. Contracted.
  1c. Sole: uniformly pale.

2. *Milax gagates   130
  2a. Extended: usually slatey-grey. Mucus colourless. Rather smooth.
  2b. Contracted.
  2c. Sole: uniformly pale.

3. Milax nigricans   130
Mediterranean
  3a. Extended: darker than *M. gagates*, tubercles coarser.
  3b. Contracted.
  3c Sole: uniformly brownish.

4. *Milax budapestensis   131
Mainly in cultivated places, a serious pest.
  4a. Extended: very slender when fully stretched.
  4b. Contracted: C-shape characteristic (not hump).
  4c. Sole: central strip dark.

5. Milax rusticus   131
C. Europe, mainly in wild places.
  5a. Extended: large, pinkish, very distinctly spotted with black.
  5b. Contracted.
  5c. Sole.

6. *Boettgerilla pallens   131
Small, pale grey. Very worm-like when fully extended.

L. flavus Penis long and convoluted, spermatheca duct joins vagina.

L. pseudoflavus Penis shorter and simply curved. Spermatheca duct joins base of penis.

L. tenellus Very similar in general outline to *L. pseudoflavus* (clearly distinct on external characters).

L. nyctelius Similar to *L. pseudoflavus* and *L. tenellus*, but with proportionately longer penis.

L. marginatus Penis with short tapering flagellum. Some mountain forms have a longer flagellum, but never as long as the penis itself. (This form is sometimes regarded as a distinct species, *L. rupicola*). Spermatheca usually about the same size as penis.

L. macroflagellatus Penis short, and with long, slightly tapered flagellum as long or longer than penis itself. Spermatheca usually much longer than penis.

†*L. valentianus* Penis with short cylindrical or bulbous flagellum, not tapering.

†Greenhouse alien only (see p. 211).

DEROCERAS   LAEVE (Müller 1774)   Pl. 14
Syn. *Agriolimax laevis* (Müller)
Description. Small slug – extended length 1.5–2.5 cm. Translucent, chestnut to very dark brown, usually with darker flecks. Mantle lighter, extending for nearly half the body-length, and with fewer and larger concentric rings compared to other *Deroceras* species. Rim of respiratory pore slightly paler than mantle. Keel short and truncated. Sole pale brown, body and foot mucus thin and colourless. For internal characters see p. 146.
Similar species. *D. sturanyi* and *D. caruanae* (p. 143).
Habitat. Very wet places – fens, river-banks, wet woodland and meadows, sometimes found immersed.
Range. Holarctic.
Distribution. Map 164. Nearly throughout, but scarce in northernmost Scandinavia.

DEROCERAS   STURANYI (Simroth 1894)   Pl. 14
Description. Small to medium slug – extended length 3–4 cm. Translucent, pale cream to dark brown, without darker flecks, but with sometimes thin whitish streaks on the sides. Mantle large, about half length of body, *margin of respiratory pore not conspicuous*. Sole pale, darker in central region, body and foot slime thin and colourless. For internal characters see p. 146.
Similar species. *D. laeve, D. caruanae* (p. 143), *D. agreste* (p. 143).
Habitat. Usually in damp places, also in gardens, waste ground and damp roadside ditches. Not as wet-loving as *D. laeve*.
Range. European (originally probably E. European only).
Distribution. Map 165. Poorly known: not uncommon in S. and E. Germany, and apparently spreading; isolated sites in S. Sweden (mainly Gotland) and in Holland.

*DEROCERAS CARUANAE (Pollonera 1891) **Pl. 14**
Syn. *D. pollonerai* (Simroth)
Description. Small to medium slug, extended length 2.5–3.5 cm. Slightly translucent, light to medium brown, sometimes greyish to black often with darker flecks. Mantle about a third of length of body, *pale margin of respiratory pore conspicuous*. Head and neck in front of mantle unusually long when extended. Keel short and truncated. Sole greyish, body and foot mucus colourless. Particularly active and aggressive, lashing tail from side to side and often snapping at other individuals. For internal features see p. 146.
Habitat. Gardens, parks and waste ground, and also in hedges and fields in some areas near the sea.
Range. European (originally probably in S.W. only).
Distribution. Map 166. Common in open sites in Ireland, W. Britain and W. France. Elsewhere mainly in gardens and greenhouses northwards to Sweden and Finland. Spreading rapidly.

*DEROCERAS AGRESTE (Linné 1758) **Pl. 14**
Syn. *Agriolimax agrestis* (Linné)
Description. Medium slug – extended length 3.5–5.0 (rarely to 6.0) cm. Body and mantle pale buff, occasionally browner and greyer, lacking reticulation of darker spots or flecks, and with rather fine tubercles. Head and tentacles usually darker. Respiratory pore with slightly paler rim. Sole white to cream, mucus colourless or milky-white especially when irritated. For internal features see p. 146. (This species was often confused with *D. reticulatum* in the past.)
Habitat. Meadows, wet montane pastures and wild places, especially in mountainous regions; to 2400 m in the Alps.
Range. W. Palaearctic.
Distribution. Map 167. Mainly northern, eastern, and montane, but exact distribution uncertain owing to confusion with *D. reticulatum*.

*DEROCERAS RETICULATUM (Müller 1774) **Pl. 14**
Syns. *Agriolimax reticulatus* (Müller), *A. agrestis* of most older authors (*non* Linné)
Description. Medium slug – extended length 3.5–5.0 (rarely 6.0) cm. Body ranging from pale cream through browns to slate-grey, and usually, but not always, with a dense pattern of darker flecks, especially in the grooves between tubercles. Tubercles large and distinct. Rim of respiratory pore slightly paler than mantle. Keel short and truncate, sole pale, mucus colourless or white when irritated. For internal characters see p. 146.
Similar species. Easily confused on external characters with *D. agreste* and *D. rodnae* (p. 146).
Habitat. Agricultural land, hedges, gardens, and grassland. A major pest of many crops. Probably the most abundant slug in lowland areas.
Range. European.
Distribution. Map 168. Nearly throughout, scarce in N. Scandinavia where it is mainly synanthropic.

144

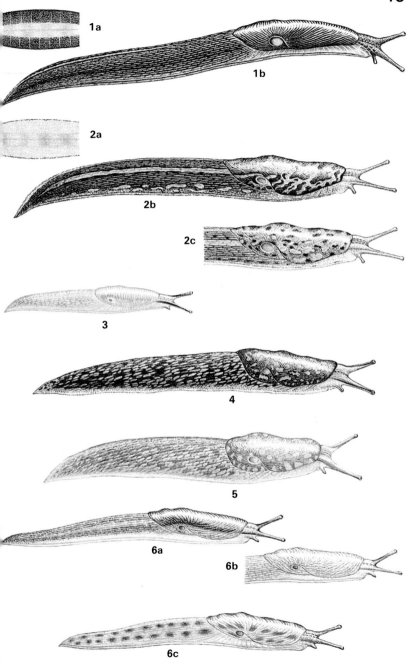

13

1a

1b

2a

2b

2c

3

4

5

6a

6b

6c

14

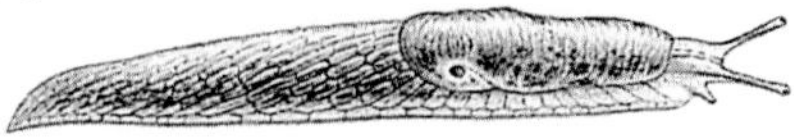

1a

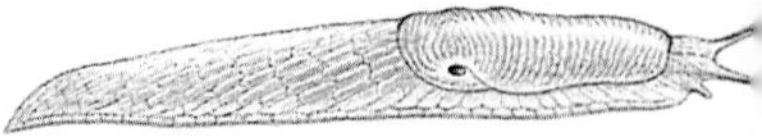

1b

2

3

4

5

6

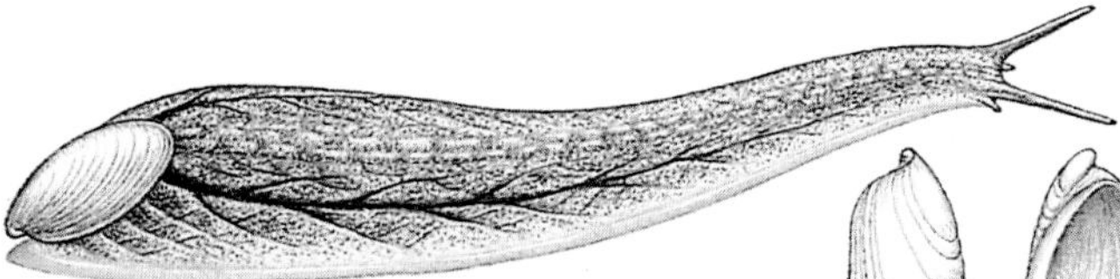

7a

7b  7c

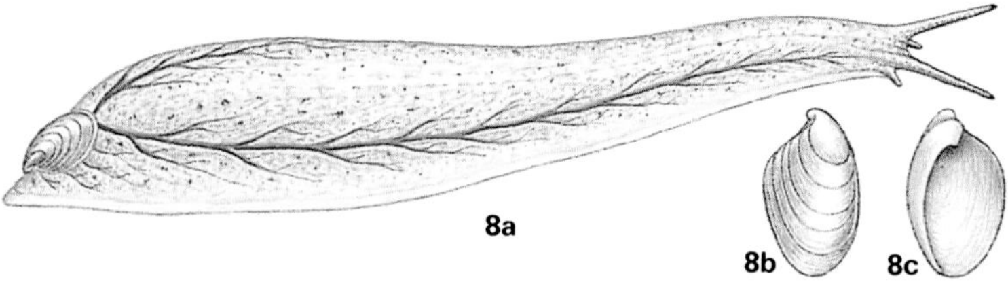

8a

8b 8c

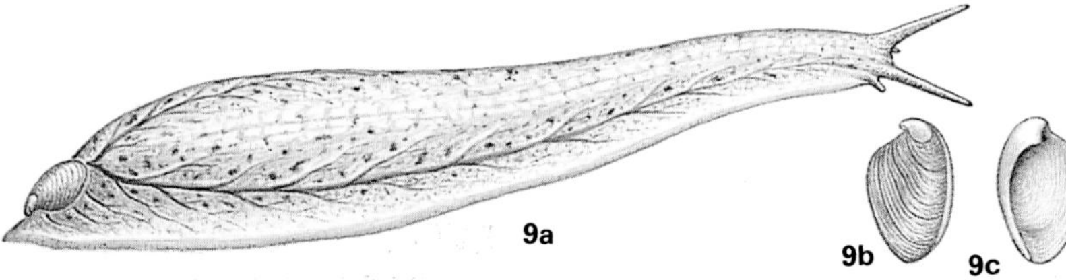

9a

9b 9c

Family LIMACIDAE Plate 14
See also plate 13
(life size)

Deroceras species can be difficult to name from their external appearance alone. For anatomical characters see p. 146.

1. *Deroceras reticulatum* 143
The commonest slug in N.W. Europe. A major pest.
   1a. Typical speckled form.
   1b. Pale form.

2. *Deroceras laeve* 142
Common in marshes. Very small. Dark chestnut-brown to black.

3. *Deroceras agreste* 143
Usually a pale uniform oatmeal (never speckled).

4. *Deroceras caruanae* 143
Very lively and aggressive. Greyish-brown, slightly translucent. Margin of respiratory pore conspicuous.

5. Deroceras rodnae 146
C. Europe, in woods. Like *D. reticulatum*; separable only by dissection.

6. Deroceras sturanyi 142
Mainly C. Europe. Brown, slightly translucent. Respiratory pore inconspicuous.

Family TESTACELLIDAE
(life size, except shells)

7. *Testacella maugei* 173
   7a. Living animal: points of origin of lateral grooves widely separated.
   7b-c. Shell (× 1½): large, oblong, strongly convex.

8. *Testacella haliotidea* 173
   8a. Living animal: points of origin of lateral grooves *just* separated.
   8b-c. Shell (× 2): much smaller than *T. maugei*.

9. *Testacella scutulum* 174
   9a. Living animal: usually yellow. Junction of lateral grooves just visible.
   9b-c. Shell (×2): small and flat.

DEROCERAS RODNAE Grossu & Lupu 1965   Pl.14

Description. Small to medium slug – extended length 3.0–4.0 cm. Body pale yellow, or cream, usually with small dark flecks especially common on the sides. Head darker, tentacles always dark, keel short and truncate. Sole pale, translucent in the central part, body mucus milky-white when irritated. For internal characters see below. See also note below.

Similar species. Easily confused with *D. reticulatum* (p. 143).

Habitat. Damp places in woods, both deciduous and conifer, and also in montane grassland (above *c.* 1000 m).

Range. C. European.

Distribution. Map 169. Poorly known, a very few sites in C. and S. Germany, Switzerland and E. France (Vosges).

Deroceras praecox Wiktor 1966 is very similar to *D. rodnae*. It is recorded from W. Poland and N. Czechoslovakia and may well be found in S.E. Germany. Its chief distinguishing feature is that the proximal end of the penis is coiled into a small spiral. The appendices are much like those of *D. rodnae* or *D. reticulatum*. Externally, it is usually paler than *D. rodnae*, and has larger flecks, when these are present.

INTERNAL DIAGNOSTIC CHARACTERS OF *DEROCERAS* SPECIES

The most important characters in this genus are the shape of the penis and its appendages.

Deroceras sturanyi has no appendages, but the penis is swollen proximally, giving it a characteristic hammer-shaped appearance.

D. laeve has a long and sinuous penis with a variable, but simple appendage. Some individuals are nearly entirely female, with vestigial male organs.

D. caruanae has 4–6 long, thin and slightly serrated appendages, and the proximal end of the penis is bilobed.

D. agreste has a single, simple penial appendage without swellings or lobes.

D. reticulatum has a complex penial appendage, with 1–4 processes, knobbly or lobed in appearance. They are much shorter and wider than those of *D. caruanae*, but the variation in size and shape is considerable.

D. rodnae has a complex penial appendage, usually with 2–3 rather knobbly processes. It could be confused with that of *D. reticulatum*. In cases of doubt, the sarcobelum or stimulator, inside the penis, should be examined – it is shaped rather like a flattened axe-head in *D. rodnae*, but it is roughly conical in *D. reticulatum*.

Note. *D. sturanyi*, *D. laeve* and *D. caruanae* are usually distinguished from the others externally by their darker colour and colourless body slime. *D. agreste* is never heavily reticulate.

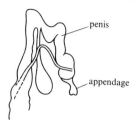

Deroceras laeve, normal form

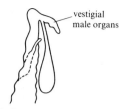

D. laeve, 'female' (aphallic) form

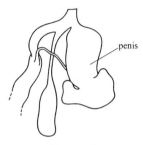

D. sturanyi

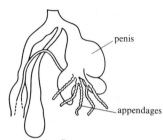

D. caruanae

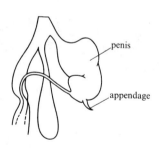

D. agreste

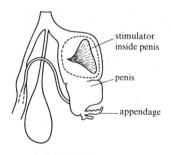

D. reticulatum

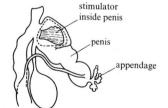

D. rodnae

Distal genitalia of Deroceras

Family **EUCONULIDAE**

The shell in this family is small and top-shaped, usually thin and glossy, with numerous rather narrow whorls. The mouth-edge is thin and simple, and the umbilicus is either minute or entirely closed. The under surface of the shell often carries very delicate spiral striations.

The Euconulidae live in damp situations in most parts of the world. They are represented in Europe by the genus *Euconulus* only.

*****EUCONULUS FULVUS** (Müller 1774)
Syn. *E. trochiformis* (Montagu)

Description. br. 2.8–3.5 mm. Shell squatly conical, with about 5½ whorls, the last slightly keeled at the periphery (more strongly so in the juvenile). Mouth crescentic; mouth-edge simple, thin and brittle. Umbilicus just perceptible. Spiral striae on base absent or very faint, even under high magnification (cf. *E. alderi*). Shell pale yellowish-brown, translucent, with a slightly silky gloss.

The body is pale.

Habitat. Catholic: widespread in deciduous and coniferous woods, grasslands, marshes; usually in fairly moist places.

Range. Holarctic.

Distribution. Map 170. Throughout.

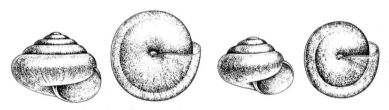

Euconulus fulvus × 7   *E. alderi* × 7

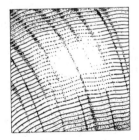

Microsculpture on base of *Euconulus alderi*

*EUCONULUS ALDERI (Gray 1840)
Syn. *E. fulvus* var. *alderi* Gray
Description. br. 2.3–2.8 mm. Shell closely similar to *E. fulvus*, but smaller and slightly darker; spiral striae on base *more distinct* under high magnification. Shell glossy rather than silky.
     The body is *dark*; in life the shell consequently appears almost black.
Habitat. Usually in wetter places than *E. fulvus*; characteristic of marshes.
Range. Probably Holarctic.
Distribution. No European map; British map 170a. Probably throughout, but more local than *E. fulvus*.

Family **FERUSSACIIDAE**

The shell is rather small, pale, glossy and translucent, generally of a slender fusiform shape with a blunt apex and a relatively large but narrow last whorl. The mouth-edge is simple and delicate. The base of the columella is usually truncate, and the columella itself often bears a spiral fold.
     Members of this rather small family live in many parts of the world, mostly in warm climates. They are often blind and subterranean in habit.

*CECILIOIDES ACICULA (Müller 1774)
Syn. *Caecilianella acicula* (Müller)
Description. 4.5–5.5 × 1.2 mm. Shell very narrow and slender, with 5½ feebly-convex whorls tapering to a blunt apex. Mouth forming about a third of the total height; columella obliquely truncate at base; a columellar fold sometimes present in juveniles. Shell colourless, delicate, glassy and transparent when fresh, after death quickly becoming white and opaque.
     The body is colourless, and eyes are absent.
Habitat. Subterranean, living well below the surface among plant roots or in the crevices of rocks, mostly on calcareous soils; more commonly found dead in flood rubbish, or in ant hills.
Range. Mediterranean and W. European.
Distribution. Map 171. Widespread, but absent from Scotland and N. Ireland, and not extending beyond southernmost Scandinavia (Sweden to 58°N). Widely distributed by man.

Cecilioides acicula × 7

CECILIOIDES JANI (De Betta & Martinati 1855)

Syn. *C. aciculoides* of many authors (*non* Cristofori & Jan)

Description. 5–7 × 1.9 mm. Shell similar to *C. acicula*, but larger and relatively much broader, and with the mouth forming about half the total height; columella more clearly truncate at base.

Habitat. Subterranean, among rocks, and in the soil at the base of old walls.

Range. Mediterranean.

Distribution. Map 172. S. Switzerland (S. Ticino) only.

Cryptazeca monodonta × 7

Cecilioides jani × 7

CRYPTAZECA MONODONTA (Folin & Bérillon 1876)

Description. 3.5–4 × 1.7 mm. Shell conical-oval, rather like a very small *Cochlicopa* or *Azeca*, with 5 almost flat-sided whorls, the last forming about two-thirds of the total height. Inner margin of mouth with a raised callus having a well-defined edge; columella obliquely truncate at base, giving the appearance of a small columellar tooth. Shell rather thin, pale yellowish-brown, very glossy and translucent.

Habitat. Moist places among rocks and leaf litter.

Range. W. Pyrenean.

Distribution. Map 173. Very rare: Basses Pyrénées only (Cambo, Bayonne).

Family **SUBULINIDAE**

In the Subulinidae the shell is narrowly conical and tapering, often of moderate size and composed of a large number of weakly-convex whorls. The base of the columella may be truncate. The mouth is generally rounder than in the Ferus- saciidae, and there is no columellar fold. The animal is usually a pale lemon-yellow colour.

The Subulinidae are almost exclusively tropical. Apart from several greenhouse aliens (see pp. 211–212), they are represented in Europe by one species only.

RUMINA DECOLLATA (Linné 1758)   **Pl. 11**
Description. 22–35 (occasionally 40) mm. Juvenile slender and tapering, concave-sided, apex bluntly rounded reflecting the very large size of the egg (2.5 mm). Adult sub-cylindrical, with 3–6 whorls only, the earlier-formed whorls being lost by *deliberate truncation*, the apical opening being sealed by a shelly plate. Shell thick, opaque, pale brown or cream, rather glossy, growth-lines crossed by irregular spiral striations.
Habitat. Dry open places: waste ground, scrub, grassy screes; mostly on calcareous soils.
Range. Mediterranean.
Distribution. Map 174. A common Mediterranean species, just extending into S.W. France (Lot et Garonne, Gers, Haute Garonne); elsewhere as an occasional adventive.

Family CLAUSILIIDAE

This large family is very distinctive: the shell is nearly always sinistral, of moderate size (commonly 10–15 mm), and is fusiform or club-shaped, with a gradually tapering spire made up of many whorls. Frequently the shell is ribbed. The mouth is relatively small and pear-shaped, with slightly expanded lips. Internally there is a

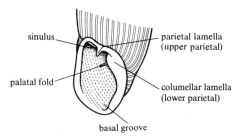

Frontal view of mouth of a clausiliid (*Laciniaria biplicata*)

more or less complex system of narrow teeth (often called folds, plicae or lamellae), only partly visible from outside. In frontal view the inner lip usually carries two distinct lamella-like teeth (here called the *parietal lamella* and the *columellar lamella*), between which there may be some minor additional (*interlamellar*) teeth. Deeply-set within the upper part of the mouth there is a *spiral lamella*, more or less in line with the parietal lamella and sometimes continuous with it. Usually there is also a *subcolumellar lamella*, partly hidden behind the base of the columellar lamella. Within the outer lip there may be a further series of narrow *palatal* teeth,

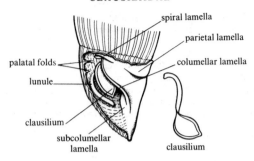

Side view of mouth of a clausiliid (*Laciniaria biplicata*), with the palatal area broken away to show the internal folds and the clausilium

often visible as sub-parallel white lines through the back of the last whorl. Sometimes there is additionally a transverse crescentic ridge (the *lunule*), set convex-side forwards in the palate about half a whorl back from the mouth; this also can often be seen externally (p. 153).

Internally, the Clausiliidae are characterized by a flexible spoon-shaped calcareous plate (the *clausilium*), the upper attenuated end of which is fixed to the columella. When the animal is crawling the clausilium is pushed elastically out of the way into a groove between the columellar and the subcolumellar lamellae, but on retraction the expanded end springs out against the palate and blocks entry into the shell. The lower margin of the clausilium is usually rounded or bluntly pointed and fits into the concavity of the lunule (when present); sometimes it is notched (e.g., in *Cochlodina*), in which case the indentation fits over one of the palatal folds. The exact function of the clausilium is uncertain, but it may help to prevent the entry of predatory insects and other small animals.

In addition to the true teeth, there may be more or less well defined patches of callus within the mouth, especially on the palate.

The Clausiliidae occur in the western Palaearctic region, in South America, and in S.E. Asia. In Europe they attain their maximum diversity in the Balkans and the Caucasus, where there are at least 150 described species. Geographical subspeciation is common. They become rarer to the west, only six species occurring in the French Pyrenees, six in Britain, and three in Ireland. They live mainly in woods and among rocks, normally hiding in crevices or under ground litter, but emerging in damp weather or at night and climbing high up on bare surfaces to graze on algae or lichens. Old living shells may become whitened or eroded, or covered with a green film. A few species are ovo-viviparous, in N.W. Europe notably *Balea perversa*, *Laciniaria biplicata* and *Macrogastra ventricosa*.

The following artificial key offers a guide to the genera occurring within our area. It is based mainly on external appearances, though internal shell characters are also referred to where they may be important for accurate diagnosis. The presence of a lunule can often be detected externally in fresh empty shells, particularly by holding

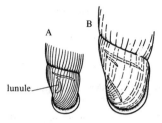

Rear view of last whorls of clausiliids having (A) a lunule (*Macrogastra plicatula*), and (B) no lunule (*Cochlodina laminata*). The palatal folds can also be seen through the translucency of the shells.

them against a strong light; it appears as a diffuse crescentic mark, but should not be confused with the lower edge of the clausilium, which may be seen as a narrow curved *line*. In cases of doubt, and for a proper examination of other internal features (e.g., the spiral lamella) the shell must be broken away with a needle, or pair of fine, strong forceps.

A natural classification of the clausilias into subfamilies is difficult, and cannot be made using shell characters alone. *Balea* and *Laciniaria*, for example, are placed in a common subfamily (Baleinae) because of their very similar anatomy, though their shells are strikingly different.

1. Shell conical, without teeth or a clausilium (sometimes with a minute parietal denticle) *Balea*, p. 172
   Shell fusiform or club-shaped, with teeth and a clausilium. **2**

2. Last whorl projecting strongly, like a spout (W. Pyrenees only) *Laminifera*, p. 154
   Last whorl not spout-like. **3**

3. Mouth triangular, very acutely pointed at base; shell smooth (Bavarian Alps only) *Erjavecia*, p. 159
   Mouth not triangular. **4**

4. Apex (first 2 whorls) distinctly conical; shell very small (8 mm), with sharp, widely-spaced ribs. *Ruthenica*, p. 158
   Apex not conical. **5**

5. Shell smooth or only bluntly-ribbed, rather translucent; parietal lip closely attached to previous whorl; parietal and spiral lamellae separate. **6**
   Shell distinctly ribbed; parietal lip more or less detached from previous whorl. **8**

6. Shell very large (>17 mm), with a row of raised white papillae along the suture; a lunule present. *Itala*, p. 157
   Shell smaller (< 17 mm), with no white papillae; no lunule. **7**

7. Shell medium-sized (12–17 mm); clausilium notched
    at base.   *Cochlodina*, p. 155
    Shell small (10–12 mm); clausilium simple (S. Swit-
    zerland only)   *Charpentieria*, p. 158

8. Mouth broadly expanded below, usually lacking a
    basal groove.   **9**
    Mouth narrower, always with a distinct basal groove,
    and often slightly pointed externally.   **10**

9. Lip with a rib-like thickening running round just
    inside the mouth, interrupted basally by a slight
    notch (Bavarian Forest only)   *Vestia*, p. 172
    Lip without a rib-like thickening; columellar lamella
    complexly forked, in oblique view often like a
    recumbent K ($\times$); parietal and spiral lamellae
    united.   *Macrogastra*, p. 162

10. Shell small (8–14 mm), ribbing usually blunt and often
    fine.   **11**
    Shell larger (15–18 mm), ribbing sharp and distinct;
    parietal and spiral lamellae separate.   **13**

11. A lunule present; parietal and spiral lamellae united.   *Clausilia*, p. 165
    Lunule absent or rudimentary.   **12**

12. Shell small (9–11 mm), brown, club-shaped; base of
    mouth indistinctly pointed; spiral lamella rudimen-
    tary, not united with parietal lamella.   *Neostyriaca*, p. 168
    Shell small (9–10 mm), pale greenish, bluntly
    fusiform; base of mouth distinctly pointed; parietal
    and spiral lamellae united.   *Fusulus*, p. 159

13. No palatal callus or visible lower palatal fold.   *Laciniaria*, p. 169
    A distinct palatal callus and/or lower palatal fold.   *Bulgarica*, p. 170

Subfamily **LAMINIFERINAE**

LAMINIFERA PAULI (Mabille 1865)
Description. 13–15 × 2.7–3 mm. Spire slender, tapering gradually to a rather
acutely pointed apex. Last whorl detached, projecting freely *well beyond the rest of
the shell*. Mouth well-rounded below, with a deep sinulus above; parietal lamella
strong; columellar lamella inconspicuous; 3–5 interlamellar folds; no palatal folds.
Ribs rather sharp, fairly widely spaced.
Habitat. Shaded places in woods and among rocks.
Range and distribution. Map 175. Rare: known only from a few places in the
foothills of the French Pyrenees (Basses Pyrénées) south of Bayonne.

Laminifera pauli × 4

Cochlodina laminata × 4

Subfamily ALLOPIINAE

*COCHLODINA LAMINATA (Montagu 1803)   **Pl. 11**
Syn. *Marpessa laminata* (Montagu)
Description. 15–17 × 4 mm. Shell broadly fusiform, with 11–12 whorls, apex rather blunt and rounded. Mouth-edge bluntly thickened, white, reflected, closely attached to previous whorl in parietal area. Parietal and columellar lamellae strongly developed; a small subcolumellar lamella; 3–4 palatal folds, of which 2 (1st and 3rd) are usually clearly visible in the mouth; palatal callus very feeble. No lunule. Shell yellowish-brown, glossy and rather translucent, with faint irregular growth-lines only.
Habitat. Shaded places in woods and scrub under ground litter; in wet weather often climbing trunks. Attaining 1900 m in the Swiss Alps.
Range. European.
Distribution. Map 176. Widespread, becoming scarcer to the west (rare in W. France, Ireland, Wales, Scotland) and absent from much of Scandinavia; rare in the S. Alps.

COCHLODINA FIMBRIATA (Rossmässler 1835)
Description. 14–16 × 4 mm. Shell closely similar to *C. laminata*, but distinguished by a more or less strongly developed white *rib-like palatal callus* a little way within the mouth, running round parallel with the growth-lines. Lower (3rd) palatal fold shorter than in *C. laminata*, scarcely visible in frontal view, and usually failing to meet the palatal callus. Shell usually paler than in *C. laminata*, often with the

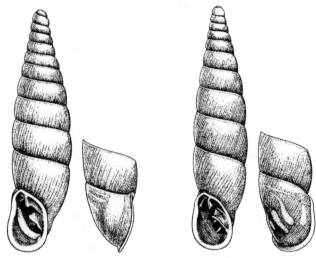

Cochlodina fimbriata × 4   *C. costata* × 4

growth-lines a little more regular and better defined, especially on the earlier whorls.

Habitat. Moist shaded places in woods and among rocks; calciphile; exclusively montane.

Range. Alpine.

Distribution. Map 177. French and Swiss Alps and Jura; also scattered localities in the mountains of S.W. Germany from the S. Black Forest to the Allgäuer Alps.

COCHLODINA COSTATA (Pfeiffer 1828)

Syns. *C. commutata* (Rossmässler), *C. ungulata* (Rossmässler), *C. silesiaca* (Schmidt)

Description. 14–16 × 3.2–3.5 mm. Shell externally similar to *C. laminata* and *C. fimbriata*. Palatal callus absent or weak, shorter than in *C. fimbriata*; 3–4 palatal folds, the 2nd (clearly visible only from behind through shell) curving sharply downwards about half a whorl back from the mouth and ending in a *white thickening*. Shell usually slightly less smooth than in *C. laminata* or *C. fimbriata*, and often darker and richer in colour.

This is a very variable species, divided into several geographical races. Other forms (including the type), which occur outside our area, may differ from the German race described above (subspecies *franconica* Ehrmann) in being larger, in having a coarsely ribbed sculpture, and in the palatal callus and teeth being more strongly developed.

Habitat. Moist shaded places in woods and among rocks; montane.

Range. E. Alpine, Carpathian and Dinaric.

Distribution. Map 178. A small area in the mountains of C. Germany only (Wiesent valley, Franconian Switzerland).

COCHLODINA COMENSIS (Pfeiffer 1849)

Description. 11.5–13 × 3.3–3.6 mm. Shell relatively short and squat, mouth broad and expanded below. Parietal and columellar lamellae both very strongly developed, the latter *sharply twisted* close to the lip; 4 palatal folds, of which 2 are clearly visible in the mouth; palatal callus irregularly developed. Shell very pale yellowish, rather translucent, with strong regular growth-ridges forming distinct close-set blunt ribs.

Habitat. Rocks, old walls, woods and scrubby places.

Range. S. Alpine.

Distribution. Map 179. S. Switzerland (S. Ticino) only.

Cochlodina comensis × 4   *C. orthostoma* × 4

COCHLODINA ORTHOSTOMA (Menke 1830)

Description. 12–13 × 3 mm. Shell relatively narrow and cylindrical, the later whorls not swelling out (cf. *C. laminata*). Parietal lamella rather weak, columella lamella very strong. Palatal folds deeply-set and not usually visible in frontal view; palatal callus parallel with outer lip, usually rather thin, not linked to palatal folds. Shell translucent, yellowish-brown (often tinged with green), glossy, with rather strong and distinct *regular blunt ribs*.

Habitat. Deciduous woods and moist shaded rocky places; often on tree trunks. Mainly montane.

Range. C. and E. European.

Distribution. Map 180. Local in S. and C. Germany (north to Thuringia) and in N.E. Switzerland; one locality in S. Finland (Karjalohja).

ITALA ITALA (Martens 1824)

Syns. *Delima itala* (Martens), *D. punctata* (Michaud), *D. braunii* (Rossmässler)

Description. 16–22 × 4–4.5 mm. Shell very large, mouth-edge white, strongly reflected. Inner lip with 3 lamellae (parietal, columellar, subcolumellar); 1 palatal fold only (upper), scarcely visible in frontal view. Lunule present, clearly visible through shell. Shell rather dull, scarcely translucent, dark reddish-brown, with a spiral row of *raised white papillae* near the suture; earlier whorls with rather strong and regular growth-ridges, later whorls almost smooth.

Habitat. Mainly rocks and old walls, but also in deciduous woods.

Range. S. Alpine.

Distribution. Map 181. Native only in S. Switzerland (Ticino) and in S.E. France (Isère, Hautes Alpes); introduced in several places north of the Alps, often apparently with vines (Geneva, Zurich, Basel, Weinheim, Heidelberg).

Charpentieria diodon × 4

Itala itala × 3

CHARPENTIERIA DIODON (Studer 1820)

Description. 10–12.5 × 2.8 mm. Shell with about 9 rather regularly enlarging whorls; apex blunt; mouth relatively large and rather squarish, with expanded lips. Columellar lamella prominent, simple; parietal lamella small; upper palatal fold just visible in frontal view. Palatal callus feeble or absent. No lunule. Shell pale yellowish-brown, glossy and very translucent, almost smooth, with only faint irregular growth-lines.

Habitat. Moist places among rocks; montane.

Range. S.W. Alpine.

Distribution. Map 182. Rare: near Gondo and Iselle in S. Switzerland (Valais) only.

Subfamily CLAUSILIINAE

RUTHENICA FILOGRANA (Rossmässler 1836)

Syn. *Graciliaria filograna* (Rossmässler)

Description. 7–9 × 2–2.2 mm. Shell very small, strongly swollen in the middle and

with the last 2 whorls narrowing markedly to a small mouth; apex *conical*, ending in a *sharp point*. Parietal and columellar lamellae weak; a palatal callus present, ending basally in a denticle-like tooth, and separated from a small subcolumellar fold by a gutter-like groove (usually only clearly seen in oblique view). No lunule. Shell pale yellowish-brown, with very sharp and narrow *widely-spaced* ribs.
Habitat. Ground litter and stones in woods (not a climbing species); calciphile; mainly montane.
Range. E. European.
Distribution. Map 183. Mountains of easternmost Germany (Bavarian Forest, Thuringian Forest, Erzgebirge, E. Harz); also a very few isolated localities in S. Germany (Swabian and Franconian Jura) and in Switzerland (S. of L. Constance).

Ruthenica filograna × 4   *Fusulus varians* × 4

FUSULUS VARIANS (Pfeiffer 1828)
Description. 9–9.5 × 2.2 mm. Shell small and rather evenly fusiform; mouth distinctly pointed below, corresponding externally with a strong basal crest. Parietal lamella distinct but but rather weak; columellar lamella inconspicuous, scarcely reaching lip; sometimes 1 or more small interlamellar folds. A strong white rib-like palatal callus present, united basally to a palatal fold, which is then separated from the subcolumellar fold by a very marked gutter-like groove, running out at the base of the mouth. No lunule. Shell pale yellowish or greenish-brown, rather glossy and translucent, with close-set fairly regular blunt ribs.
Habitat. Moist shaded woodland, under ground litter and stones; montane.
Range. E. Alpine and W. Carpathian.
Distribution. Map 184. Mountains of East Germany (Erzgebirge); isolated sites in the Bavarian Alps (S. of the Chiemsee) and in Franconian Switzerland.

ERJAVECIA BERGERI (Rossmässler 1836)
Description. 10.5–12 × 2.3–2.5 mm. Mouth *triangular*, the lowest point corresponding externally to a strongly raised basal crest and internally with a deep groove. Lips thickened and expanded, parietal lip clearly detached from previous whorl. Parietal lamella small but distinct; other teeth inconspicuous in frontal view. Lunule vestigial. Shell dark reddish-brown (often weathering to a pale grey), dull, virtually smooth.

160

Plate 15

Family HELICIDAE
Subfamily HELICELLINAE
See also plates 16 and 24
(1 and 2 ×2, 3-8 ×3)

1. ***Candidula intersecta** 177
Ribbing distinct. Mouth-rib strong. Umbilicus symmetrical.
   1a-b. Colour variants.
   1c-e. Typical form.

2a-c. ***Candidula gigaxii** 177
Ribbing closer and finer than in *C. intersecta*; last whorl broader.
Umbilicus eccentric.

3a-b. **Candidula unifasciata** 176
Small and white. Ribbing fine, blunt, may appear smooth at first
glance.

4a-b. **Helicella apicina** 182
Mediterranean only. Mouth large, without internal rib. Hairy when
young.

5a-c. **Trochoidea geyeri** 182
C. Europe. Ribbing coarse, sharp, irregular. Mouth-rib weak or
absent. For anatomy see Fig., p. 183.

6a-c. **Helicopsis striata** 183
C. Europe. Very like *Trochoidea geyeri*, often confused. For
anatomy see Fig., p. 183.

7. ***Trochoidea elegans** 182
Mainly Mediterranean. Distinctively conical.

8a-b. **Helicella conspurcata** 182
Mediterranean, in relatively shady places. Hairy when young.

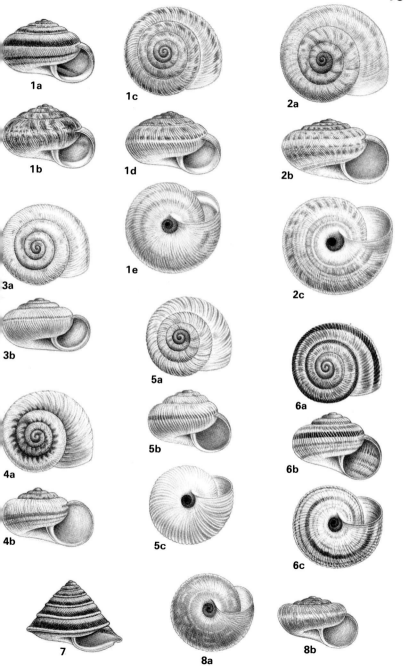

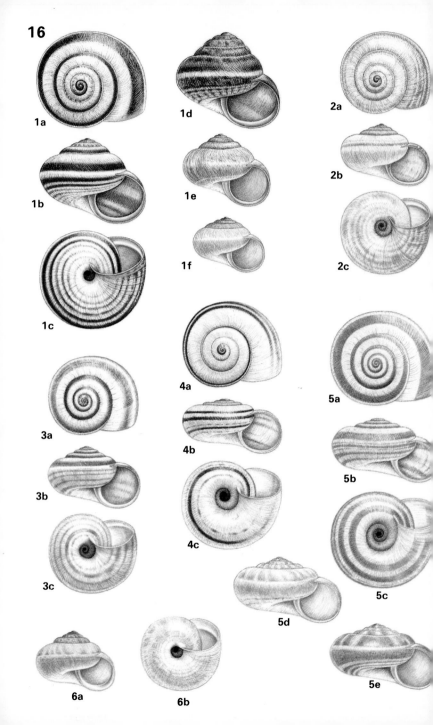

16

1a 1b 1c 1d 1e 1f

2a 2b 2c

3a 3b 3c

4a 4b 4c

5a 5b 5c 5d 5e

6a 6b

Family HELICIDAE
Subfamily HELICELLINAE
See also plates 15 and 24

($\times 1\frac{1}{2}$)

Plate 16

1. ***Cernuella virgata**   177
Common in British Isles and France. Globular, umbilicus small.
Highly polymorphic.
    1a-c. Typical form.
    1d-f. Size and colour variants.

2a-c. **Cernuella aginnica**   178
Mainly S. France. Flatter than *C. virgata*, umbilicus wider.

3a-c. **Cernuella neglecta**   179
Mainly S. France. Flatter than either *C. virgata* or *C. aginnica*.
Umbilicus still wider.

4a-c. **Helicella obvia**   179
C. Europe (not in west). Very white. Flat above, last whorl very
broad.

5. ***Helicella itala**   179
W. Europe. Last whorl narrower than in *H. obvia*, umbilicus wider.
    5a-c. Typical form.
    5d-e. Colour variants.

6a-b. **Helicella bolenensis**   179
Rare, mainly Mediterranean. White, globular, with fine growth-
ridges.

Habitat. Screes and rocks, usually in warm exposed situations; calciphile; montane.
Range. E. Alpine.
Distribution. Map 185. Calcareous Alps of S.E. Bavaria, from Berchtesgaden to the R. Inn.

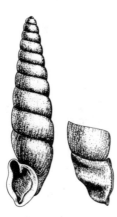

Erjavecia bergeri × 4

Macrogastra ventricosa × 4

MACROGASTRA VENTRICOSA (Draparnaud 1801)   Pl. 11
Syns. *Clausilia ventricosa* Draparnaud, *Iphigena ventricosa* (Draparnaud)
Description. 17–19 × 4–4.3 mm. The largest *Macrogastra*; spire narrow and tapering, later whorls broadening rapidly, often giving a distinctly club-shaped outline to the shell. Mouth rounded below, internally with a *slight* basal groove. Columellar lamella bifid towards lip and also internally; no interlamellar folds. Palatal callus very weak or absent; no visible palatal folds. Shell reddish-brown, with blunt well-defined regular ribs (about 5 per mm on penultimate whorl) crossed by very fine spiral striations.
Habitat. Mainly woods, under leaf litter, logs and mossy rocks.
Range. C. European.
Distribution. Map 186. E. France, S. Belgium, Switzerland, Germany (rare in N. German plain), Denmark, southernmost Norway and Sweden.

MACROGASTRA LINEOLATA (Held 1836)
Syns. *Clausilia lineolata* Held, *Iphigena lineolata* (Held)
Description. 13–16 × 3.3–3.7 mm. Shell rather similar to *M. ventricosa*, but considerably smaller. Mouth well-rounded below, without a basal groove. Columellar

lamella bifid both inwardly and towards lip, giving a clear ⅄-form; 1–2 weak interlamellar folds; a moderately developed palatal callus present, becoming thicker basally, where it often forms an *ill-defined white ridge* (false palatal fold) running back into the mouth. Shell reddish-brown, with blunt regular ribs (about 5–6 per mm on penultimate whorl).

Habitat. Moist woodland, under leaf litter, logs and stones, and among mossy rocks; mainly montane, attaining 1400 m in the Swiss Alps.

Range. W.C. European and Alpine.

Distribution. Map 187. E. France (Isère to Ardennes), Switzerland, S. Belgium, S. Holland (Limburg), local in S., S.W., and C. Germany as far north as the Thuringian Forest and the Harz (absent from most of Bavaria); also an isolated area on the German Baltic coast and in the Danish islands.

Macrogastra lineolata × 4   *M. densestriata* × 4

MACROGASTRA DENSESTRIATA (Rossmässler 1836)

Syns. Clausilia densestriata Rossmässler, *Iphigena densestriata* (Rossmässler)

Description. 12–13.5 × 3–3.2 mm. Outline similar to *M. lineolata*, but shell a little smaller and individual whorls slightly less tumid. Mouth well-rounded below. Columellar lamella very prominent, projecting into the mouth in a quadrant-like curve, the lower end clearly bifid over lip but not bifid internally; 3–4 distinct interlamellar folds. Palatal callus moderately developed, becoming thicker basally and joined by a well-defined narrow palatal fold. Shell reddish-brown, much more closely and finely ribbed than *M. lineolata* (about 8–9 ribs per mm on penultimate whorl).

Habitat. Moist shaded rocks, usually in woodland; calciphile; montane.

Range. E. Alpine and Dinaric.

Distribution. Map 188. Calcareous Alps of S.E. Bavaria (near Reichenhall).

MACROGASTRA BADIA (Pfeiffer 1828)

Syns. *Clausilia badia* Pfeiffer, *Iphigena badia* (Pfeiffer), *I. mucida* (Rossmässler)
Description. 12–14 × 3–3.2 mm. Shell rather evenly fusiform (not markedly club-shaped), mouth broad and well-rounded below. Columellar lamella bifid internally, the two ridges remaining sub-parallel; externally not bifid (or only weakly so), the main lower edge running abruptly at an angle into the columella, the upper branch alone reaching the lip; 1–3 weak interlamellar folds. Palatal callus thin but distinct, running round parallel with the growth-lines; no visible palatal folds. Shell reddish-brown, usually rather glossy, finely but bluntly ribbed (about 8 ribs per mm on penultimate whorl).
Habitat. Moist woods, under ground litter and on tree trunks and mossy rocks; montane.
Range. E. Alpine.
Distribution. Map 189. S. Bavaria (Bavarian Forest, Berchtesgaden Alps, Allgäuer Alps).

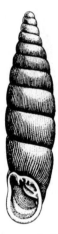

Macrogastra badia × 4   *M. plicatula* × 4

MACROGASTRA PLICATULA (Draparnaud 1801)

Syns. *Clausilia plicatula* Draparnaud, *Iphigena plicatula* (Draparnaud)
Description. 11–14 × 3 mm. Shell usually rather slender (not strongly tumid in the middle). Mouth well-rounded below, without a basal groove. Columellar lamella clearly ⋊-shaped, the 2 external branches about equally developed and extending out onto the lip; 1–3 interlamellar folds. Palatal callus rather thin, frequently divided into a basal crescentic area and a second patch below the sinulus. No visible palatal folds. Shell reddish-brown, with characteristically sharp and rather *widely-spaced* ribs (about 5–6 per mm on penultimate whorl).
Habitat. Woods, rocks, damp shaded places generally; attaining over 2000 m in the Swiss Alps.
Range. C. European.

Distribution. Map 190. Common throughout most of Germany and Switzerland; also E. France, S. Belgium, Denmark, S. Scandinavia.

*MACROGASTRA ROLPHII (Turton 1826)

Syns. *Clausilia rolphii* Turton, *Iphigena rolphii* (Turton)

Description. 11–14 × 3.4–3.6 mm. Shell relatively short and squat, the later whorls broadening out markedly. Mouth well-rounded below, but furnished internally with a clear basal groove; outer lip often sharply indented immediately below the sinulus. Columellar lamella ⅃-shaped, external branches short and weak; 1–3 rudimentary interlamellar folds. No palatal callus; no visible palatal folds. Shell reddish-brown, with rather blunt ribs, about 7 per mm on penultimate whorl.

Habitat. Moist deciduous woods, hedgebanks, among moss; always in ground litter (not a climbing species).

Range. W. European.

Distribution. Map 191. S. England, France, Belgium, S. Holland (Limburg); local in N.W. Germany as far east as the R. Weser.

Clausilia parvula × 4

Macrogastra rolphii × 4

CLAUSILIA PARVULA Férussac 1807

Description. 8–9.5 × 2–2.2 mm. Shell *very small and slender*. Mouth furnished internally with a clear basal groove. Columellar lamella weak; a palatal callus present, joined basally to a distinct narrow white palatal fold running back into the mouth. Shell with very close and delicate striation-like ribbing only, making it appear *smooth* to the naked eye.

Habitat. Moderately moist places among rocks and screes, old walls, woods, hedgebanks; calciphile; attaining 2400 m in Switzerland (Valais).

Range. C. European.

Distribution. Map 192. E. France, Switzerland, Belgium, S. Holland (Limburg), S. and C. Germany (not in the N. German plain); occasionally adventive in England.

*CLAUSILIA BIDENTATA (Ström 1765)

Syns. *C. nigricans* (Maton & Rackett), *C. rugosa* of British authors

Description. 9–12 × 2.3–2.7 mm. Shell larger than *C. parvula*, generally rather slender. Columellar lamella weak, sometimes bifurcating feebly onto the lip; occasionally 1–2 rudimentary interlamellar folds (usually none). Basal groove and adjacent palatal fold well developed. Shell dark reddish-brown or blackish when fresh (but like other Clausiliidae often bleached pale grey), frequently showing irregular transverse white streaks near the suture; finely and regularly ribbed (about 11 ribs per mm on penultimate whorl), with a delicate spiral striation visible under high magnification.

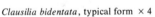

Clausilia bidentata, typical form × 4   *C. bidentata*, form *rugosa* × 4

The relationship of this very variable species with closely allied forms occurring in southern France is not clear. *Clausilia rugosa* Draparnaud and *C. pyrenaica* Charpentier, which tend to replace typical *C. bidentata* in the Mediterranean region and in the Pyrenees respectively, differ in having coarser sculpture and more strongly developed folds.

Habitat. Moderately moist places, among rocks, old walls, woods, hedgebanks; rare above 1000 m.

Range. N. European.

Distribution. Map 193. Widespread in the British Isles, France, Belgium, Holland, Switzerland (Vaud, Valais), C. and N. Germany, Denmark, S. Scandinavia (coastally to 70°N in Norway).

*CLAUSILIA DUBIA Draparnaud 1805

Syn. *C. cravenensis* Taylor

Description. 11–14 (occasionally 16) × 2.7–3.2 mm. Shell closely similar to *C. bidentata*, but larger and relatively broader. Lower margin of columellar lamella often showing a distinctly notched or stepped profile as viewed frontally; no interlamellar folds. Ribs slightly more widely-spaced than in *C. bidentata* (8–10 per mm on penultimate whorl); spiral micro-striation rather distinct.

This is a very variable species, in which many geographical races have been distinguished.

Habitat. Characteristically on moist shaded rocks and old walls, more rarely in woodland; calciphile; attaining 2400 m in Switzerland (Valais).

Range. C. European.

Distribution. Map 194. Highly discontinuous: N. England, S. and E. France, Switzerland, S. Belgium, Holland, Germany (absent from most of the N. German plain), local in the Danish islands and S. Scandinavia.

Clausilia dubia × 4

C. cruciata × 4

CLAUSILIA CRUCIATA Studer 1820

Description. 9–11 (occasionally 14) × 2.3–2.5 mm. Shell rather stumpy and evenly fusiform (not markedly club-shaped), the upper part of the spire straight-sided or only feebly concave in outline. Mouth small and narrowly rhomboidal; columellar lamella bifid both internally and also towards lip, sometimes producing the appearance of a St Andrew's cross (✕) in oblique view; generally 1–2 interlamellar folds. Palatal callus usually strongly developed, united basally to a strong lower palatal fold. Shell with rather *coarsely-spaced* ribs (about 6–7 per mm on penultimate whorl); spiral micro-striation very faint.

Habitat. Mainly in moist shaded woodland, under ground litter or on tree trunks; above the tree-line in rocky open habitats. Principally montane, attaining 2400 m in Switzerland (Valais).

Range. Alpine and N. European.

Distribution. Map 195. Very discontinuous: Vosges, Jura, Alps, mountains of S. and C. Germany as far north as the Harz; scattered localities in C. Scandinavia, to about 65°N in Sweden and Finland.

CLAUSILIA PUMILA Pfeiffer 1828

Description. 12–13 × 3–3.4 mm. Shell somewhat similar to *C. cruciata*, but usually larger and with a more club-shaped outline produced by the concave and tapering form of the upper part of the spire. Columellar lamella rather indistinctly bifid towards lip; usually 1–2 interlamellar folds. Palatal callus normally *feebly developed or absent* (cf. *C. cruciata*); lower palatal fold relatively weak and not strongly raised. Sculpture similar to *C. cruciata*: ribs rather coarsely-spaced (about 6 per mm on penultimate whorl); spiral micro-striation almost imperceptible.

Habitat. Damp woods, mainly in ground litter and under fallen logs (not a strongly climbing species).

Range. C. and E. European.

Distribution. Map 196. Eastern half of Germany (not in the Rhineland or in S. Bavaria), Denmark, southernmost Sweden.

Neostyriaca corynodès × 4

Clausilia pumila × 4

NEOSTYRIACA CORYNODES Held 1836

Syn. *Graciliaria corynodes* (Held)

Description. 9–11 × 2.2–2.4 mm. Shell superficially similar to *Clausilia parvula*, but slightly larger and usually more club-shaped. Lower margin of columellar lamella forming a smooth curve, dying rather abruptly into the side of the mouth, not bifid towards lip. Palatal callus *very prominent and white*, running round parallel to the outer lip and ending suddenly at the base as a ridge adjacent to a deep gutter-like groove (cf. the form of the lower palatal fold in *C. parvula*). No lunule. Shell dull, dark reddish-brown, with very close and faint ribbing (appearing smooth to the naked eye).

Habitat. Damp rocks and screes; calciphile; exclusively montane, though rare above 1200 m.

Range. Alpine.

Distribution. Map 197. Mainly in the northern calcareous Alps from France (rare), through Switzerland to S.E. Bavaria; local in the Swiss Jura (mainly east of Basel); a few places in the mountains of S.W. Germany (S. Black Forest, S. Swabian Jura).

Neostyriaca strobeli × 4

NEOSTYRIACA STROBELI (Porro 1838)

Syn. *Graciliaria strobeli* (Porro)

Description. 9–11 × 2.5–2.8 mm. Shell rather swollen in the middle, with a narrow spire and with the last 2 whorls contracting markedly towards the relatively small mouth. Palatal callus strongly developed, often divided into an upper denticle-like patch below the sinulus, and a basal portion united to a strong lower palatal fold; basal groove distinct. Shell reddish or yellowish-brown, often rather translucent, with regular strong ribs (about 7 per mm on penultimate whorl), their crests often streaked with white near the suture.

Habitat. Damp places among rocks and ground litter; not above 700 m.

Range. S. Alpine.

Distribution. Map 198. S. Switzerland (Ticino) only, around Lake Lugano.

Subfamily BALEINAE

LACINIARIA PLICATA (Draparnaud 1801)

Description. 15–18 × 3.3–3.6 mm. Shell tall and narrow (12–13 whorls), with a gradually tapering spire; outline of later part rather cylindrical. Mouth-edge rather expanded and distinctly detached all round, projecting beyond the previous whorl. Outer lip with *6–9 strong denticle-like folds* (very occasionally reduced or absent); 2–3 interlamellar folds; little palatal callus; no lower palatal fold. Shell dull, ribs rather sharp and close (6–7 per mm on penultimate whorl), their crests often whitened towards the suture.

Habitat. Mainly damp rocks and old walls in open habitats; less often in woods.

Range. C. and E. European.

Distribution. Map 199. E. France (Jura, Vosges, Ardennes), Switzerland; local in Germany (absent from most of the N. German plain and from the S.E.); scattered localities around the coasts of the southern Baltic (Danish islands, Gotland, N.E. Germany).

Laciniaria plicata × 4   *L. biplicata* × 4

LACINIARIA BIPLICATA (Montagu 1803)

Description. 16–18 × 3.8–4 mm. Size and shape rather similar to *L. plicata*, but broader in the later whorls. Mouth slightly pointed below, with a very distinct internal basal groove. Columellar lamella rather weak, often bifid onto the lip as two small denticles; no interlamellar folds. Palatal callus virtually absent; no lower palatal fold. Ribs sharp, slightly coarser and more widely-spaced than in *L. plicata* (5–6 per mm on penultimate whorl), their crests often whitened.

Habitat. Shaded places in woods, herbage, or among rocks; frequent on the floodplains of rivers; more rarely in dry exposed habitats.

Range. C. European.

Distribution. Map 200. N.E. France (Nord, Pas de Calais), Belgium, Holland, Germany, N. Switzerland; also widely scattered localities in S. England, Denmark, S. Norway, S. Sweden (in these areas probably spread by man).

BULGARICA CANA (Held 1836)

Syn. *Laciniaria cana* (Held)

Description. 15–18 × 3.6–3.9 mm. Shell similar to *Laciniaria biplicata* in size and general appearance. Columellar lamella simple (never bifid); no interlamellar folds.

Palatal callus *moderately well developed*, often divided into an upper patch below the sinulus and a lower ridge-like thickening (false palatal fold) running inwards near the base of the mouth; basal groove very distinct. Ribs slightly more widely spaced than in *L. biplicata* (4–5 per mm on penultimate whorl), often with whitened crests; fine spiral microsculpture rather distinct.

Habitat. Moist woodland, under ground litter and on tree trunks; principally montane.

Range. C. and E. European.

Distribution. Map 201. Highly discontinuous: local in the N. Alpine foreland region from Lake Constance to S.E. Bavaria; scattered localities in mountains of S. and C. Germany; Baltic coast of N.E. Germany; one locality in Finland (Koli, 63° 10′N).

Bulgarica cana × 4   *B. vetusta* × 4

BULGARICA VETUSTA (Rossmässler 1836)

Syns. *Laciniaria vetusta* (Rossmässler), *L. festiva* (Küster)

Description. 15–16 × 3.2 mm. Shell rather slender, with the last whorl and mouth noticeably tall and narrow; basal groove distinct. Columellar lamella simple (not bifid), rather inconspicuous and deeply-set; no interlamellar folds. Palatal callus feeble; lower palatal fold *very distinct*, running up into the mouth along the left border of the basal groove. Ribs strong and widely spaced (4–5 per mm on penultimate whorl), often with whitened crests; spiral microsculpture virtually absent.

This is a geographically variable species: the typical form, which occurs outside our area, differs from the German race described above (subspecies *festiva* Küster) in having a stronger palatal callus, and finer, closer ribbing.

Habitat. Moist rocks and screes, usually in fairly open places.
Range. S.E. European.
Distribution. Map 202. Rare: a few widely scattered localities in the mountains of C. Germany (Upper Franconia, Thuringia, S. Saxony).

VESTIA TURGIDA (Rossmässler 1836)

Syns. *Laciniaria turgida* (Rossmässler), *Pseudalinda turgida* (Rossmässler)
Description. 14–15 × 3.6–3.8 mm. Shell rather conical and stumpy, with tumid whorls; mouth broad, well-rounded below. Columellar lamella weak, sometimes bifid towards lip. Palatal callus developed as a slight but distinct *rib-like thickening set just within the mouth*, interrupted basally by a slight notch. Shell pale yellowish-brown, rather glossy, with bluntly rounded ribs, often becoming virtually smooth in the last whorl.
Habitat. Very moist woodland, under logs and ground litter; montane.
Range. Carpathian.
Distribution. Map 203. Rare: known only from a small area in the mountains of the Bavarian Forest close to the Czech frontier.

Vestia turgida × 4

Balea perversa × 4

*BALEA PERVERSA (Linné 1758)

Description. 8–10 × 2.2 mm. Shell narrowly conical, with a gently bowed outline; suture deep, slightly channelled. Mouth rather squarish, either without teeth, or with a very small parietal denticle only; outer lip delicate, slightly thickened and expanded (cf. juveniles of other Clausiliidae!). No clausilium. Shell pale brownish or greenish, with close irregular growth-ridges, often giving a rather silky polish.
Habitat. Characteristic of dry exposed places among rocks and on old stone walls;

less commonly on trees (only very occasionally found in ground litter). Attaining 2400 m in Switzerland (Valais).
Range. W. European.
Distribution. Map 204. Widespread, but becoming rarer to the east, and scarce in the N. German plain; mainly coastal in Scandinavia (in Norway to 68°N, in Finland to 63°N); Iceland.

Family **TESTACELLIDAE**

Slugs with a small external shell at the hind end, which covers the mantle. In all other slugs in W. Europe there is no external shell, and the mantle is just behind the head. There are two grooves running forward from the mantle on the upper surface, from which oblique side branches descend on each side. See also *Daudebardia* (p. 126).

The Testacellidae occur mainly around the western Mediterranean and the Atlantic coasts and islands. There is only one genus, *Testacella,* with three species in our area, where they are largely associated with man. They are carnivorous, preying on earthworms, and they are very extensible. There is no jaw, but the radular teeth are sharp, long and backward-directed, thus ensuring a good grip on the prey.

Periods of activity are short, and partly subterranean, and the slugs hide underground in cold or dry weather. Consequently, they are some of the hardest species to find. Association with man in gardens and rubbish heaps appears to be due to the well manured and worm-rich soils these provide.

*TESTACELLA MAUGEI Férussac 1819   **Pl. 14**
Syn. *Testacella haliotoides* Lamarck
Description. Medium to large slug, extended length 6–10 cm. Brown, speckled with black above, with a double row of conspicuous tubercules, and paler sides. Foot fringe and sole brighter, often pink or orange. Points of origin of lateral grooves *about 5 mm apart at mantle. Shell larger than other species*, oblong and convex, 12–16 mm long, 6–7 mm wide. There are a number of colour varieties – grey, greenish-brown, rufous and black.
Habitat. Nearly always in gardens or other well-manured ground.
Range. W. European (Atlantic).
Distribution. Map 205. S. Ireland, S.W. Britain, westernmost France.

*TESTACELLA HALIOTIDEA Draparnaud 1801   **Pl. 14**
Syn. *Testacella europaea* Roissy
Description. Large slug, extended length 8–12 cm, usually dull creamy-white or yellow above, usually with whitish foot-sole. Points of origin of lateral grooves at front edge of mantle *close together, but distinct*. Shell small and nearly triangular, slightly convex or flat; upper end of columella bluntly rounded, 7–8 mm long, 5–6 mm wide.
Habitat. Mostly in parks and gardens, but also in fields and vineyards in the south.
Range. W. European and W. Mediterranean.
Distribution. Map 206. Ireland, Britain, France (mainly in W.); also occasionally

in gardens in W. Switzerland, W. Germany (Heidelberg, Frankfurt) and Denmark (E. Jutland).

*TESTACELLA SCUTULUM Sowerby 1821   **Pl. 14**
Description. Large slug, extended length 8–12 cm. Yellow speckled with black or brown, foot fringe and sole usually orange. Lateral grooves join *before reaching common origin at front edge of mantle*. Shell nearly triangular and flattened (sometimes concave), upper end of columella sharply truncate. Periostracum thicker and less easily abraded than in *T. haliotidea*. 6–7 mm long, 4 mm wide.
Habitat. Mostly in parks and gardens.
Range. W. European.
Distribution. Map 207. Ireland, Britain and W. France.

Family **BRADYBAENIDAE**

Members of this family resemble the Helicidae (p. 175) in external appearance, most having large, globular shells, but they differ internally. It is a predominantly Asian family, and there is only one species in our area, *Bradybaena fruticum*, which closely resembles a number of the Helicidae.

*BRADYBAENA FRUTICUM (Müller 1774)   **Pl. 20**
Syns. *Eulota fruticum* (Müller), *Fruticicola fruticum* (Müller)
Description. 10–19 × 13–23 mm. Shell globular to slightly depressed, conical or slightly convex above, with 5–6½ convex whorls with deep sutures. Rounded below, with a medium umbilicus (one-sixth to one-fifth width of shell), which is slightly eccentric and very slightly obscured by the reflected columellar lip. Mouth rounded or slightly elliptical, with a white internal rib and a feeble lip, only everted basally. Shell white to pale greeny-yellow, sometimes with a faint darker band at the periphery. Growth-ridges rather coarse and irregular, crossed by much finer spiral striations.
Similar species. *Monacha cantiana* (p. 184) has shallower sutures and smaller umbilicus; *Euomphalia strigella* (p. 197) has a larger and more eccentric umbilicus and a lip everted round most of the mouth.
Habitat. In damp places – hedges, scrub, fields, on the edges of woods; usually absent from open sunny places. Attaining 1700 m in the Alps.
Range. C. and E. European and Asian.
Distribution. Map 208. Eastern France, Switzerland, Belgium, S. Netherlands (Limburg), S. E. England (Kent, possibly extinct), Germany, Denmark and E. Scandinavia, north to 66°N in Finland.

Family **HELICIDAE**

This family contains the largest European snails, and is the most successful, with 68 species occurring in our area. The centre of distribution is the Mediterranean, and there are many more species in the south of our area than in the north.

The shells of Helicidae are usually medium to very large in size, thick, and often brightly coloured, but there is an immense range of size, shape and colouring between, and sometimes within species. Members of the family are found in a very wide range of habitats, but there are within it groups of species which share features of habitat, size and way of life. These groups correspond approximately to the classification of the family into subfamilies, and the general features of each are described below.

Subfamily **HELICELLINAE**   pages 176–184. Plates 15, 16, 24.

All but two of the sixteen species in this group are typically found in dry open habitats such as dunes, open grassland and rocky hillsides. Many rest in the open, attached to rocks or plants, and they have thick white shells, often with variable patterns of darker blotches and bands. Most are medium sized, with globular or flattened shells, but the two *Cochlicella* species (Plate 24) are spire-shaped.

Two species, *Helicella conspurcata* and *H. apicina* (Plate 15) live in damper and shaded habitats, and are dull brown and hairy, resembling members of the subfamily Hygromiinae, which are mostly woodland species.

The group is very southern in distribution, and the northern parts of our area have few native species. Human activity in draining and clearing the land has made more suitable habitats, and many species have spread or been introduced northwards. Only one of the seven British species is certainly native.

Most species in the group can be identified by their shells, but internal characters are given for a few where difficulties can arise.

Subfamily **MONACHINAE**   pages 184–185. Plates 20, 22.

The three species in this group are often regarded as part of the Helicellinae, but in habits and appearance they are intermediate between that group and the Hygromiinae. Two species, *Monacha cantiana* and *M. cartusiana*, are typically found in rather open places, and like some Helicellinae, *M. cantiana* has been spread north of its original range. The other species, *Ashfordia granulata*, more closely resembles the Hygromiinae, with a northern distribution, hairy shell and a preference for damp habitats.

Subfamily **HYGROMIINAE**   pages 185–197. Plates 17–20, 23.

The 25 species in this group are mostly small to medium sized, with brown shells (often hairy), although some species have paler colour variants. In general, they are woodland snails, extending into hedges and other shady places, and also into open habitats where these are cool and moist, especially in the extreme west and in mountain pastures. When resting, they usually hide under logs or vegetation.

The greatest diversity of species in this group is to be found in central Europe, and especially in the Alps, where there are many local forms. The genus *Trichia* has the greatest number of such forms, and their status is sometimes obscure. More details are given on page 191. Internal characters are given for the few difficult identifications.

Subfamily **HELICODONTINAE** pages 197–198. Plate 22.

This group of four species is somewhat intermediate between the Hygromiinae and the Ariantinae. Shells are medium sized, flattened and usually hairy, and all are woodland species. They have a rather southerly distribution, and only one species, *Helicodonta obvoluta*, is widespread, and even it is absent from much of the north.

Subfamily **ARIANTINAE** pages 192–202. Plates 20–22.

The twelve species of this group have in common a preference for damp habitats, but are otherwise rather diverse. *Chilostoma* species, medium to large, flattened species, live in open but rocky ground, and avoid exposure by hiding in crannies and fissures and under boulders, only emerging in wet weather. They are southerly and montane in distribution, with species peculiar to the Alps and Pyrenees. *Isognomostoma* species are flattened, brown, hairy snails, very like *Helicodonta*, living in woods.

The remaining three species are each very distinct. *Arianta arbustorum*, a large globular species, is common in damp habitats over most of Europe; *Helicigona lapicida*, a very flattened species, is more local and has habits similar to *Chilostoma*, while *Elona quimperiana* is confined to the S.W. seaboard of our area.

Subfamily **HELICINAE** pages 202–205. Plates 23, 24.

The eight species in this group are all large and globular or slightly flattened, and many of them are very variable in shell colour and pattern. Included are the largest European snail *Helix pomatia* and the common garden snail *Helix aspersa*. Like the Helicellinae, the group is most successful in the Mediterranean area, but its species are found in more shaded habitats – hedges, vineyards, parkland and gardens, as well as woods. Only one species, *Cepaea hortensis*, is native in all the countries of our area, but several others are widely distributed, *H. aspersa* and *H. pomatia* having been spread by man.

Details of internal characters are given only for two species of *Cepaea* which are sometimes confusing.

Subfamily **HELICELLINAE**

CANDIDULA UNIFASCIATA (Poiret 1801)   **Pl. 15**
Syns. *Helicella candidula* (Studer), *Helicella rugosiuscula* (Michaud)
Description. 3–6 × 5–9 mm. Shell globular, depressed, with a conical spire of 5–6 convex whorls with deep sutures, only slightly angled at the periphery. Umbilicus moderately wide, deep and slightly eccentric. Mouth oval, flattened above and below, and with a small internal rib. Shell white or whitish, opaque, usually with

one dark spiral band just above the periphery, and with fine, rather blunt, regular transverse ribbing. Some banding variants can occur (banding sometimes absent). **Similar species.** *Candidula gigaxii* is larger, has less convex whorls and shallower sutures, and is usually more depressed. *C. intersecta* has less regular and coarser ribbing, and is more keeled at the periphery.
Habitat. Dry, open or rocky places, including dunes. Attaining 2000 m in the Alps.
Range. W. and C. European.
Distribution. Map 209. France (rare in N.), Belgium. Netherlands (mainly Limburg), Switzerland, Germany (rare on N. plain) and S. Baltic coasts from E. Denmark to Gotland.

*CANDIDULA INTERSECTA (Poiret 1801) Pl. 15
Syn. *Helicella caperata* (Montagu)
Description. 5–8 × 7–13 mm. Shell globular but strongly depressed, with a convex spire of 5–6½ slightly convex whorls with shallow sutures, slightly angled at the periphery. Umbilicus moderately wide and deep, slightly eccentric. Mouth nearly circular, with a white internal rib. Shell opaque, white to ginger, often with darker spiral bands and blotches, and with marked, irregular transverse ribbing. Shell colour and pattern very variable, with bands blotched, interrupted, fused, colourless or completely absent, so that completely white or brown shells may be found.
Similar species. *Candidula unifasciata* (p. 176). *C. gigaxii* is more depressed, with a broader last whorl, has finer ribbing and a more eccentric umbilicus. *Trochoidea geyeri* (p. 182) and *Helicopsis striata* (p. 183) are less flattened above and below, have coarser ribbing, deeper sutures and no (or an incomplete) rib round mouth.
Habitat. Dry and open sites, especially dunes and grassland. Buries in fine weather, when hard to find.
Range. W. European.
Distribution. Map 210. British Isles, W. and N. France, Belgium, Netherlands and scattered sites in N. Germany, Denmark and southernmost Sweden.

*CANDIDULA GIGAXII (Pfeiffer 1850) Pl. 15
Syns. *Helicella gigaxii* (Pfeiffer), *H. heripensis* (Mabille)
Description. 4–8 × 6–15 mm. Shell strongly depressed above, with a low conic/convex spire of 5–5½ slightly convex whorls with shallow sutures, scarcely angled at the periphery. Umbilicus moderately wide, and eccentric, mouth round with a slight internal rib. Shell white or pale opaque brown, usually with some thin, interrupted brown spiral bands, and with fine and rather regular transverse ribbing.
Similar species. *C. unifasciata* (p. 176), *C. intersecta*.
Habitat. Dry open sites, usually calcareous. Frequently with *Cernuella virgata* and in slightly more covered places than *C. intersecta*.
Range. W. European.
Distribution. Map 211. S.E. Britain, W. and C. France, Belgium, W. Netherlands and a few isolated inland sites in Germany (Brunswick, Thuringia) and C. Ireland.

*CERNUELLA VIRGATA (da Costa 1778) Pl. 16
Syns. *Helicella virgata* (da Costa), *H. maritima* (Draparnaud), *H. variabilis* (Draparnaud)
Description. 6–19 × 8–25 mm. Shell globular, with a high convex spire of 5–7 convex whorls with moderate sutures and a narrow umbilicus, partly obscured by

the reflected columellar lip. Mouth round, with an internal rib which may be white or brown. Shell white or ginger, usually with dark brown spiral bands, which may be diluted, interrupted, blotched or fused, and sometimes lack pigment. Growth-ridges rather irregular. This species is very variable in size, shape and colouration of the shell.

Similar species. *Helicella bolenensis* (p. 179) usually lacks bands, is yellowish-white with stronger, more regular growth-ridges. *Cernuella neglecta* and *C. aginnica* are more depressed and have larger umbilici.

Habitat. Moderately dry and open calcareous sites, dunes, grassland and hedgerows.

Range. Mediterranean and W. European.

Distribution. Map 212. British Isles (mainly S.), France (mainly W.), coasts of Belgium and Netherlands.

CERNUELLA AGINNICA (Locard 1894)   Pl. 16

Syns. *C. augustiniana* of Dutch authors (*non* Bourguignat), *Helicella cespitum* of Belgian authors (*non* Draparnaud).

Description. 6–11 × 8–18 mm. Shell globular, slightly depressed, with a low coni-cal spire of 5–6 convex whorls with deep sutures. Umbilicus moderately wide (*c.* one-sixth–one-fifth shell width), mouth round, with a thin whitish internal rib. Shell thick, white, usually with rather broken up dark spiral bands, and fine, rather regular growth-ridges.

Similar species. *C. virgata* (p. 177). *C. neglecta* is more depressed, has a larger umbilicus, more oval mouth, and less marked growth-ridges.

Habitat. Dry open habitats, including dunes.

Range. Mediterranean.

Distribution. Map 213. S. France north to Vienne and Rhône; also a few sites on the coast of Belgium and W. Netherlands. Exact distribution uncertain due to con-fusion with both *C. virgata* and *C. neglecta*.

CERNUELLA NEGLECTA (Draparnaud 1805)   Pl. 16

Syn. *Helicella neglecta* (Draparnaud)

Description. 6–10 × 9–18 mm. Shell markedly depressed, with a low convex spire of 5–6 whorls with shallow sutures. Umbilicus wide (*c.* one-quarter – one-fifth shell width). Mouth slightly oval, with a thin, sometimes pinkish internal rib. Shell thick, white usually with brown spiral bands (mostly below the periphery), nearly smooth, with fine and irregular growth-ridges.

Similar species. *C. virgata* (p. 177), *C. aginnica*. *Helicella itala* (p. 179) is flatter above, has a rounder mouth and a wider umbilicus.

Habitat. Open dry sites – roadsides, screes and rocky places.

Range. Mediterranean.

Distribution. Map 214. Mainly S. France (Rhône and Garonne valleys); elsewhere casually introduced in widely scattered sites in N. France, Switzerland, Germany (upper Rhine, Saale and Unstrut valleys), Belgium, Netherlands and S.E. England (Kent, now extinct).

*HELICELLA ITALA (Linné 1758)   **Pl. 16**
Syn. *H. ericetorum* (Müller)
Description. 5–12 × 9–25 mm. Shell very depressed above, convex below, with a
very low spire of 5½–6½ slightly convex whorls with shallow sutures. Umbilicus
very wide (*c*. one-third width of shell). Last whorl turns down slightly, but abruptly
at the mouth, which is slightly elliptical, and usually lacks a clearly defined internal
rib. Shell white or pale ginger (very rarely, pale pink), usually with dark brown
spiral bands, nearly smooth, with fine, irregular growth-ridges. Shell colour and
pattern very variable.
Similar species. *H. obvia* has a smaller umbilicus, and a broader last whorl not
descending abruptly at the mouth. *Cernuella neglecta* (p. 178).
Habitat. Dry exposed habitats – dunes, screes and calcareous grassland. Attaining
2000 m in the Alps and Pyrenees.
Range. W. European.
Distribution. Map 215. British Isles (in N. coastal only), France, Belgium, Netherlands, N. Switzerland, Denmark and Germany (rare in E. and on N. plain).

HELICELLA OBVIA (Menke 1828)   **Pl. 16**
Syn. *H. candicans* (Pfeiffer)
Description. 7–10 × 14–20 mm. Shell extremely depressed above, with spire
scarcely rising above last whorl, with 5–6 rather flattened whorls with shallow sutures.
Umbilicus wide (*c*. quarter of width of shell), mouth slightly elliptical, and without
clearly defined rib. Last whorl scarcely descends at mouth. Shell opaque and white,
often with brown spiral bands, especially at and below the periphery. Nearly
smooth, growth-ridges fine and irregular.
Similar species. *H. itala*.
Habitat. Dry exposed sites, similar to those occupied by *H. itala*. Attaining over
2000 m in the Alps.
Range. S.E. European.
Distribution. Map 216. E. half of Germany (W. to Lübeck, Brunswick and Heidelberg), Switzerland, and occasional colonies further west (Hamm, Westphalia;
Montigny, Dordogne).

HELICELLA BOLENENSIS (Locard 1882)   **Pl. 16**
Syn. *H. bolli* (Steusloff)
Description. 6.5–11.5 × 8–14 mm. Shell globular, slightly depressed, with a convex spire of 5½ convex whorls with deep sutures. Umbilicus moderately wide,
slightly obstructed by reflected columellar lip. Mouth somewhat elliptical, and with
a thick white internal rib. Shell thick, yellowish or white, unbanded or with faint
spiral bands at and below the periphery and with marked regular growth-ridges.
Similar species. *Cernuella virgata* (p. 177). *Candidula intersecta* (p. 177) is more
coarsely and irregularly ribbed, is shouldered at the periphery and has shallower
sutures.
Habitat. Dry exposed grassland.
Range. W. Mediterranean.
Distribution. Map 217. Rare: A few isolated sites in S.W. France (Haute Garonne),
East Germany (Neu-Brandenburg), W. Germany (Würzburg, Ochsenfurt a. Main,
Ludwigshaven a. Rhein).

Plate 17
Family HELICIDAE
Subfamily HYGROMIINAE
See also plates 18-20, 23
($\times 2\frac{1}{2}$)

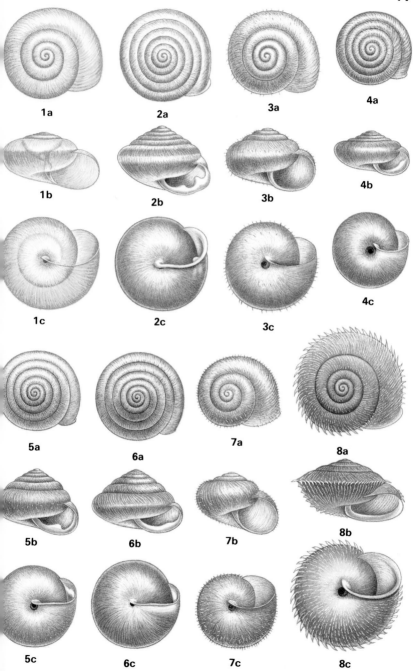

17

1a 2a 3a 4a

1b 2b 3b 4b

1c 2c 3c 4c

5a 6a 7a 8a

5b 6b 7b 8b

5c 6c 7c 8c

18

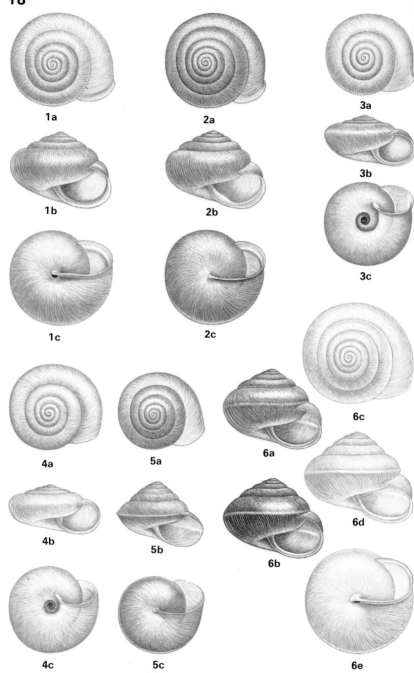

1a 2a 3a

1b 2b 3b

3c

1c 2c

6c

4a 5a 6a

6d

4b 5b 6b

4c 5c 6e

Family HELICIDAE
Subfamily HYGROMIINAE
See also plates 17, 19, 20, 23
(×2)

Plate 18

1a-c. Perforatella incarnata   186
C. Europe, common. Reticulate microsculpture characteristic (see Fig., p. 186).

2a-c. Perforatella vicina   187
N. Bavaria (Franconia) only. Umbilicus virtually sealed.

3a-c. Perforatella umbrosa   187
S. Germany, montane. Thin and translucent. Lip sharply everted. Fine microsculpture characteristic (see Fig., p. 187).

4a-c. Perforatella glabella   186
S. France only, montane. Thin and very translucent. No everted lip.

5a-c. *Hygromia cinctella   190
Mainly Mediterranean. Strongly keeled, with white spiral band on periphery. No mouth-rib.

6. *Hygromia limbata   191
Common in W. France. Periphery with a pale spiral band. Thin everted lip and strong mouth-rib.
   6a-b. Colour variants.
   6c-e. Typical pale form.

HELICELLA CONSPURCATA (Draparnaud 1801)   Pl. 15

Description. 3–5 × 5–8 mm. Shell depressed above, convex below, with a low conical spire of 5–6 whorls with moderate sutures, slightly shouldered at the periphery. Umbilicus small and circular. Mouth oval, lacking internal rib. Shell opaque brown, sometimes whitish, flecked with white, and sometimes with faint darker spiral bands. Transverse ribbing marked and slightly irregular. Juveniles covered with fine, slightly curved hairs, usually worn off in adults (hair-pits visible with microscope).

Habitat. In relatively shaded places – under stones and on trees and logs, unlike most Helicellinae.

Range. W. Mediterranean.

Distribution. Map 218. A common Mediterranean species, occasionally recorded inside our area in S. France (Basses Pyrénées).

HELICELLA APICINA (Lamarck 1822)   Pl. 15

Description. 3.5–5 × 6.5–9 mm. Shell very depressed above, with a very low spire of 4–5 convex whorls with deep sutures. Umbilicus wide (c. a quarter of width of shell). Mouth rounded, but slightly flattened above, lacking an internal rib. Shell thick, greyish-white, with brown spotting near the sutures. Dark spiral bands weak and interrupted, sometimes absent. Growth-ridges distinct but irregular, most pronounced on last whorl. Juveniles sparsely covered with short hairs – few or none remain on adults.

Habitat. In slightly damp sites – meadows, under litter and stones, mostly in cultivated areas.

Range. Mediterranean.

Distribution. Map 219. A common Mediterranean species, extending just inside our area in S. France (Haute Garonne).

*TROCHOIDEA ELEGANS (Gmelin 1791)   Pl. 15

Syns. *Helicella elegans* (Gmelin), *Helix terrestris* Donovan

Description. 5–8 × 7–10 mm. Shell conical above, very flattened below, with 6–7 sharply keeled, overlapping, flattened whorls. Umbilicus small and circular. Mouth very flattened above and below, with a notch at the keeled periphery. Shell white or whitish, usually with dark spiral bands, rarely brown all over, and with fine regular growth-ridges.

Habitat. Dry exposed sites – grassland, dunes and screes.

Range. Mediterranean.

Distribution. Map 220. A common Mediterranean species, extending into S.W. France along the valley of the Garonne, and occasionally as an adventive in N. France. Well established in a few sites in S.E. England.

TROCHOIDEA GEYERI (Soós 1926)   Pl. 15

Syn. *Helicella geyeri* (Soós)

Description. 3.5–5 × 5–8 mm. Shell globular, slightly depressed with convex whorls, rounded at the periphery. Umbilicus moderately large, mouth rounded and with a very weak internal rib only. Shell whitish, often with dark, interrupted spiral bands, and with very coarse, irregular and interrupted transverse ribbing.

Similar species. *Candidula intersecta* (p. 177). *Helicopsis striata* (p. 183) is *very* similar in external appearance, but has a larger protoconch (c. 1.5mm wide to *T*.

geyeri 1.0 mm), less interrupted ribbing and a slightly larger umbilicus. Internally, *H. striata* has four dart-sacs, *T. geyeri* two rudimentary ones only.

Habitat. Dry, open calcareous areas with short vegetation or rocks.

Range. C. European.

Distribution. Map 221. Rare: isolated localities in N.E. France, S. Belgium, Switzerland (Lake Geneva basin), Germany (Württemberg, Franconia, Thuringia) north to Hannover; also Isle of Gotland. Full distribution uncertain owing to confusion with *H. striata*.

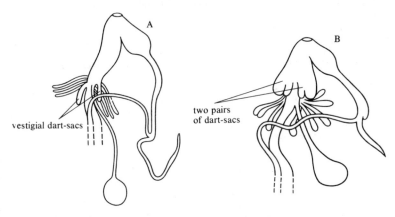

Distal genitalia of   A, *Trochoidea geyeri*   B, *Helicopsis striata*

HELICOPSIS STRIATA (Müller 1774)   **Pl. 15**

Syn. *Helicella striata* (Müller)

Description. 4.5–6.5 × 6–9 mm. Shell globular, slightly depressed with convex whorls, well-rounded at the periphery. Umbilicus moderately large, mouth rounded and with a very weak internal rib only. Shell whitish, often with dark interrupted spiral bands and with coarse and slightly irregular transverse ribbing.

Similar species. *Candidula intersecta* (p. 177), *Trochoidea geyeri* (p. 182).

Habitat. Dry and open areas, especially with rocks, also field-edges.

Range. C. European.

Distribution. Map 222. Rather rare: E. France (Vosges), C. Germany north to Harz mountains, also Isle of Öland. Full distribution uncertain due to confusion with *Trochoidea geyeri*.

*COCHLICELLA ACUTA (Müller 1774)   **Pl. 24**

Syn. *C. barbara* of some older British authors (*non* Linné)

Description. 10–20 (rarely 30) × 4–7 mm. Shell a *very* elongated cone, with 8–10 slightly convex whorls with moderate sutures. Umbilicus minute, obscured by reflected columellar lip. Mouth elliptical, taller than broad, lacking internal rib. Shell white or ginger, often with darker bands and blotches, colour and pattern very variable. Growth-ridges irregular and rather weak.

Habitat. Maritime, usually in dunes and coastal grassland, occasionally calcareous ground inland.
Range. Mediterranean and Atlantic.
Distribution. Map 223. Atlantic coasts of Ireland (inland occasionally in S.), Britain, France and Belgium; occasionally as an adventive elsewhere.

*COCHLICELLA BARBARA (Linné 1758)   Pl. 24

Syns. *C. ventricosa* (Draparnaud), *C. ventrosa* (Férussac)
Description. 8–12 × 5–8 mm. Shell an elongated cone of 7–8 *very* slightly convex whorls with shallow sutures. Umbilicus minute and partly obscured by columellar lip. Mouth elliptical and lacking internal rib. Shell thick and white, with some variation in colour and banding as in *C. acuta*. Growth-ridges slightly more pronounced than in *C. acuta*, especially on last whorl.
Habitat. Dry exposed sites near the sea, especially dunes, occasionally inland in S. France.
Range. Mediterranean.
Distribution. Map 224. A common Mediterranean species, occasionally straying north into our area (Basses Pyrénées, Haute Garonne), and also established on Channel coast of France and Belgium (between Gravelines and La Panne) and in S.W. England (Torquay).

Subfamily **MONACHINAE**

*MONACHA CARTUSIANA (Müller 1774)   Pl. 20

Syn. *Theba cartusiana* (Müller)
Description. 6–10 × 9–17 mm. Shell depressed globular, with 5½–6½ convex whorls rising in a flattened cone, and with a slightly shouldered periphery. Umbilicus minute, partly obscured by reflected columellar lip. Mouth elliptical, with a thickened internal rib. Shell usually creamy-white, sometimes brown or reddish near the mouth, and often with traces of translucent pale brown spiral bands, most conspicuous near the mouth.
Similar species. *M. cantiana* is larger, less depressed, with a rounder mouth and a larger umbilicus.
Habitat. Widespread in grassland, hedges, roadsides etc., not usually in woods. Rare above 500 m. Restricted to dry sunny sites at the north of its range.
Range. Mediterranean and S.E. European.
Distribution. Map 225. France, W. and S. Switzerland; and locally in S.E. England, the Low Countries and W. Germany (Rhine valley); occasionally adventive elsewhere.

*MONACHA CANTIANA (Montagu 1803)   Pl. 20

Syns. *Theba cantiana* (Montagu), *Monacha cemenelea* (Risso)
Description. 11–14 × 16–20 mm. Shell globular, slightly depressed, with 5½–6 convex whorls in a low conical spire, with a rounded periphery. Umbilicus small (one-seventh to one-ninth of breadth of shell), slightly obscured by reflected columellar lip. Mouth nearly circular, with a white internal rib. Shell creamy-white, often darkening to reddish-brown near the mouth, and sometimes with rather diffuse, wide, reddish spiral bands most noticeable near the mouth.

Similar species. *M. cartusiana* (p. 184); *Euomphalia strigella* (p. 197) and *Bradybaena fruticum* (p. 174) have a larger umbilicus.

Habitat. Roadside verges, hedges, waste ground and scrub, occasionally dunes. Not in woods.

Range. Mediterranean and N.W. European.

Distribution. Map 226. S. and E. Britain, extreme N.E. and S.W. France (absent from central areas), Belgium, Netherlands and coast of N.W. Germany.

*ASHFORDIA GRANULATA (Alder 1830) Pl. 22

Syn. *Monacha granulata* (Alder)

Description. 5–7 × 7–9 mm. Shell globular, with 5½–6 convex whorls with deep sutures. Umbilicus minute, and partly obscured by reflected columellar lip. Mouth rounded above, flattened below, with internal rib thin or absent. Shell slightly glossy, thin, translucent, whitish to pale brown, covered with fine straight hairs with bulbous bases.

Similar species. *Trichia 'hispida'* group, especially *T. plebeia* (p. 194) has curved hairs, better developed internal rib and lip, and shallower sutures. *Perforatella rubiginosa* (p. 190) has curved hairs and shallower sutures.

Habitat. Woods, hedges, marshes and damp shaded places generally.

Range. W. European (virtually British Isles only).

Distribution. Map 227. Widespread but local in Britain, scarce in Ireland; also Channel Islands and Brittany (Finistère).

Subfamily HYGROMIINAE

*ZENOBIELLA SUBRUFESCENS (Miller 1822) Pl. 17

Syns. *Hygromia subrufescens* (Miller), *H. fusca* (Montagu)

Description. 4–6 × 6–10 mm. Shell globular, slightly depressed, with a low convex spire of 4½–5 convex whorls with moderate sutures, slightly shouldered above the periphery. Umbilicus minute, partly covered by reflected columellar lip. Mouth slightly elliptical, usually lacking internal rib, or with thin white thickening. Shell thin and flexible, feebly calcified, transparent and slightly glossy, usually pale brown, with very fine irregular growth-ridges.

Similar species. *Perforatella glabella* (p. 186) is more depressed, has a larger umbilicus and minute scales on the shell.

Habitat. In woodland, shady and well vegetated river banks, and especially in montane regions.

Range. W. European (Atlantic).

Distribution. Map 228. W. Britain and Ireland, and near Atlantic coasts of France.

PERFORATELLA BIDENTATA (Gmelin 1788) Pl. 17

Syn. *P. bidens* (Chemnitz)

Description. 5–7 × 6.5–8.5 mm. Shell low conical above, slightly flattened below, with 7–8 tightly coiled convex whorls with shallow sutures, the last whorl slightly angled above the periphery. Umbilicus minute and nearly sealed by reflected columellar lip. Mouth angular, flattened above and below, and with a glossy white everted lip armed internally with one palatal and one basal tooth. Shell opaque, pale brown, usually with a whitish spiral band at the periphery, growth-ridges distinct and rather regular.

Similar species. *Trichia edentula* (p. 196) has no teeth, and is more convex above.

Habitat. Woodland – in litter and on logs.

Range. E. European.

Distribution. Map 229. Discontinuous: scattered localities in S.E. and C. Germany as far north as Schleswig-Holstein, also in E. Denmark, southernmost Sweden (including Öland and Gotland), S. Finland and E. France (Alps, Vosges).

PERFORATELLA INCARNATA (Müller 1774)   Pl. 18

Syn. *Monacha incarnata* (Müller)

Description. 9–11 × 13–16 mm. Shell slightly depressed globular, with a low slightly convex spire of convex whorls with rather shallow sutures. Umbilicus narrow (less than one-tenth of breadth of shell) and partly obscured by reflected lip. Mouth elliptical, with a thin everted lip and a strong internal rib. Shell opaque, yellowish-brown, slightly paler at the periphery, with irregular growth-ridges and a very fine reticulated sculpture, giving the shell a dull sheen.

Similar species. *P. vicina* (p. 187). *Hygromia limbata* (p. 191) and *Monacha cantiana* (p. 184) lack the reticulated sculpture.

Habitat. Woods, hedges and other damp places to 1500 m.

Range. C. European.

Distribution. Map 230. Widespread, to C. France in the west, and southernmost Sweden to the north.

Microsculpture of shell of *Perforatella incarnata*

PERFORATELLA GLABELLA (Draparnaud 1801)   Pl. 18

Syns. *Monacha glabella* (Draparnaud), *Monachoides glabella* (Draparnaud)

Description. 5–8 × 7–14 mm. Shell depressed convex above, convex below, with a spire of 5–6 slightly convex whorls with shallow sutures, the last very slightly angled at the periphery. Umbilicus rather narrow (*c.* one-eighth to one-ninth of breadth of shell). Mouth elliptical, with a thin internal rib but no lip. Shell thin, transparent, yellowish-brown, and slightly glossy, with fine irregular growth-lines and cross-shaped scales (microscope).

Similar species *Zenobiella subrufescens* (p. 185).

Habitat. Meadows, hedges and scrub in warm places, usually in calcareous montane regions.

Range. W. Mediterranean.

Distribution. Map 231. S.E. France (Isère, Hautes Alpes).

PERFORATELLA VICINA (Rossmässler 1842)   **Pl. 18**
Syn. *Monacha vicina* (Rossmässler)
Description. 8.5–11.5 × 12–15.5 mm. Shell globular, conic/convex above, with
6–6½ convex whorls with moderate sutures. Umbilicus more or less completely
sealed by reflected lip. Mouth with a white internal rib. Shell translucent, pale
yellowish-brown, slightly paler and more opaque at the periphery, with fine, blunt
growth-ridges and a fine granular sculpturing giving the shell a dull sheen.

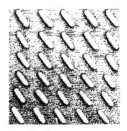

Microsculpture of shell of *Perforatella vicina*

Similar species. *P. incarnata* (p. 186) is more depressed above, has an open
umbilicus and a finer pattern of reticulation. *Hygromia limbata* (p. 191) lacks the
reticulation, has less convex whorls and shallower sutures, and has an open (but
very small) umbilicus.
Habitat. Montane forests.
Range. Carpathian.
Distribution. Map 232. Isolated in N. Bavaria (N. Franconian Jura and Franconian
Switzerland).

PERFORATELLA UMBROSA (Pfeiffer 1828)   **Pl. 18**
Syns. *Monacha umbrosa* (Pfeiffer), *Zenobiella umbrosa* (Pfeiffer)
Description. 5.5–7 × 10–13 mm. Shell depressed, with a very low conical spire of
convex whorls with moderate sutures, the last whorl angled and slightly thickened
at the periphery. Umbilicus wide (*c.* half breadth of shell) deep and eccentric.
Mouth very elliptical, flattened above and below, with a thin everted lip, and a thin

Microsculpture of shell of *Perforatella umbrosa*

Plate 19

Family HELICIDAE
Subfamily HYGROMIINAE
See also plates 17, 18, 20, 23
(3 and 8 ×3, remainder ×2)

Trichia can be hard to name. There is great variability and many species are ill-defined, especially in the Alps. Note that juveniles are normally hairy, though hairs are often rubbed off or lost with age.

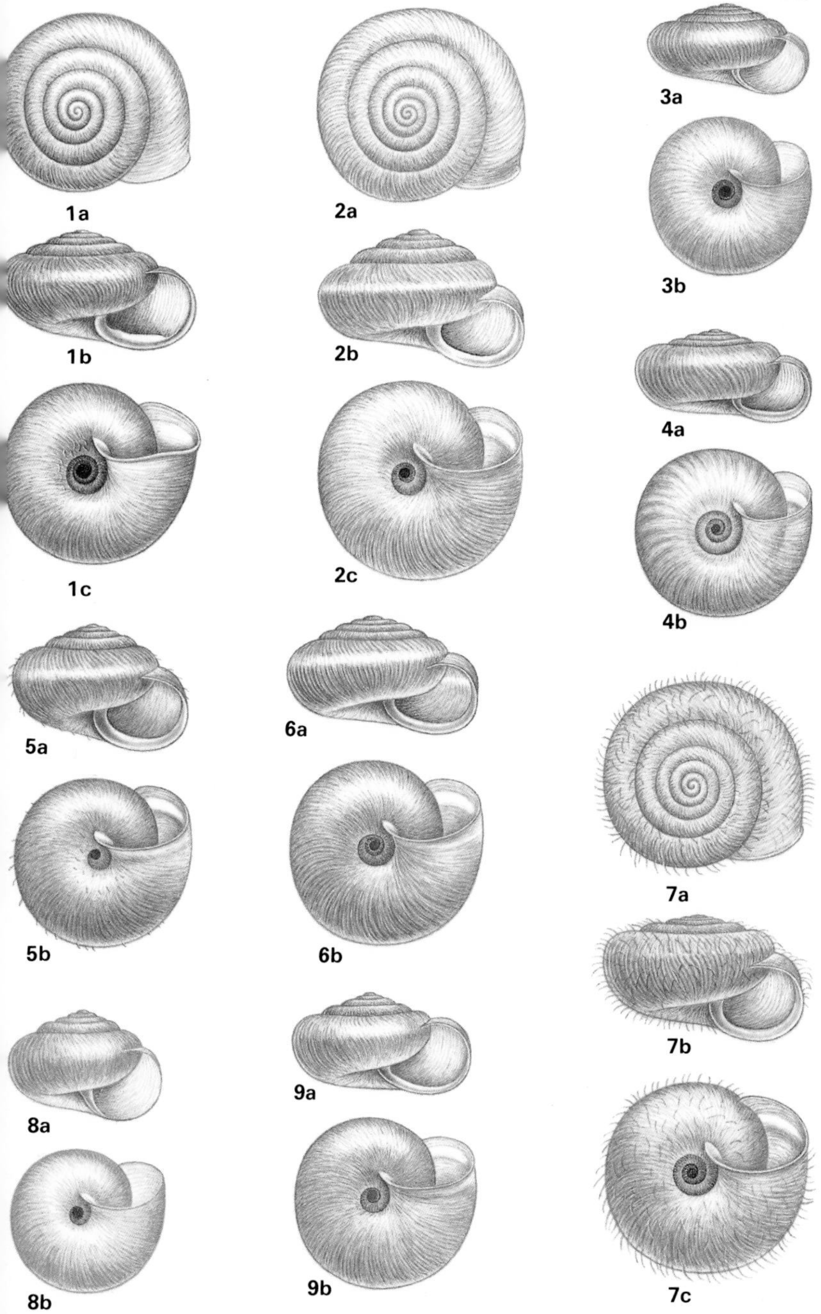

1a

1b

1c

2a

2b

2c

3a

3b

4a

4b

5a

5b

6a

6b

7a

7b

7c

8a

8b

9a

9b

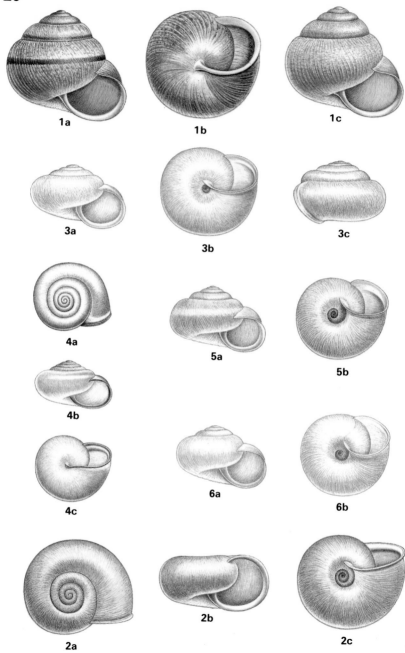

1a 1b 1c

3a 3b 3c

4a 5a 5b

4b

4c 6a 6b

2a 2b 2c

Family HELICIDAE
Subfamily ARIANTINAE
See also plates 21 and 22
($\times 1\frac{1}{2}$)

Plate 20

1. ***Arianta arbustorum** 199
Shell flecked or mottled. A small umbilical chink, unlike *Cepaea* (plate 23).
1a-b. Typical form.
1c. Pale bandless variant.

2a-c. **Elona quimperiana** 199
Rare, old woods in Brittany and W. Pyrenees.

Subfamily MONACHINAE
See also plate 22
($\times 1\frac{1}{2}$)

3a-c. ***Monacha cantiana** 184
Common in England, in waste ground. Creamy-white. Hairy when young.

4a-c. ***Monacha cartusiana** 184
Common in S. France. Smaller than *M. cantiana*, more tightly coiled. Umbilicus minute.

Subfamily HYGROMIINAE
See also plates 17–19, 23
($\times 1\frac{1}{2}$)

5a-b. **Euomphalia strigella** 197
Mainly C. Europe. Lip everted, with strong internal rib. Umbilicus large.

Family BRADYBAENIDAE
($\times 1\frac{1}{2}$)

6a-b. ***Bradybaena fruticum** 174
Common except in west, in damp places. Globular with distinct spiral striations. Often greeny-yellow.

internal rib below. Shell rather thin, slightly translucent, pale brown with fine, blunt growth-ridges and a finely sculptured surface giving the shell a shagreened appearance.

Similar species. *Trichia striolata* (p. 194) has a smaller umbilicus and rougher and more opaque shell, and lacks the sculpturing. *Trichia villosa* (p. 195) is hairy, and lacks the sculpturing.

Habitat. Montane deciduous woodlands.

Range. E. Alpine and Carpathian.

Distribution. Map 233. Mountains of S.E. Germany (E. Bavaria, Thuringia, S. Saxony), also isolated in Swabia (Biberach).

PERFORATELLA RUBIGINOSA (Schmidt 1853) Pl. 17

Syns. *Monacha rubiginosa* (Schmidt), *Monachoides rubiginosa* (Schmidt)

Description. 4.5–5 × 6–8 mm. Shell globular, convex above with 4½–5 convex whorls with moderate sutures, rounded at the periphery. Umbilicus small and partly obscured by reflected columellar lip. Mouth slightly oval and lacking internal rib. Shell thin, translucent, pale brown and slightly glossy, with fine irregular growth-ridges and short, curved hairs, often worn with adults.

Similar species. *Ashfordia granulata* (p. 185). The *Trichia hispida* group (p. 191), especially *T. plebeia*, which has longer hairs and a perceptible internal rib and a slight lip when adult.

Habitat. Woods, marshes, meadows and other damp habitats, mainly along river valleys.

Range. E. European and Siberian.

Distribution. Map 234. Mostly Germany: Danube valley, middle and lower Rhine valley, N. German plain E. to Rügen; also in the Rhine valley in Netherlands, and in S. Sweden (Öland, Gotland).

PYRENAEARIA CARASCALENSIS (Férussac 1821) Pl. 23

Description. 6.5–10 × 10–16 mm. Shell depressed, globular, with a convex spire of 5–5½ rapidly expanding, slightly convex whorls with rather shallow sutures, the last slightly shouldered at the periphery. Umbilicus narrow and deep, slightly obscured by reflected columellar lip. Mouth large and oval, without lip, and only traces of internal rib. Shell opaque, pale brown, often blotchy, growth-ridges strong and irregular, with traces of reticulate sculpturing on the uppermost whorls.

Habitat. High montane grassland and scrub from 700–3000 m.

Range. Pyrenean.

Distribution. Map 235. W. and C. Pyrenees, from Ariège to the Atlantic.

*HYGROMIA CINCTELLA (Draparnaud 1801) Pl. 18

Description. 6–7 × 10–12 mm. Shell globular, slightly depressed, conical above with 5–6 flattened whorls and very shallow sutures, strongly keeled at the periphery. Umbilicus minute, almost closed by reflected columellar lip. Mouth elliptical, mouth-edge simple and lacking internal rib. Shell slightly translucent, yellowish-white to pale brown, with a thin white spiral band at the keel, growth-ridges fine and rather regular.

Habitat. Woods, hedgerows and orchards.

Range. Mediterranean.

Distribution. Map 236. S.E. France. extending up Rhône valley into Switzerland

(Geneva basin); also near the Atlantic in S.W. France and well established as an introduction in S.W. England (S. Devon).

*HYGROMIA LIMBATA (Draparnaud 1805)   Pl. 18
Syn. *H. odeca* (Locard)
Description. 9–11 × 12–17 mm. Shell globular, conico-convex above, with 5–6 slightly convex whorls and shallow sutures. Umbilicus very small (less than one-tenth of width of shell) and partly obscured by reflected columellar lip. Mouth elliptical, with a thin everted lip and a strong internal rib. Shell slightly glossy and translucent, growth-lines fine and regular; creamy-white to dark brown, often with white or dark spiral bands, usually at the periphery.
Habitat. Woods, hedges and damp herbage up to 2500 m.
Range. S.W. European.
Distribution. Map 237. Common in S.W. and W. France from the Pyrenees to the Channel. Scattered localities in C. France, and well established as an introduction in S. Britain (Devon, Worcestershire); occasionally adventive elsewhere.

Genus TRICHIA
Within this genus there are four well known species of whose identity there is no doubt – *T. villosa*, *T. biconica*, *T. edentula* and *T. unidentata*, and one newly described, but distinct, species *T. graminicola*, which has a very restricted distribution.

There are also two groups of forms, containing many described species, but the distinctions between them are small and not always reliable. The commonest and most widespread member of each group is described in detail, and the others are described with references to the common form.

TRICHIA HISPIDA group (members of this group frequently retain hairs on the shell when adult).
*1) TRICHIA HISPIDA (Linné 1758)   Pl. 19
Syns. *Fruticicola hispida* (Linné), *Hygromia hispida* (Linné), *Trichia concinna* (Jeffreys)
Description. 5–6 × 5–12 mm. Shell slightly depressed convex above, flattened below, with 6–7 moderately convex whorls, rounded or very slightly keeled at the periphery. Umbilicus variable (from one-eighth to one-quarter of width of shell), mouth slightly elliptical, flattened below and with a thin, slightly reflected lip and an internal rib, most raised and whitened below. Shell brown to cream, with irregular growth-ridges; slightly glossy and translucent and covered with short curved hairs, usually remaining in the umbilicus if worn from the rest of the shell. Shells variable in shape and hairiness, those from wetter and cooler habitats tend to be higher, hairier and to have a smaller umbilicus.
Similar species. *Trichia striolata* group.
Habitat. Catholic, absent from very dry sites but widespread elsewhere. Ascends to *c.* 2000 m in Alps and Pyrenees.
Range. European.
Distribution. Map 238. Common as far N. as S. Scotland and S. Scandinavia, being entirely associated with man near its northern limits (Norway to 69°N, Finland to 67°30').

Plate 21

Family HELICIDAE
Subfamily ARIANTINAE
See also plates 20 and 22
$(1–3, 7 \times 1¼; 4–6 \times 1½)$

1a-d. **Chilostoma zonatum** 201
Mainly S. Switzerland, montane. Mouth rather rounded.

2a-d. **Chilostoma achates** 201
E. Switzerland, S.E. Bavaria, montane. More flattened than *C. zonatum*.

3a-c. **Chilostoma cingulatum** 199
S. Switzerland, S. Bavaria. Very flattened. White, with a single distinct band. Often on stone walls and ruins.

4a-c. **Chilostoma squamatinum** 200
S.W. France, common. Small and brown.

5a-c. **Chilostoma desmoulinsi** 200
C. Pyrenees only. Flatter than *C. squamatinum*, distinctly keeled.

6a-c. **Chilostoma glaciale** 201
French Alps only. Coarse regular ribbing.

7a-c. **Chilostoma alpinum** 202
French Alps only. Larger than *C. glaciale*, more finely ribbed. No spiral band.

21

1a

2a

3a

1b

2b

3b

1c

2c

3c

1d

2d

4a

5a

6a

7a

4b

5b

6b

7b

4c

5c

6c

7c

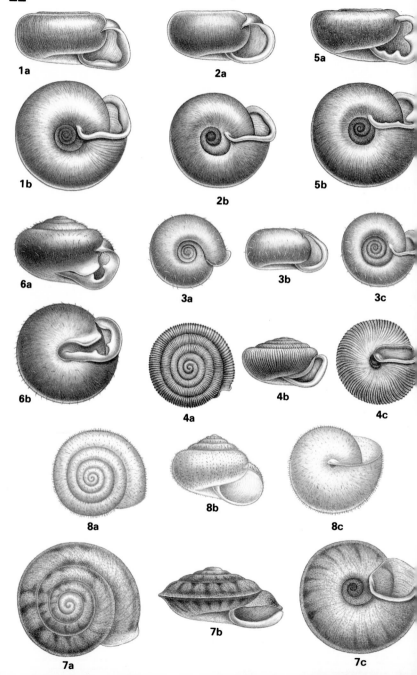

1a

2a

5a

1b

2b

5b

6a

3a

3b

3c

6b

4a

4b

4c

8a

8b

8c

7a

7b

7c

Family HELICIDAE
Subfamily HELICODONTINAE

Plate 22

1a-b. *Helicodonta obvoluta* ×2   198
Mainly C. Europe, common. Blunt tooth-like thickenings on lip.

2a-b. Helicodonta angigyra ×2½   198
S. Alps only. No blunt thickenings on lip. Umbilicus strongly eccentric.

3a-c. Drepanostoma nautiliforme ×3   197
S. Switzerland only.

4a-c Trissexodon constructus ×3   198
Basses Pyrénées only, rare.

Subfamily ARIANTINAE
See also plates 20 and 21

5a-b. Isognomostoma holosericum ×2½   202
Alps and S. Germany, mainly in coniferous woods. Strong triangular teeth on outer lip. Often densely hairy.

6a-b. Isognomostoma isognomostoma ×2½   202
C. Europe, common in montane woods. Strong parietal tooth. Often densely hairy.

7a-c. *Helicigona lapicida* ×2   199
Very sharply keeled. Often in crevices of rocks and walls.

Subfamily MONACHINAE
See also plate 20

8a-c. *Ashfordia granulata* ×3   185
Mainly British Isles. Densely hairy. Umbilicus minute.

*2) TRICHIA PLEBEIA (Draparnaud 1805)   **Pl. 19**
Syns. *Fruticicola sericea* (Draparnaud, *non* Müller), *Trichia liberta* of British
authors (*non* Westerlund).
Description. 5–7 × 7–10 mm. More globular than *T. hispida*, with 5–6 whorls and a
smaller umbilicus and denser hairs. Internal rib weak. Forms intermediate between
this species and *T. hispida* are quite common.
Habitat. As for *T. hispida*, often in wetter sites.
Range. C. European.
Distribution. Map 239. France, C. England, Switzerland, S. Germany E. to
Thuringia and Saxony. Exact distribution uncertain due to confusion with
T. hispida.

3) TRICHIA SUBERECTA (Clessin 1873)   **Pl. 19**
Description. 4–5 × 5–7 mm. A small form with a range of shape variation similar to
T. hispida. Distinguished from other *Trichia* internally by having 6 rather than 8
branches to the mucus glands.
Range, Distribution and Habitat. Map 240. Rare, found between 1000 and 2000 m in
the extreme east of Switzerland (Engadine), in the Alpine foreland region of S.
Germany (S.W. Swabian Alps), and in W. Austria; also a single record from the
N.W. Italian Alps (Upper Aosta valley).

The **TRICHIA STRIOLATA** group (members of this group usually lack hairs
when fully adult.)
*1) TRICHIA STRIOLATA (Pfeiffer 1828)   **Pl. 19**
Syns. *Fruticicola striolata* (Pfeiffer), *Hygromia striolata* (Pfeiffer), *H. rufescens* of
British authors (*non* Pennant).
Description. 6.5–9 × 11–14 mm. Shell slightly depressed convex and conical
above, flattened below with 6 convex whorls with moderately deep sutures. Last
whorl angled at the periphery, which may be thickened to form a pale and more
opaque spiral band. Umbilicus medium (one-eighth to one-fifth of width of shell),
mouth elliptical, slightly flattened below, with a slightly reflected lip below, and a
thickened internal rib. Shell opaque or slightly translucent, with rather coarse and
irregular growth-ridges, and hairless when adult. Colour variable from dark red-
brown to creamy-yellow.
Similar species. *T. hispida* group are smaller, usually hairy, and less angled at the
periphery. *Perforatella umbrosa* (p. 187), *T. villosa* (p. 195).
Habitat. Woods, hedges, roadsides and waste ground; gardens (widely spread by
man). Usually in damp and shaded places.
Range. N.W. European.
Distribution. Map 241. British Isles, N.E. France, the Netherlands (Rhine delta),
southern half of Germany (mainly in river valleys and lowlands). Occasionally
adventive elsewhere.

2) TRICHIA MONTANA (Studer 1820)   **Pl. 19**
Syn. *Fruticicola striolata montana* (Studer)
Description. 5–7 × 9–12 mm. Usually less angled at the periphery, with a mouth
less flattened below, and with more convex whorls and deeper sutures than *T.
striolata*, but not always distinguishable. Separated from *T. striolata* by small
differences in internal anatomy, having longer dart-sacs and flagellum.

Habitat. Woods and rocky ground between 400 and 1600 m.
Range. N. Alpine.
Distribution. Map 242. French and Swiss Jura and Alps, and in the S. German Alps.

3) TRICHIA CAELATA (Studer 1820)   **Pl. 19**
Syn. *Fruticicola caelata* (Studer)
Description. 4 × 8 mm. Shell smaller, flatter and more glossy and translucent than typical *T. striolata*. Distinguished internally from *T. striolata* and *T. montana* by very short dart sacs.
Habitat, Range and Distribution. Map 243. Rocky limestone areas between 500 and 1300 m in the upper Birs valley, S. of Basel, Swiss Jura only.

4) TRICHIA CLANDESTINA (Hartmann 1821)   **Pl. 19**
Description. 6–7 × 10–11 mm. Shell with more rapidly expanding whorls, and with fewer exposed to view in the umbilicus than *T. striolata* and *T. montana*. Distinguished internally by very short flagellum.
Habitat, Range and Distribution. Map 244. Only between 400 and 1000 m in mountains N.E. of Zurich, Switzerland.

TRICHIA GRAMINICOLA Falkner 1973   **Pl. 19**
Description. 4.5–5.5 × 9¼–11 mm. Shell very depressed, often almost flat above, flattened below, with 5–5½ whorls with moderately deep sutures, and the last slightly shouldered at the periphery. Umbilicus wide and deep (*c*. one-fifth to one-quarter of width of shell), mouth oblique elliptical, flattened above and below, mouth-edge very slightly everted, and with a white internal rib behind. Shell brown, slightly glossy and translucent, growth-ridges irregular.
Similar species. The flattest forms of *T. hispida* (p. 191) are less flattened and shouldered, and have a less oblique mouth. Internally *T. graminicola* differs from all forms of *T. hispida* in having a much longer vaginal neck.
Habitat. In pine woods with grassy field-layer.
Range and Distribution. Map 245. Described in 1973, this species has so far been found only from one mountain near Blumberg, South Baden, S.W. Germany.

TRICHIA VILLOSA (Studer 1789)   **Pl. 19**
Syn. *Fruticicola villosa* (Studer)
Description. 6–8 × 10–14 mm. Shell depressed above, with a low, blunt, spire and convex whorls. Umbilicus wide and deep (*c*. one-fifth of width of shell). Mouth elliptical, flattened below and above, and with a weak internal rib *c*. 1 mm behind the peristome. Last whorl slightly shouldered at the periphery. Shell opaque, pale yellowish-brown, with moderately irregular growth-ridges and covered with long curved hairs (up to 1 mm long).
Similar species. *T. striolata* (p. 194) lacks hairs, is less flattened and has a higher spire and a thicker internal rib. *T. graminicola* is flatter above, smaller and less hairy. *Perforatella umbrosa* (p. 187).
Habitat. Damp and shaded places in mountainous regions (usually from 500–2000 m in the Alps).
Range. N.W. Alpine.
Distribution. Map 246. E. France (Vosges, Jura, Alps), Switzerland (Jura, N.

Alps), S. Germany from upper Rhine valley to S.E. Bavaria. Also occasionally elsewhere as a deliberate or accidental introduction.

TRICHIA BICONICA (Eder 1917)   Pl. 17
Syn. *Fruticicola biconica* (Eder)
Description. 2.5–3.5 × 5–6 mm. Shell flattened above, spire a very low cone of 5–5½ tightly coiled convex whorls with deep sutures. Last whorl angled at the periphery and flattened below. Umbilicus narrow, circular and deep (*c.* one-eighth of width of shell). Mouth flattened above and below, elliptical with the mouth-edge weakly everted below and a thin whitish internal rib behind it. Shell opaque pale brown, with coarse, blunt and widely spaced irregular growth-ridges above, smoother below.
Habitat, Range and Distribution. Map 247. Apparently endemic in one locality in Switzerland (Bannalpass, Nidwalden), on grassy limestone screes at about 2000 m.

TRICHIA UNIDENTATA (Draparnaud 1805)   Pl. 17
Syn. *Fruticicola unidentata* (Draparnaud)
Description. 5–6 × 6–8 mm. Shell high and convex above, flattened below, with 6–7 tightly coiled convex whorls, rounded at the periphery. Umbilicus *c.* one-eighth of width of shell. Mouth elliptical, flattened below, with a simple mouth-edge and a small white or pinkish internal rib with a single, thick basal tooth. Shell thin, opaque, yellowish to reddish-brown, with fine growth-ridges, and many long (*c.* 0.5 mm), curved hairs often worn from old shells, but leaving small basal tubercles.
Similar species. *T. edentula* and *Perforatella bidentata* (p. 185) have a smaller umbilicus and are angled at the periphery, and differ in number of teeth.
Habitat. Montane woods, usually 500–2000 m.
Range. E. Alpine and Carpathian.
Distribution. Map 248. N.E. Switzerland (E. of Basel); S. Germany (mainly in the Alpine foreland region, with a few scattered localities as far N. as the R. Main); Erzgebirge in East Germany. Doubtful in France (Jura mountains and Isère).

TRICHIA EDENTULA (Draparnaud 1805)   Pl. 17
Syn. *Fruticicola edentula* (Draparnaud)
Description. 4.5–5.5 × 7–8 mm. Shell steeply conical-convex above, flattened below, with 7–8 tightly coiled whorls, the last angled at the periphery. Umbilicus minute, and nearly sealed by reflected columellar lip. Mouth very elliptical, flattened below with a slightly reflected lip below the periphery, and an internal rib, somewhat thickened basally. Shell opaque brown with a pale band round the periphery, and with rather coarse growth-ridges and short, fine hairs (usually lost in adults).
Similar species. *T. unidentata*. *Perforatella bidentata* (p.'185).
Habitat. Montane forests from 500–2000 m.
Range. W. Alpine.
Distribution. Map 249. S. French and Swiss Jura and N. Alps; S. Vosges; Alpine foreland region of S. Bavaria and in the Bavarian Forest.

*PONENTINA SUBVIRESCENS (Bellamy 1839)   **Pl. 17**
Syns. *Trichia subvirescens* (Bellamy), *Hygromia revelata* (Gray, *non* Férussac), *Ponentina montivaga* (Westerlund)
Description. 4–6.5 × 5–8 mm. Shell globular, slightly depressed, with 4–4½ rapidly expanding convex whorls. Umbilicus small, and partly covered by the reflected columellar lip. Mouth large and round, with a very weak or no internal rib. Shell dull greenish-yellow, with blunt irregular growth-ridging; slightly translucent and covered with short soft hairs (often much worn in adults).
Habitat. Grassland and rocky areas, usually damp and close to the sea.
Range. S.W. European (Atlantic).
Distribution. Map 250. Coastal areas of W. France (in Loire valley as far as E. as Tours), Channel Islands, S.W. England and S. Wales (Pembroke).

EUOMPHALIA STRIGELLA (Draparnaud 1801)   **Pl. 20**
Description. 10–12 × 12–18 mm. Shell globular, conical/convex above, with 5–6 convex whorls with well marked sutures. Rounded below with a large, somewhat eccentric umbilicus (*c.* one-quarter of width of shell), last whorl descending abruptly at the mouth, which is slightly elliptic with a white, everted lip and a thick white internal rib. Shell yellowish to light brown, often with a paler and more opaque zone at the periphery, growth-ridges strong but irregular.
Similar species. *Monacha cantiana* (p. 184), *Bradybaena fruticum* (p. 174).
Habitat. Hedgerows, scrub, rocky ground and open woods – in moderately exposed and sunny places, up to *c.* 2600 m in the Alps (Graubünden).
Range. C. European.
Distribution. Map 251. C. and S.E. France, Switzerland, Germany (mainly in S., occasionally in lower Rhine valley and N. German plain), E. Denmark and E. Scandinavia to about 63°N.

CILIELLA CILIATA (Studer 1820)   **Pl. 17**
Description. 4–6 × 9–12 mm. Shell low conical above with a spire of flattened whorls with very shallow sutures, sharply keeled at the periphery. Convex below, umbilicus small and slightly obscured by the reflected lip. Mouth very oblique and oval with a pale everted lip and an internal rib. Shell dull brown, with oblique radial lines of lamellae which are enlarged to form a single row of spines at the periphery (these may be partly lost in adults).
Habitat. Montane habitats – grassy slopes, stream sides and rocks up to 1700–2000 m in the Alps.
Range. S. and W. Alpine.
Distribution. Map 252. S. Switzerland (Valais, Ticino, Graubünden) and S.E. France (Savoie, Hautes Alpes).

Subfamily **HELICODONTINAE**

DREPANOSTOMA NAUTILIFORME Porro 1836   **Pl. 22**
Description. 3–4 × 5–7 mm. Shell flattened above and below, compressed, with a deeply sunken spire of 5 rapidly expanding whorls, the last of which partly obscures the previous one. Convex or very slightly angled at the periphery. Umbilicus wide

and shallow. Mouth unequally crescentic, wider below than above, with a weak, slightly everted lip and a thin brown internal rib. Shell slightly translucent brown, dull, virtually smooth and sparsely covered with thin hairs.
Habitat. Under stones and fallen leaves in shady places.
Range. S. Alpine.
Distribution. Map 253. S. Switzerland (Ticino) only.

*HELICODONTA OBVOLUTA (Müller 1774)   Pl. 22
Description. 5–7 × 11–15 mm. Shell flat above, with a slightly sunken spire of 5–6 tightly coiled whorls. Shallowly convex at the periphery and flattened below. Umbilicus wide and deep. Mouth angled, flattened above and below, with a white everted lip and low blunt thickenings in the basal and mid outer regions. Shell opaque brown, growth-ridges irregular; densely covered with hairs when young (adults may be completely hairless).
Similar species. *Helicodonta angigyra* has an umbilicus becoming abruptly eccentric at the last whorl, is smaller, and lacks the thickenings on the lip. The last whorl descends abruptly at the mouth. *Isognomostoma holosericum* (p. 202) does not have a sunken spire, has fewer and wider whorls, and triangular teeth.
Habitat. Hedgerows and woodland, especially on calcareous soils, up to *c.* 1500 m in the Alps. Restricted to woodlands at the edge of its range.
Range. C. European.
Distribution. Map 254. S.E. England (Sussex, Hampshire), France (rare in W.), S. Belgium, S. Netherlands (Limburg), Switzerland, S. half of Germany (isolated colonies in Schleswig–Holstein).

HELICODONTA ANGIGYRA (Rossmässler 1835)   Pl. 22
Description. 4–5 × 9–10 mm. Shell flat above, with a very slightly sunken spire of 6–7 very tightly coiled whorls with deep sutures. Periphery slightly convex, flattened below with a wide, deep umbilicus becoming markedly eccentric at the last whorl. Last whorl turns down abruptly at the mouth. Mouth flattened above and below, angled, with a white everted outer lip slightly thickened centrally to form a callus. Shell opaque reddish-brown with fine irregular growth-ridges and covered (especially when young) with thin stiff hairs.
Similar species. *H. obvoluta. Isognomostoma holosericum* (p. 202) has fewer, wider whorls and triangular teeth.
Habitat. Woods and scrub, especially in moutains, up to *c.* 1400 m.
Range. S. Alpine.
Distribution. Map 255. French Alps (Savoie), S. Switzerland (Ticino).

TRISSEXODON CONSTRICTUS (Boubée 1836)   Pl. 22
Description. 3–4 × 7–8 mm. Shell very flattened above, convex below, with a marked shoulder above the periphery, with a very low spire of 5½–6½ flattened and tightly coiled whorls. Umbilicus small. Mouth very narrow and crescent-shaped, with a white and everted lip and a long crescentic parietal lamella partly obscuring the mouth. Shell opaque brown, with marked, regular, lamella-like transverse ribs.
Habitat. Under stones and litter in damp and shady scrub.
Range. Pyrenean.
Distribution. Map 256. Rare, a few localities in Basses Pyrénées only.

Subfamily **ARIANTINAE**

ELONA QUIMPERIANA (Férussac 1821)   **Pl. 20**
Description. 10–12 × 20–30 mm. Shell flat above, with a slightly sunken spire of 5–6 rapidly expanding convex whorls with moderate sutures, convex below, and rounded at the periphery. Umbilicus wide and deep. Mouth nearly round, slightly flattened below, with a white everted lip. Shell thin, translucent, pale yellowish-brown, with weak and irregular growth-ridging.
Habitat. Moist woods and scrub and shady and damp herbaceous areas.
Range. W. European (Atlantic).
Distribution. Map 257. Very local: a few places in Finistère, Côtes du Nord, Basses Pyrénées only.

*ARIANTA ARBUSTORUM (Linné 1758)   **Pl. 20**
Syn. *Helicigona arbustorum* (Linné)
Description. 10–22 × 14–28 mm. Shell globular, with a convex or conical spire of 5–6 slightly convex whorls with rather shallow sutures. Umbilicus a tiny crescentic slit almost closed by reflected columellar lip. Mouth nearly round, with a white, everted lip. Shell opaque, brown or yellow, usually with a dark brown spiral band at the periphery, and nearly always with extensive paler flecking over the shell. At high altitudes the shell is usually small and more conical; the largest shells are usually somewhat flattened.
Habitat. Widespread – meadows, herbage, woods and hedgerows, but always in damp places, and very restricted in areas with dry climate and good drainage. Attaining 2700 m in the Alps.
Range. W. and C. European.
Distribution. Map 258. Throughout N.W. and C. Europe, but becoming rare in the extreme west and south; absent from S. Ireland, and rare in N.E. Scandinavia.

*HELICIGONA LAPICIDA (Linné 1758)   **Pl. 22**
Description. 7–9 × 12–20 mm. Shell flattened above and below, with a low, slightly convex spire of 5½ slightly convex whorls with very shallow sutures. Very sharply keeled at the periphery. Umbilicus wide and deep, mouth elliptical, notched by the keel, and with a thin white everted lip. Shell pale to medium brown opaque, with a pattern of darker radial blotches and with moderately coarse, irregular growth ridges. Also a distinctive granular microsculpture, giving a shagreened appearance. Colour and blotching can vary considerably.
Habitat. In holes and crevices in rocky ground, stone walls, and also in old woodland and hedgerows. Attaining *c.* 1600 m in the Alps (Valais).
Range. W. and C. European.
Distribution. Map 259. Widespread, reaching S.E. Britain and S. Scandinavia, but scarce in N. European plain. Isolated in S. Ireland (Fermoy, Co. Cork, possibly introduced).

CHILOSTOMA CINGULATUM (Studer 1820)   **Pl. 21**
Syns. *Helicigona cingulata* (Studer), *H. preslii* (Rossmässler)
Description. 10–12 × 20–27 mm. Shell very flattened above, with 5 convex, rapidly expanding whorls and moderate sutures. Umbilicus large; last whorl turning down

sharply at the mouth which is elliptical and very oblique. Mouth-edge with a lip strongly everted below, backed by a white internal rib below only. Shell white to creamy-white with a single brown spiral band just above the periphery.

Habitat. Under calcareous rocks and walls up to *c*. 1500 m.

Range. Mainly S. Alpine.

Distribution. Map 260. S. Switzerland (Ticino), S. Bavaria (mainly in the Allgaüer Alps). Introduced in a few places in S. Germany as far north as Staffelstein (Franconian Switzerland) and Nähstein (Thuringia).

Note: *Chilostoma planospira* (Lamarck 1822), a S. Alpine species nowhere native within our area, occurs with *C. cingulatum* as an introduction at one locality in S. Germany (ruins of Donaustauf, near Regensburg), where a large colony has flourished since 1850. *C. planospira* closely resembles *C. zonatum* (see below), but has a slightly more compressed shell with a flatter spire, and the main brown spiral band lies inside a well-defined paler and more translucent area, above and below which there may be further faint dark bands.

CHILOSTOMA SQUAMATINUM (Moquin-Tandon 1856)   Pl. 21
Syn. *C. corneum* (Draparnaud)

Description. 6–8 × 12–15 mm. Shell somewhat flattened conical-convex above, with 5–6 convex whorls with deep sutures, the last slightly angled at the periphery. Umbilicus large. Last whorl turning down sharply at the mouth, which is elliptical, flattened below and above; mouth-edge markedly everted to form a white lip. Shell pale to dark brown, and slightly glossy, with a single dark brown spiral band at the periphery (inconspicuous in dark brown shells) often set in a wider pale band.

Similar species. *C. desmoulinsi* is flatter above, more angled at the periphery, has less convex whorls, shallower sutures, a more oblique mouth, and a lip forming a continuous circle round the mouth.

Habitat. Holes and crevices in rocks, screes and walls, usually seen on the surface only in wet weather.

Range. S.W. European.

Distribution. Map 261. The Pyrenees, S. and C. France north to Brittany along the Atlantic seaboard.

CHILOSTOMA DESMOULINSI (Farines 1834)   Pl. 21

Description. 5–6 × 13–15 mm. Shell flattened above, with a very low convex spire of 5½–6 weakly convex whorls with shallow sutures, the last clearly angled at the periphery. Umbilicus large; last whorl turns down sharply at the mouth, which is very elliptical and oblique, with the mouth-edge everted into a white lip which continues over the parietal area to make a complete circle round the mouth in fully adult shells. Shell yellowish to dark brown, slightly glossy with a faint trace of a dark spiral band at the periphery.

Similar species. *C. squamatinum.*

Habitat. In cracks and crevices in rocks and screes between 600–2800 m.

Range. E. Pyrenean.

Distribution. Map 262. Ariège and Hautes Pyrénées.

CHILOSTOMA ZONATUM (Studer 1820)   **Pl. 21**
Syns. *Helicigona zonata* (Studer), *Chilostoma foetens* (Studer)
Description. 9–13 × 18–26 mm. Shell slightly flattened above, with a low convex spire of 5 convex whorls with moderate sutures, the last rounded at the periphery. Umbilicus large; last whorl turning down abruptly at the mouth, which is less elliptical and oblique than in other *Chilostoma* species, and which has an everted white lip at the periostome. Shell yellowish to greenish-brown, slightly glossy, with moderately distinct, irregular growth-ridges and a brown spiral band at the periphery.
Similar species. This species is part of a complex of geographically replacing forms in the Alps, being the westernmost form. It is distinguished from the eastern *C. achates* by being less flattened, having more convex whorls, a less oblique mouth, and a greenish colour.
Habitat. Damp, often non-calcareous rocky places in montane regions, from 800–2900 m.
Range. S.W. Alpine.
Distribution. Map 263. French Alps (scarce), S. Switzerland (mainly in Valais and Ticino, and not E. of the upper Rhine valley).

CHILOSTOMA ACHATES (Rossmässler 1835)   **Pl. 21**
Syns. *Helicigona ichthyomma* (Held), *H. cisalpina rhaetica* (Strobel)
Description. 7–12 × 17–29 mm. Shell very flattened, with very low conical spire (sometimes nearly flat) of 5 weakly convex whorls with moderate sutures, the last slightly shouldered at the periphery. Umbilicus large; last whorl turning down abruptly at the mouth which has a white everted lip at the peristome. Shell glossy, slightly translucent whitish-brown, with a dark brown spiral band at the periphery below which is a parallel pale band, often almost white, growth-ridges rather fine and irregular. The form in Basse Engadine is larger and with higher spire than that in the upper Rhine valley.
Similar species. *C. zonatum.*
Habitat. Rocks and screes from 900–2300 m.
Range. E. Alpine.
Distribution. Map 264. E. Switzerland (Basse Engadine and upper Rhine valleys) and S.E. Bavaria (mainly in the Berchtesgaden Alps).

CHILOSTOMA GLACIALE (Férussac 1821)   **Pl. 21**
Description. 6–8 × 12–16 mm. Shell flattened above with very low convex spire of 5–5½ convex whorls with moderate sutures, very slightly or not shouldered at the periphery. Umbilicus large, last whorl turning down slightly at the mouth, which is slightly oval with an everted white lip. Shell opaque, whitish, with a single spiral brown band just above the periphery; and with rather coarse regular transverse ribbing and very fine spiral sculpturing.
Similar species. *C. alpinum* (p. 202) is larger, less flattened, more shouldered at the periphery, lacks the spiral band and is less coarsely and more irregularly ribbed.
Habitat. Rocky scrub and screes in the Alps to 2500 m.
Range. S.W. Alpine.
Distribution. Map 265. French Alps (Haute Savoie, Savoie, Isère, Hautes Alpes).

CHILOSTOMA ALPINUM (Férussac 1821)   Pl. 21

Description. 9–12 × 15–22 mm. Shell somewhat flattened above, with a low convex-conical spire of 5–5½ slightly convex whorls with moderate sutures, slightly keeled or shouldered at the periphery. Umbilicus large, mouth elliptical with a white everted lip. Shell yellowish-white, often flecked and streaked with moderate and irregular growth-ridging. Specimens from lower altitudes (800–1500 m) tend to be flatter and more often flecked than those above.

Similar species. *C. glaciale* (p. 201).

Habitat. Calcareous meadows, scrub and rocky areas in the Alps from 800–2800 m.

Range. S.W. Alpine.

Distribution. Map 266. French Alps (Haute Savoie, Savoie, Isère, Hautes Alpes).

ISOGNOMOSTOMA ISOGNOMOSTOMA (Schröter 1784)   Pl. 22

Syn. *Isognomostoma personatum* (Lamarck)

Description. 4–7 × 7–11 mm. Shell depressed globular, with a low, blunt convex spire of 5–6 convex whorls with moderate sutures, and rounded at the periphery. Flattened below, with a tiny crescentic opening at the umbilicus, which is nearly sealed by the reflected lip of the mouth. Outer edge of mouth sharply everted, and backed internally by a paler rib supporting one basal and one mid-outer palatal tooth. Parietal face of mouth-edge with a broad lamella (only fully developed in completely adult shells). Shell opaque, smooth and brown, with long slightly curved hairs (often partly eroded in old shells).

Habitat. Montane woodlands from 300–1700 m.

Range. Alpine and Carpathian.

Distribution. Map 267. Montane regions of C. Europe north to Harz mountains, the Sauerland and the Eifel; S. Belgium (Ardennes), E. France (Alps, Jura, Vosges).

ISOGNOMOSTOMA HOLOSERICUM (Studer 1820)   Pl. 22

Description. 5–6 × 9–12 mm. Shell completely flat, or very slightly raised above, with 4½–5 convex whorls and well marked sutures; periphery shouldered just below the upper surface, sides convex below to a flattened base. Umbilicus wide and deep. Mouth angular, flattened above and below, with a white everted lip with one or two basal and one mid-outer triangular teeth. Shell opaque brown, growth-ridging fine and irregular and with a dense covering of short hairs.

Similar species. *Helicodonta obvoluta* (p. 198). *Helicodonta angigyra* (p. 198).

Habitat. Montane conifer forests, often on non-calcareous soils, usually from 1000–2000 m.

Range. Alpine and Carpathian.

Distribution. Map 268. French and Swiss Alps and Jura and a few scattered localities in the mountains of S. and E. Germany (Bavarian Alps, Bavarian Forest, Erzgebirge, Franconian Switzerland, N. Franconian Jura).

Subfamily HELICINAE

*THEBA PISANA (Müller 1774)   Pl. 24

Syn. *Euparypha pisana* (Müller)

Description. 9–20 × 12–25 mm. Shell slightly depressed globular, with 5½–6 slightly convex whorls with shallow sutures. Umbilicus narrow, and partly obscured by reflected columellar lip. Mouth elliptical, with an internal rib, and often with a pinkish flush. Shell white, ginger or rarely pink, the growth-ridges crossed by fine spiral striations and often with a varied pattern of dark spiral bands which are often dilute, transparent, interrupted or fused. Juveniles have a sharp keel at the periphery, but in adults the periphery is only very slightly shouldered.

Similar species. *Cernuella virgata* (p. 177) has a larger umbilicus, deeper sutures, and lacks the spiral striations.

Habitat. Dry, exposed sites, usually near the sea, and frequently on dunes (almost exclusively so at the N. of range). Sits out on plant stems in dry weather.

Range. Mediterranean.

Distribution. Map 269. A common Mediterranean species, established in numerous places along the Atlantic coasts of France, Belgium, the Netherlands, S.W. England (Cornwall), S. Wales, and E. Ireland. Occasionally adventive elsewhere in England, France and Switzerland.

EOBANIA VERMICULATA (Müller 1774)   Pl. 24

Description. 14–27 × 22–30 mm. Shell depressed globular, with 5–6 slightly convex whorls and shallow sutures. Umbilicus completely sealed by reflected lip. Mouth flattened above and below, last whorl turning down abruptly at the peristome, with a strong white, everted lip. Shell thick, creamy-white, with irregular growth-ridges and a finely reticulated surface, and with up to 5 variable dark brown bands, often fused or interrupted or with a pattern of whitish reticulation superimposed.

Habitat. Fields, hedgerows, gardens and vineyards.

Range. Mediterranean.

Distribution. Map 270. Common in Mediterranean regions, coming just within our area in S. France (upper Rhône valley, upper Garonne valley); occasionally adventive elsewhere.

CEPAEA VINDOBONENSIS (Férussac 1821)   Pl. 23

Description. 17–21 × 20–25 mm. Shell globular, with a conical spire of 5½–6 convex whorls. Umbilicus completely closed by lip. Mouth with a strong thickened lip, dark brown at the columella fading round to the suture where it is nearly white. Shell whitish or dull yellow, with fine, rather regular growth-ridges and up to 5 dark spiral bands, the upper two of which are usually thin and weakly pigmented.

Similar species. *C. nemoralis* is more brightly coloured, usually has a uniformly dark lip, has a less ribbed shell and is more flattened below.

Habitat. Scrub and bushes on warm valleys and slopes.

Range. S.E. European.

Distribution. Map 271. East Germany (upper Elbe valley, N. to Meissen).

*CEPAEA NEMORALIS (Linné 1758)   Pl. 23

Syn. *Helix nemoralis* Linné

Description. 12–22 (rarely 28) × 18–25 mm (rarely 32). Shell globular, slightly depressed, with a rather conical spire of 5½ convex whorls. Umbilicus completely sealed by lip (rarely very slightly open). Thickened lip usually dark brown, occasionally white or intermediate. Shell brightly coloured, glossy, with growth-ridges rather weak and irregular and with 0–5 dark spiral bands. This species and *C.*

hortensis (below) are the most variable in colour and banding pattern of all N.W. European helicid snails.

Similar species. *C. vindobonensis* (p. 203). *C. hortensis* is usually smaller, and less conical above, and usually has a white lip. In areas where lip colour is variable, dissection is necessary – *C. hortensis* has bifurcated blades to the dart while those of *C. nemoralis* are simple. *C. hortensis* usually has 4 or more branches of each mucus gland, *C. nemoralis* 3 or less. *C. sylvatica* has a pale brown lip darkest at the columella, is more coarsely growth-ridged, and has a small blunt projection on the columellar lip.

Habitat. Very varied, woods, hedges, scrub, grassland and dunes. Attaining *c.* 1200 m in the Alps and 1800 m in the Pyrenees.

Range. W. European.

Distribution. Map 272. Widespread, northwards to C. Scotland and coastal areas of S. Norway, Sweden and Finland; spread by man near its northern limits.

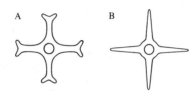

Cross section of darts of   A, *Cepaea hortensis*   B, *C. nemoralis*

*CEPAEA HORTENSIS (Müller 1774)   **Pl. 23**

Syn. *Helix hortensis* Müller

Description. 10–17 × 14–20 (rarely 22) mm. Shell slightly depressed globular, with a low convex spire of *c.* 5–5½ whorls. Umbilicus completely sealed by lip. Mouth with a white thickened lip (occasionally brown). Shell brightly coloured, glossy, with growth-ridges rather weak and irregular and with 0–5 spiral bands. This species, like *C. nemoralis* (p. 203) is exceptionally variable in shell colour and banding pattern.

Similar species. *C. nemoralis* (p. 203). *C. sylvatica* usually has some pigment in the lip, has coarser growth-ridges and has a thickened projection on the columellar lip.

Habitat. Very varied – woods, grassland, hedges and dunes, but commonly in wetter or colder places than *C. nemoralis*, with which it may often be found. Attaining over 2000 m in the Alps.

Range. W. and C. European.

Distribution. Map 273. Widespread, but rarer than *C. nemoralis* in south and west and extending further north in Scotland and Scandinavia (beyond Arctic Circle in Norway, to 61°30 in Finland); also in Iceland.

CEPAEA SYLVATICA (Draparnaud 1801)   **Pl. 23**

Description. 12–16 × 18–25 (rarely 28) mm. Shell slightly depressed globular, with a convex spire of 5–6 convex whorls. Umbilicus usually completely sealed by lip. Mouth with thickened lip, brown in the columellar region becoming paler to nearly white at the suture, and with a small, blunt projection in the columellar region. Shell yellowish or whitish, with rather coarse irregular growth-ridging, and with 0–5 brown spiral bands, the upper two of which are usually small and discontinuously pigmented.

Similar species. *C. nemoralis* (p. 203), *C. hortensis* (p. 204).

Habitat. Montane forest and meadows from 500–2400 m.

Range. W. Alpine.

Distribution. Map 274. French and Swiss Alps and Jura; upper Rhine valley north to Karlsruhe and Worms; introduced in gardens at Landsberg (Lech valley).

*HELIX ASPERSA Müller 1774   Pl. 24

Description. (Rarely 20) 25–35 (rarely 40) × 25–40 (rarely 45) mm. Shell globular, with 4½–5 rapidly expanding and slightly convex whorls. Umbilicus completely sealed by lip. Mouth large, with a thickened white lip. Shell usually pale brown, occasionally yellow, with 0–5 dark spiral bands, variable and often flecked with white. There is a characteristic wrinkle-like sculpture.

Habitat. Very varied. Often associated with man in gardens and parks, especially near the edge of its range, but also in dunes, woods, rocks and hedgerows. Often a garden pest.

Range. Mediterranean and W. European.

Distribution. Map 275. Widespread in natural habitats in oceanic areas of France, Ireland and S. Britain, becoming coastal and synanthropic in N. Britain, Belgium, Netherlands, W. Switzerland and W. Germany, east to the Rhine valley. Occasionally as an adventive or garden introduction elsewhere.

*HELIX POMATIA Linné 1758   Pl. 24

Description. 30–50 × 32–50 mm. Shell very large, globular, with 5–6 convex whorls, and a tiny umbilicus partly covered by reflected lip. Mouth large, with a thickened lip which is often slightly pigmented. Shell thick, creamy-white, with coarse growth-ridges and fine spiral striae, often with rather indistinct brown spiral bands. The largest N.W. European snail.

Similar species. Confusion with empty shells of other large species imported as food is possible (especially *H. lucorum* from S.E. Europe).

Habitat. Calcicole, in woods, hedges and tall herbage, especially in vineyards as a pest. Attaining *c*. 2000 m in the Alps. 'Cultivated' as food in some areas.

Range. C. and S.E. European.

Distribution. Map 276. Widespread in C. Europe, extending westwards to C. France and S.E. England, and north to the S. Baltic coasts. Introduced in a few places in S. Norway, Sweden and Finland.

Greenhouse aliens

Many exotic snails have from time to time been reported in N.W. Europe from greenhouses, especially from the hot-houses of botanic gardens. No doubt they are accidentally brought in with plants and soil. Usually they fail to establish themselves and obviously they are not encouraged to do so. Nevertheless there are a few species which are rather characteristic of these places, and which once introduced are evidently well adapted to surviving and breeding under the unusual conditions encountered: relatively high, steady temperatures and humidities, coupled with severe human disturbance. They must have excellent powers of passive dispersal, either as eggs or as adults, and it is noteworthy that several have been widely spread by man in open habitats in warmer parts of the world. Some are ovo-viviparous, a feature no doubt useful both in assisting dispersal and in protecting the young from the effects of cultivation.

Greenhouse faunas have not yet been much studied, so that the selection of exotic species given below is provisional and the criteria for inclusion somewhat ill-defined. Furthermore, the taxonomy in some cases presents difficulties, since the original home of the species may be uncertain.

Apart from true exotics, a number of ordinary N.W. European molluscs commonly occur in greenhouses, and are sometimes able to exist in this way beyond their natural climatic limits. Some of these occurrences are mentioned in the main text of this book. Garden and other synanthropic species are obviously favoured (e.g., *Arion hortensis*, *Oxychilus draparnaudi*, *Limax flavus*, *Deroceras caruanae*). Other species fairly often recorded are *Discus rotundatus*, *Oxychilus cellarius*, *O. alliarius*, *Deroceras reticulatum*, *D. laeve*, *Boettgerilla pallens*, *Lauria cylindracea*, *Cecilioides acicula* and *Vallonia pulchella*. *Deroceras laeve* is represented by a peculiar form, externally purplish-grey rather than brown, and internally lacking a penis and vas deferens (see p. 147).

Family PLEURODISCIDAE

This family comprises only the genus *Pleurodiscus*, represented by a few species living in the eastern Mediterranean. They are ovo-viviparous.

PLEURODISCUS BALMEI (Potiez & Michaud 1838)
Syn. *Patulastra flavida* (Rossmässler)
Description. br. 8–11 mm. Shell discoidal, with 5½ regularly enlarging whorls; suture well defined; periphery slightly angled, especially in the juvenile. Mouth-edge simple, unthickened. Umbilicus wide and deep. Shell pale golden-brown, with very regular *sharp ribs* (6 per mm on last whorl), often giving a slight sparkle to the naked eye.
Original home and habitat. Mediterranean (Sicily, Sardinia, Malta, Algeria). A species of waste ground, especially among rocks.

Pleurodiscus balmei × 3

Helicodiscus parallelus × 4½

Opeas pumilum × 4

Zonitoides arboreus × 4½

Lamellaxis clavulinus × 4

Hawaiia minuscula × 5½   *Subulina octona* × 3   *Subulina striatella* × 3   *Gulella io* × 6

Plate 23

Family HELICIDAE
Subfamily HELICINAE
See also plate 24
(×1¼)

Cepaea species are extremely variable in colour and banding pattern.

1. ***Cepaea nemoralis** 203
Widespread. Usually with a brown lip (occasionally white).
1a-b. Yellow five-banded form.
1c. Brown unbanded form.
1d. Yellow form with interrupted bands.
1e. Pink midbanded form.
1f. Brown midbanded form.
1g. White-lipped form.

2. ***Cepaea hortensis** 204
Widespread. Smaller than *C. nemoralis*. Usually a white lip (sometimes coloured).
2a-b. Yellow five-banded form.
2c. Yellow unbanded form.
2d. Yellow form with transparent bands.
2e. Yellow form with fused bands and coloured lip.

3a-b. **Cepaea sylvatica** 204
Alpine. Small blunt thickening on columellar lip.

4a-b. **Cepaea vindobonensis** 203
E. Germany (Elbe valley). Whitish or dull yellow (never brightly coloured). Growth-lines rather coarse.

Subfamily HYGROMIINAE
See also plates 17–19, 20
(×1½)

5a-b. **Pyrenaearia carascalensis** 190
Pyrenees only. Lip simple. Strong growth-ridges.

23

1a 1c 1e 1b 1d 1f 1g 2a 2c 2b 2d 2e 3a 4a 5a 3b 4b 5b

24

1a   1b   2a   2b

3

4a

4b

4c

5a   5b

6a

6b

6c

Family HELICIDAE
Subfamily HELICELLINAE
See also plates 15 and 16

Plate 24

1. ***Cochlicella barbara** ×3½ 184
Mainly Mediterranean. Broadly conical. Growth-ridges rather coarse.
1a-b. Typical colour variants.

2. ***Cochlicella acuta** ×2½ 183
W. Europe, maritime. Narrower than *C. barbara*.
2a-b. Typical colour variants.

Subfamily HELICINAE
See also plate 23
(life size)

3. ***Helix pomatia** 205
The 'Roman' or 'edible snail' of commerce. The largest N.W. European species.

4.

*Theba pisana 202
Mediterranean and maritime. Very variable in colour and shape. Juveniles sharply keeled.
4a-b. Pale variant.
4c. Typical form.

5a-b. ***Helix aspersa** 205
The 'garden snail'. Common in most western areas, especially round human habitations.

6a-c. **Eobania vermiculata** 203
Common near the Mediterranean, sometimes introduced further north.

Occurrence in N.W. Europe. Greenhouses in the botanic gardens in London (Kew), Glasgow and Dublin (Glasnevin).

Family **ENDODONTIDAE** (see p. 101)

HELICODISCUS PARALLELUS (Say 1821)
Syn. *H. lineatus* (Say)
Description. br. 2.8–3.3 mm. Shell discoidal, with 4½ very closely-coiled rounded whorls separated by a rather deep suture. Mouth-edge simple, unthickened; 2–4 blunt denticles present a little way within the mouth in mature specimens. Umbilicus shallow and extremely wide, about two-fifths of the width of the base. Shell dull, pale greenish, with diagnostic sculpture of *fine parallel raised ridges* running *spirally* round the whorls.
Original home and habitat. N. America, where it is mainly a species of woods and other moist places.
Occurrence in N.W. Europe. Greenhouses in Ireland, England and Holland.

Family **ZONITIDAE** (see p. 116)

HAWAIIA MINUSCULA (Binney 1840)
Syn. *Zonitoides minusculus* (Binney)
Description. br. 2.2–2.5 mm. Shell discoidal, spire rather raised, with 4½ well-rounded whorls separated by a deep suture. Mouth almost circular, mouth-edge simple and unthickened. Umbilicus broad and deep. Shell somewhat translucent, nearly colourless, with a dull silky sheen caused by fine irregular growth-lines.

This species somewhat resembles a very large *Punctum pygmaeum* (see p. 101). It is also not unlike *Helicodiscus singleyanus* (see p. 102), a species occasionally reported from greenhouses.
Original home and Habitat. N. America (now widely spread by man elsewhere). A common and catholic species.
Occurrence in N.W. Europe. Greenhouses in several countries, including Holland, West Germany, England, Scotland, Ireland.

ZONITOIDES ARBOREUS (Say 1816)
Description. br. 4.5–5 mm. Shell discoidal, spire a little raised, with 4½ closely-coiled whorls, slightly compressed and with a hint of keeling at the periphery. Shell translucent, glossy, pale yellowish-brown, with faint irregular growth-lines.

The appearance of this species from above is very like that of *Z. excavatus* (see p. 127), but from below the umbilicus is seen to be much narrower.
Original home and habitat. N. America (now widely spread by man elsewhere). A common species of moist habitats especially in woods.
Occurrence in N.W. Europe. Frequent in greenhouses in most countries, including Iceland; very occasionally recorded living in the open as an escape.

Family **LIMACIDAE** (see p. 135)

LIMAX VALENTIANUS Férussac 1821
Syns. *L. poirieri* Mabille, *Lehmannia valentiana* (Férussac)
Description. Medium-sized slug, extended length 5–7 cm, with a yellowish-grey or yellowish-violet body and a slightly darker head, watery and gelatinous in appearance like *L. marginatus*; usually with one dark band on each side of and near to the mid-line, and sometimes a second, feebler pair lower down. Keel short. Mantle with a median darker band and a pair of lateral darker bands forming a lyre-shape. Sole pale greyish, mucus colourless. For internal features see p. 139.

Limax valentianus ×⅔

L. valentianus is virtually indistinguishable externally from *L. nyctelius* (a species also recorded from greenhouses; see p. 137). It is also similar to *L. marginatus*.
Original home and habitat. Iberian peninsula, now widely spread by man in many parts of the world. A terrestrial, not an arboreal slug, unlike *L. marginatus*.
Occurrence in N.W. Europe. Frequent in greenhouses in most countries; very occasionally recorded in the open an an escape.

Family **SUBULINIDAE** (see p. 150)

SUBULINA OCTONA (Bruguière 1789)
Description. 14–17 mm. Shell narrow and tapering, straight-sided, with 8–9 evenly rounded, somewhat tumid whorls, apex blunt. Outer lip sharp and simple; base of columella slightly but distinctly truncate. Shell colourless, glossy and translucent, growth-lines fairly well-marked, especially on the last whorl.
Original home and habitat. Tropical America; moist places in ground litter.
Occurrence in N.W. Europe. Recorded from hothouses in Britain, Ireland, Denmark and Germany (but note that many reputed occurrences require confirmation, as this species has several times been recorded in error for other species of Subulinidae).

SUBULINA STRIATELLA (Rang 1831)
Syns. *S. petrensis* (Morelet), *Homorus striatellus* (Rang)
Description. 16–24 mm. Shell superficially rather like *S. octona*, but larger, with flatter-sided, less tumid whorls, and with much stronger and more regular growth-ridges, giving a *finely ribbed* effect. Shell also less glossy.
Original home and habitat. Tropical W. Africa; moist places in ground litter.
Occurrence in N.W. Europe. Hothouses in the botanic gardens in London (Kew), Cambridge and Glasgow; sometimes a pest, feeding on the roots of plants.

LAMELLAXIS CLAVULINUS (Potiez & Michaud 1838)

Syns. *Opeas clavulinum* (Potiez & Michaud), *O. mauritianum* of some authors, *Leptiniaria urichi* (Smith)

Description. 7.5–9 mm. Shell elongate, virtually straight-sided (but first 2–3 whorls sometimes slightly bowed in outline), whorls very feebly convex, apex rather blunt. Outer lip simple and delicate; columella not truncate at base. Shell colourless, thin and translucent, glossy, with rather distinct growth-lines.

It should be noted that the taxonomy of this and of other species of this widespread tropical genus reported from European hothouses needs further elucidation.

Original home and habitat. Probably tropical E. Africa, but widely spread by man elsewhere; moist places in ground litter.

Occurrence in N.W. Europe. Hothouses in England, Scotland, Ireland and Holland.

OPEAS PUMILUM (Pfeiffer 1840)

Syn. *O. goodalli* (Miller)

Description. 5.5–7 mm. Shell narrowly conical, outline straight-sided, with about 6 feebly convex whorls, the last accounting for about half the total height; apex rather sharply pointed (cf. *Lamellaxis*). Columella not truncate. Shell translucent, colourless, *coarsely and closely striated*, often with an iridescent sheen; growth-lines strongly S-shaped, curving inwards near the suture to correspond with a marked sinus at the top of the outer lip.

Original home and habitat. Tropical C. America, but now widely dispersed by man; moist places in ground litter.

Occurrence in N.W. Europe. Hothouses in England (first reported near Bristol with Bromeliaceae about 1816), Scotland, Ireland, France, Holland, Germany, Denmark, Sweden.

Family STREPTAXIDAE

This is a large and diverse family of exclusively tropical snails, found in Africa, S. America and the Far East. They are carnivorous.

GULELLA IO Verdcourt 1974

Syn. *G. devia* of some British authors

Description. 3.5–4 mm. Shell cylindrical, with a dome-shaped apex, whorls almost flat-sided. Mouth squarish, mouth-edge white, somewhat thickened and reflected. Mouth with 4 teeth: 1 parietal, 1 palatal, 2 columellar; parietal set close to the outer lip, strong and lamella-like; palatal set rather low. Shell colourless, glossy and translucent, the growth-lines developing into rather strong widely-spaced rib-like ridges, especially on the last quarter whorl behind the outer lip.

Original home. Unknown, but almost certainly tropical Africa, where *Gulella* is represented by very many species; *G. io* is at present known only as an introduction in greenhouses in Britain and Czechoslovakia.

Occurrence in N.W. Europe. Hothouses in the botanic gardens in London (Kew), Cambridge and Edinburgh.

Bibliography and Societies

The literature on European non-marine Mollusca is immense. The following list is necessarily highly selective, being restricted to a few of the more useful and comprehensive works dealing with the species occurring within our area. Most of the older literature may be traced through them.

(a) British works

BOYCOTT, A.E. 1934. The habitats of land Mollusca in Britain. *Journal of Ecology*, vol. 22, pp. 1–38.
A classic ecological study.

ELLIS, A.E. 1926; reprinted with appendix 1969. *British Snails*. Oxford: Clarendon Press.
The standard work, still very useful. Photographic illustrations.

KERNEY, M.P. 1976. *Atlas of the non-marine Mollusca of the British Isles*. Cambridge: Institute of Terrestrial Ecology (obtainable from the Conchological Society, see p. 214).
Distribution maps of all species on a 10-kilometre grid.

QUICK, H.E. 1960. British Slugs (Pulmonata; Testacellidae, Arionidae, Limacidae). *Bulletin of the British Museum (Natural History), Zoology* vol. 6, no. 3.
A monographic treatment with much anatomical detail. Some recently segregated species are not included.

TAYLOR, J.W. 1894–1921. *Monograph of the Land and Freshwater Mollusca of the British Isles*. 3 vols + 3 parts (unfinished). Leeds: Taylor Brothers.
Incomplete and somewhat outmoded, but of permanent value for the extremely fine coloured illustrations, especially those showing variation in slugs.

(b) Continental works

ADAM, W. 1960. *Faune de Belgique. Mollusques I. Mollusques terrestres et dulcicoles*. Brussels: L'Institute royal des sciences naturelles de Belgique.
Excellent line drawings.

EHRMANN, P. 1933; facsimile reprint 1956. *Die Tierwelt Mitteleuropas. II (1). Weichtiere, Mollusca*. Leipzig: Quelle & Meyer.
A fundamental work of permanent value. Illustrated with photographs and line drawings.

GERMAIN, L. 1930–31; facsimile reprint 1962. *Faune de France, 21, 22. Mollusques terrestres et fluviatiles*. Paris: Lechevallier.
Very useful, though including many species of doubtful validity and not always reliable in detail. Fully illustrated.

GITTENBERGER, E., BACKHUYS, W. and RIPKEN, T.E.J. 1970. *De Landslakken van Nederland*. Amsterdam: Koninklijke Nederlandse Natuurhistorische Vereniging.
Excellent line drawings, and maps for all Dutch species.

LOŽEK, V. 1956. *Klíč Československých Měkkýšů* [Key to the Mollusca of Czechoslovakia] Bratislava: Vydavatel'stvo Slovenskej Académie Vied.

LOŽEK, V. 1964. Quartärmollusken der Tschechoslowakei. *Rozpravy ústředního Ústavu geolického*, vol. 31, pp. 1–374.

Both works illustrated with fine photographs.

MERMOD, G. 1930. *Catalogue des Invertébrés de la Suisse. 18. Gastéropodes*. Geneva: Museum d'Histoire Naturelle.

Comprehensive, though with few illustrations.

WIKTOR, A. 1973. *Die Nacktschnecken Polens*. Monographie Fauny Polski, vol. 1. Warsaw: Press of the Polish Academy.

A monographic treatment of most of the slugs included in this field guide, with excellent illustrations of internal organs.

ZILCH, A. & JAECKEL, S.G.H. 1962. *Ergänzung Tierwelt Mitteleuropas: Weichtiere, Mollusca*. Leipzig: Quelle & Meyer.

A useful supplement to *Ehrmann* with much geographical information, though not always reliable in detail. Illustrations crude.

PERIODICALS

The Journal of Conchology. Leeds and London, 1874 – in progress. Organ of the Conchological Society of Great Britain and Ireland.

Proceedings of the Malacological Society. London, 1893–1975; continued as *The Journal of Molluscan Studies*. 1976 – in progress. Organ of the Malacological Society of London.

There are also several continental periodicals. Two of the most important, containing many papers on non-marine Mollusca, are:

Archiv für Molluskenkunde. Frankfurt a. Main, 1869– in progress. Organ of the German Malacological Society.

Basteria. Lisse & Leiden, 1936 – in progress. Organ of the Malacological Society of the Netherlands.

BRITISH SOCIETIES

The Conchological Society of Great Britain and Ireland.

Hon. Secretary: Mrs E. B. Rands, 51 Wychwood Avenue, Luton, Beds.

The Malacological Society of London.

Hon. Secretary: Dr A. Bebbington, Bristol Polytechnic, Redland Hill, Bristol.

Both societies are concerned with all the Mollusca, including land slugs and snails. Both produce a journal (see periodicals) containing papers on molluscs and book reviews. Both hold regular lecture programmes in London, and occasionally elsewhere. The Conchological Society is particularly interested in distribution, ecology and mapping schemes. It caters for amateurs as well as professionals, and has a special section for junior members. It also produces a quarterly newsletter with a wide variety of items, produces occasional 'papers for students' on practical aspects of conchology, and organizes field excursions to places of interest. The Malacological Society caters more for professionals; its journal contains papers on the anatomy, physiology and behaviour of molluscs.

Index

Numbers in normal type refer to main descriptive texts. **Bold** numbers refer to the colour plates, *italic* numbers to the distribution maps. Synonyms are shown in *italics*.

DISTRIBUTION MAPS

Distribution maps

The European Distribution Maps on pp. 226–256 are designed to give a rough idea of the geographical ranges within N.W. Europe of the species described in this book. They should be used with caution. Though a good deal of work has gone into their construction they are based on information which is nearly always inadequate and occasionally no doubt wrong. A particular failing is that the maps usually do not discriminate between species which are common throughout their ranges and those living only in widely separated localities, so that the distribution of the rarer species tends to appear much exaggerated. In some cases isolated occurrences outside the main range are shown by dots. The exact placing of these dots should not necessarily be interpreted as marking exact sites, but is rather an indication that the species is known to occur in one or more places in the *general* area indicated. Occasionally a question mark is used to show additional areas where the species is likely to be present, though positive records are lacking.

The British Distribution Maps on pp. 260–288 show the distribution of all species marked * in the text. Here ranges may be accepted as being shown fairly accurately, though the attempt to suggest frequency by shading is necessarily somewhat subjective.

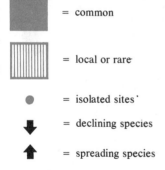

= common

= local or rare

= isolated sites

= declining species

= spreading species

MAP CAPTIONS

The map number is referred to in the main text and in the index; references to text descriptions are in normal type, and to colour plates in **bold** type.

The map number for the British distribution map is the same as that used for the full European sequence.

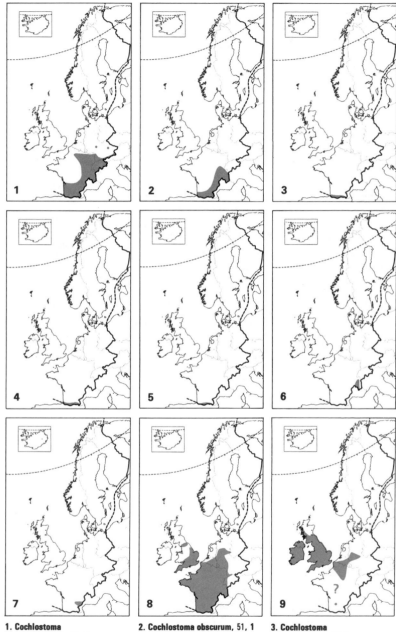

1. Cochlostoma
   septemspirale, 51, 1
4. Cochlostoma partioti, 52, 1
7. Cochlostoma patulum, 52, 1

2. Cochlostoma obscurum, 51, 1
5. Cochlostoma nouleti, 52, 1
8. Pomatias elegans, 53, 1

3. Cochlostoma
   crassilabrum, 52, 1
6. Cochlostoma apricum, 52, 1
9. Acicula fusca, 54

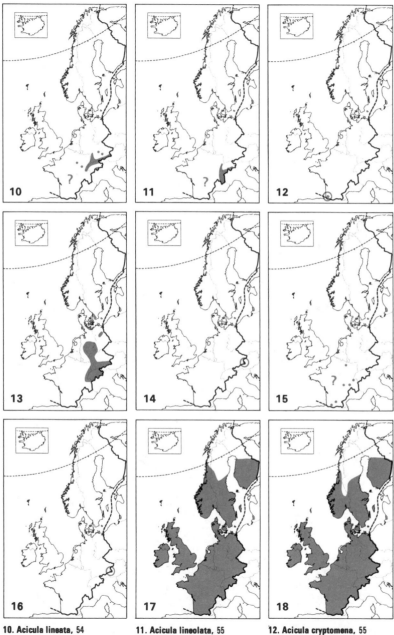

10. Acicula lineata, 54
13. Acicula polita, 55
16. Renea veneta, 56

11. Acicula lineolata, 55
14. Acicula gracilis, 56
17. Carychium minimum, 57

12. Acicula cryptomena, 55
15. Acicula dupuyi, 56
18. Carychium tridentatum, 58

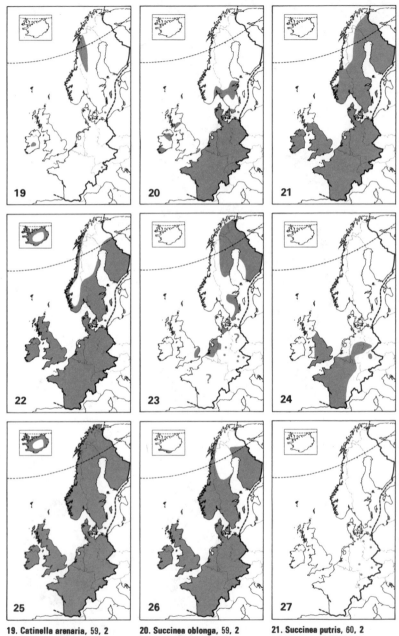

19. Catinella arenaria, 59, 2
20. Succinea oblonga, 59, 2
21. Succinea putris, 60, 2
22. Oxyloma pfeifferi, 60, 2
23. Oxyloma sarsi, 61, 2
24. Azeca goodalli, 62, 1
25. Cochlicopa lubrica, 62, 1
26. Cochlicopa lubricella, 62, 1
27. Cochlicopa nitens, 62, 1

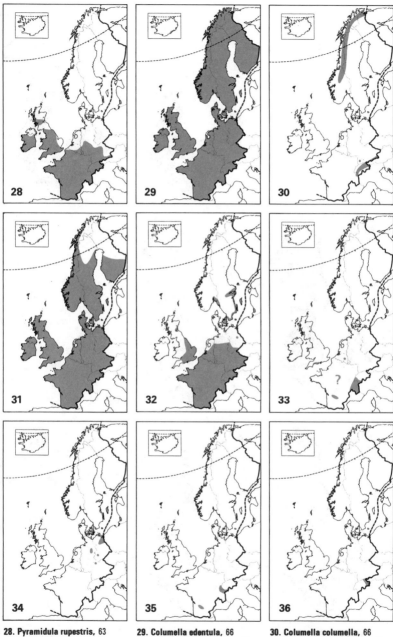

28. Pyramidula rupestris, 63
31. Columella aspera, 67
34. Truncatellina costulata, 68

29. Columella edentula, 66
32. Truncatellina cylindrica, 68
35. Truncatellina claustralis, 69

30. Columella columella, 66
33. Truncatellina callicratis, 68
36. Trancatellina monodon, 69

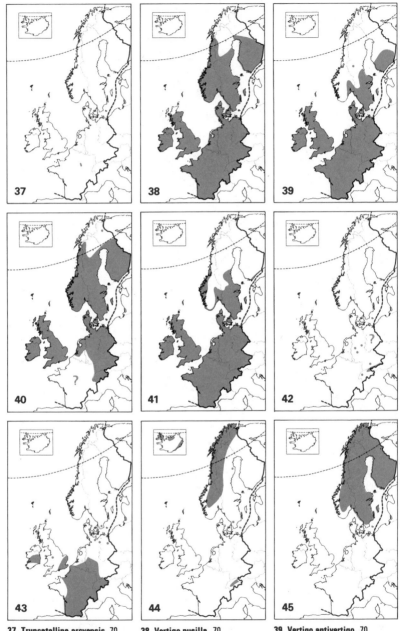

37. Truncatellina arcyensis, 70
38. Vertigo pusilla, 70
39. Vertigo antivertigo, 70
40. Vertigo substriata, 71
41. Vertigo pygmaea, 71
42. Vertigo heldi, 72
43. Vertigo moulinsiana, 72
44. Vertigo modesta, 73
45. Vertigo ronnebyensis, 73

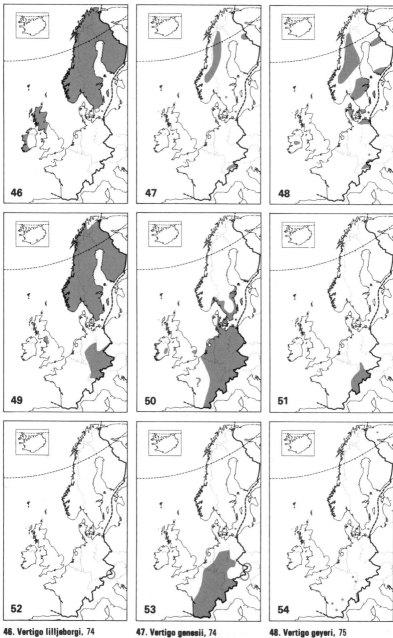

46. Vertigo lilljeborgi, 74
49. Vertigo alpestris, 75
52. Orcula gularis, 77

47. Vertigo genesii, 74
50. Vertigo angustior, 75
53. Orcula doliolum, 77, 2

48. Vertigo geyeri, 75
51. Orcula dolium, 76, 2
54. Pagodulina pagodula, 77

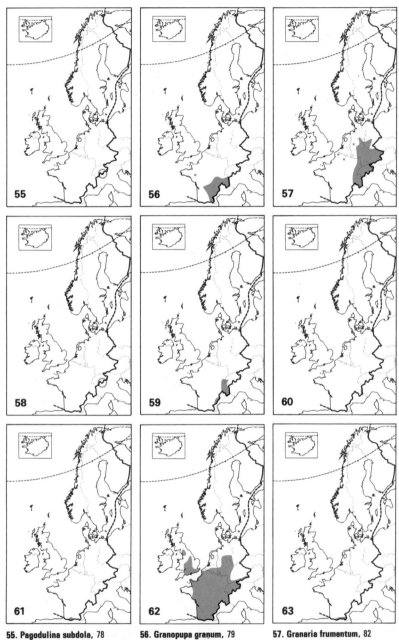

55. Pagodulina subdola, 78
58. Granaria illyrica, 82
61. Granaria braunii, 84

56. Granopupa granum, 79
59. Granaria variabilis, 83
62. Abida secale, 84, 2

57. Granaria frumentum, 82
60. Granaria stabilei, 83
63. Abida pyrenaearia, 85

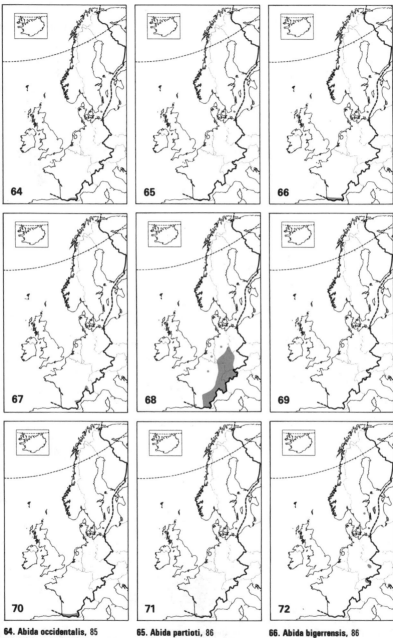

64. Abida occidentalis, 85
65. Abida partioti, 86
66. Abida bigerrensis, 86
67. Abida polyodon, 86
68. Chondrina avenacea, 87, 2
69. Chondrina megacheilos, 87
70. Chondrina bigorriensis, 88
71. Chondrina tenuimarginata, 88
72. Chondrina clienta, 89

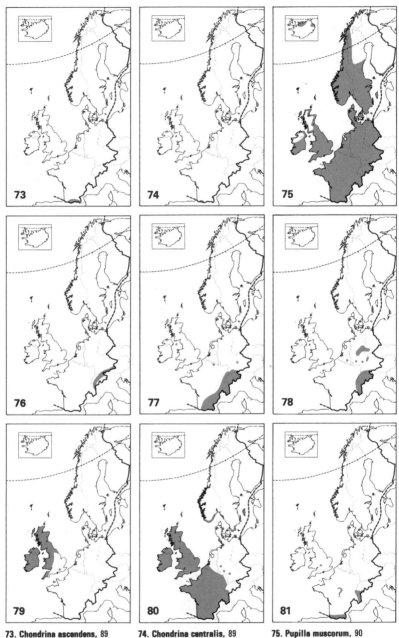

73. **Chondrina ascendens**, 89
74. **Chondrina centralis**, 89
75. **Pupilla muscorum**, 90
76. **Pupilla alpicola**, 91
77. **Pupilla triplicata**, 91
78. **Pupilla sterri**, 92
79. **Leiostyla anglica**, 92
80. **Lauria cylindracea**, 92
81. **Lauria sempronii**, 93

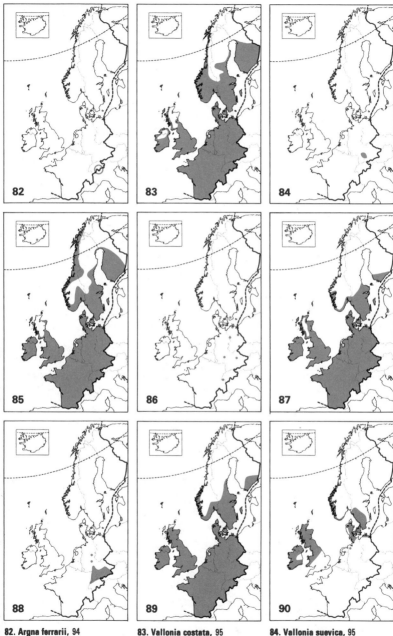

82. Argna ferrarii, 94
83. Vallonia costata, 95
84. Vallonia suevica, 95
85. Vallonia pulchella, 96
86. Vallonia enniensis, 96
87. Vallonia excentrica, 96
88. Vallonia declivis, 97
89. Acanthinula aculeata, 97
90. Spermodea lamellata, 98

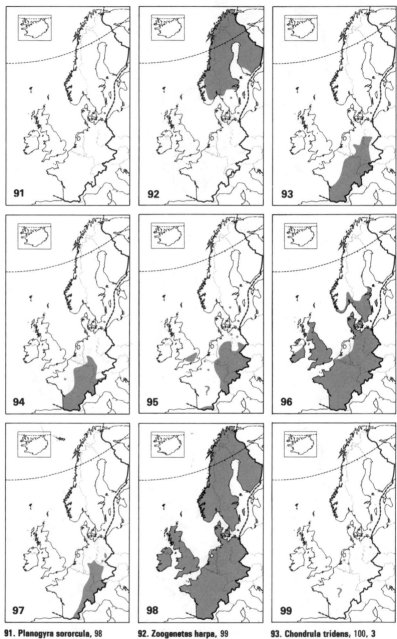

91. Planogyra sororcula, 98
94. Jaminia quadridens, 100, 3
97. Zebrina detrita, 101, 3

92. Zoogenetes harpa, 99
95. Ena montana, 100, 3
98. Punctum pygmaeum, 101

93. Chondrula tridens, 100, 3
96. Ena obscura, 100, 3
99. Helicodiscus
      singleyanus, 101

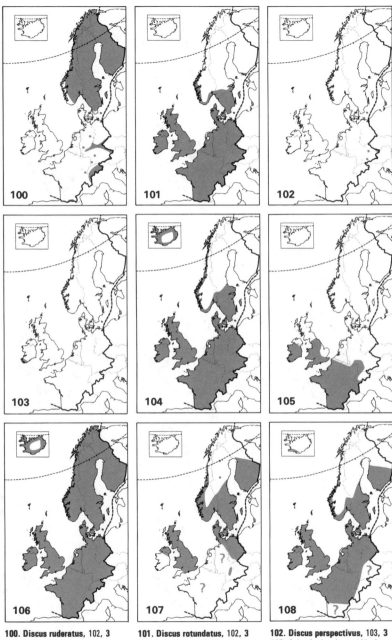

100. Discus ruderatus, 102, 3
103. Geomalacus
     maculosus, 103, 4
106. Arion subfuscus, 104, 5

101. Discus rotundatus, 102, 3
104. Arion ater, 104, 4
107. Arion fasciatus, 105, 5

102. Discus perspectivus, 103, 3
105. Arion lusitanicus, 104, 4
108. Arion circumscriptus, 105, 5

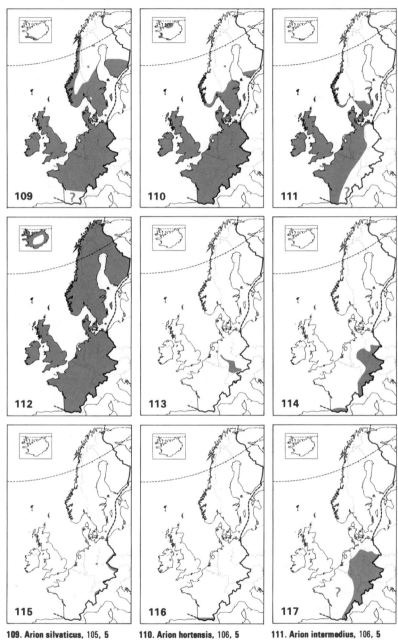

109. Arion silvaticus, 105, 5
112. Vitrina pellucida, 109, 6
115. Semilimax kotulae, 111, 6

110. Arion hortensis, 106, 5
113. Vitrinobrachium
        breve, 109, 6
116. Semilimax pyrenaicus, 111, 6

111. Arion intermedius, 106, 5
114. Semilimax semilimax, 110, 6
117. Eucobresia diaphana, 111, 7

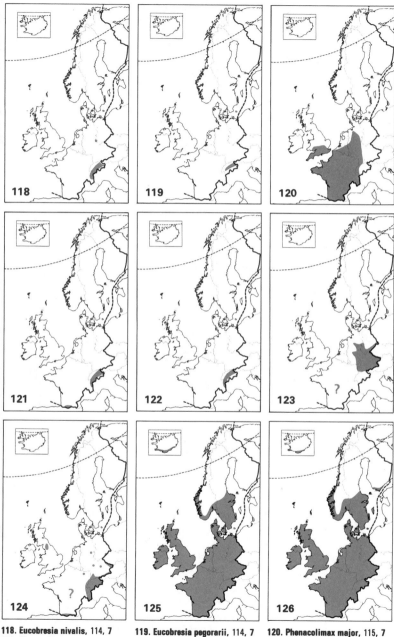

118. Eucobresia nivalis, 114, 7
121. Phenacolimax
    annularis, 116, 7
124. Vitrea subrimata, 118

119. Eucobresia pegorarii, 114, 7
122. Phenacolimax
    glacialis, 116, 7
125. Vitrea crystallina, 118, 8

120. Phenacolimax major, 115, 7
123. Vitrea diaphana, 117
126. Vitrea contracta, 119

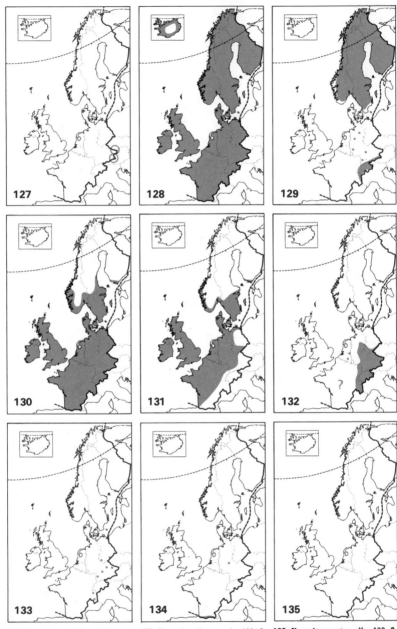

127. Aegopis verticillus, 119
130. Aegopinella pura, 120, 8
133. Aegopinella minor, 122, 8

128. Nesovitrea hammonis, 120, 8
131. Aegopinella nitidula, 121, 8
**134. Aegopinella
    epipedostoma**, 122

129. Nesovitrea petronella, 120, 8
132. Aegopinella nitens, 122, 8
**135. Aegopinella
    ressmanni**, 123, 9

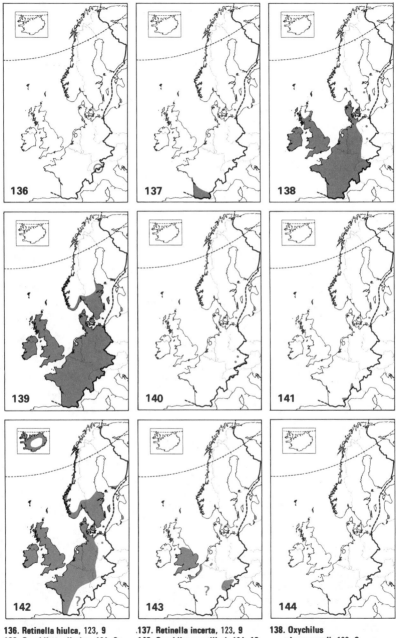

136. Retinella hiulca, 123, 9
139. Oxychilus cellarius, 124, 9
142. Oxychilus alliarius, 125, 10

.137. Retinella incerta, 123, 9
140. Oxychilus mortilleti, 124, 10
143. Oxychilus
    helveticus, 125, 10

138. Oxychilus
    draparnaudi, 123, 9
141. Oxychilus hydatinus, 124, 10
144. Oxychilus clarus, 125, 10

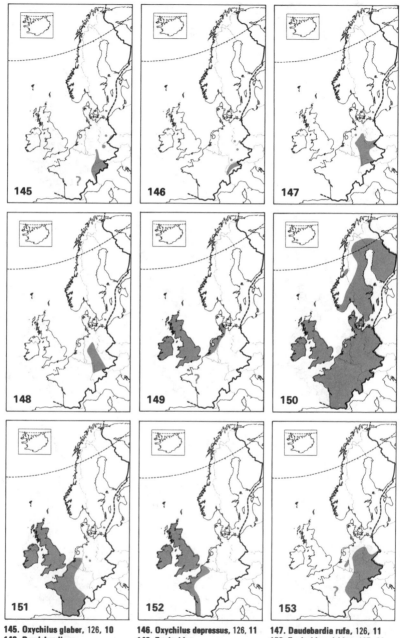

145. Oxychilus glaber, 126, 10
148. Daudebardia
     brevipes, 127, 11
151. Milax gagates, 130, 12

146. Oxychilus depressus, 126, 11
149. Zonitoides
     excavatus, 127, 11
152. Milax sowerbyi, 130, 12

147. Daudebardia rufa, 126, 11
150. Zonitoides nitidus, 127, 11
153. Milax rusticus, 131, 12

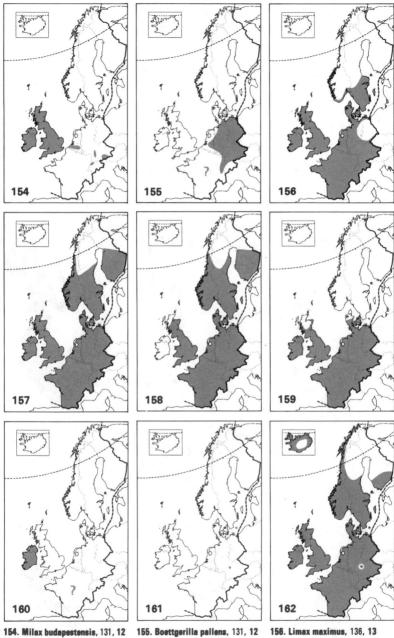

154. **Milax budapestensis**, 131, 12
155. **Boettgerilla pallens**, 131, 12
156. **Limax maximus**, 136, 13
157. **Limax cinereoniger**, 136, 13
158. **Limax tenellus**, 136, 13
159. **Limax flavus**, 137, 13
160. **Limax pseudoflavus**, 137, 13
161. **Limax nyctelius**, 137
162. **Limax marginatus**, 138, 13

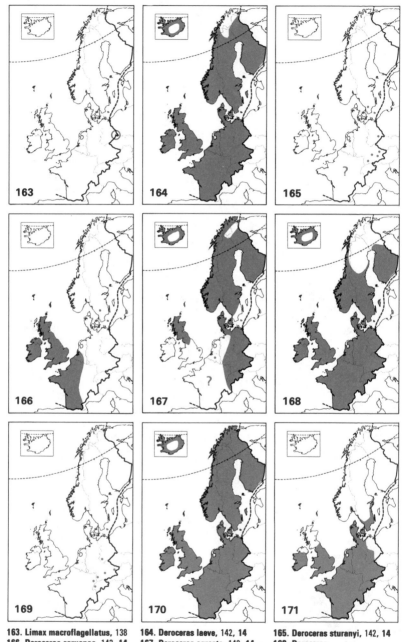

163. **Limax macroflagellatus**, 138
166. **Deroceras caruanae**, 143, 14
169. **Deroceras rodnae**, 146, 14
164. **Deroceras laeve**, 142, 14
167. **Deroceras agreste**, 143, 14
170. **Euconulus fulvus**, 148
165. **Deroceras sturanyi**, 142, 14
168. **Deroceras reticulatum**, 143, 14
171. **Cecilioides acicula**, 149

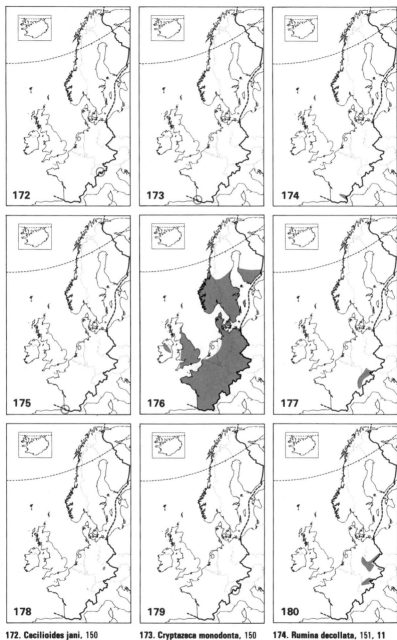

172. Cecilioides jani, 150
175. Laminifera pauli, 154
178. Cochlodina costata, 156

173. Cryptazeca monodonta, 150
176. Cochlodina
     laminata, 155, 11
179. Cochlodina comensis, 157

174. Rumina decollata, 151, 11
177. Cochlodina fimbriata, 155
180. Cochlodina orthostoma, 157

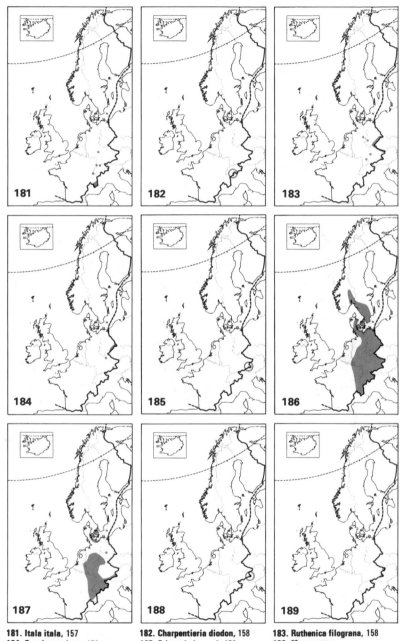

181. Itala itala, 157
182. Charpentieria diodon, 158
183. Ruthenica filograna, 158
184. Fusulus varians, 159
185. Erjavecia bergeri, 159
186. Macrogastra
     ventricosa, 162, 11
187. Macrogastra lineolata, 162
188. Macrogastra
     densestriata, 163
189. Macrogastra badia, 164

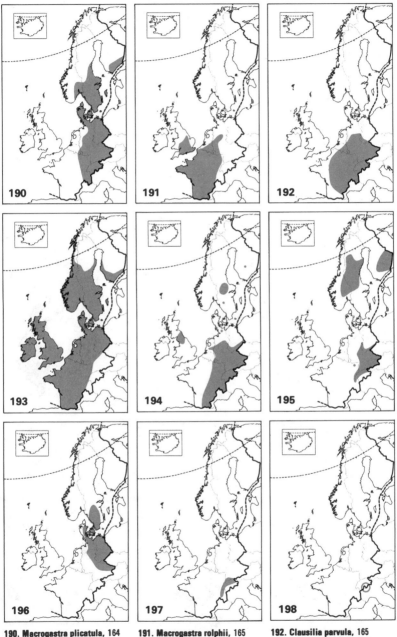

190. **Macrogastra plicatula**, 164
193. **Clausilia bidentata**, 166
196. **Clausilia pumila**, 168

191. **Macrogastra rolphii**, 165
194. **Clausilia dubia**, 166
197. **Neostyriaca corynodes**, 168

192. **Clausilia parvula**, 165
195. **Clausilia cruciata**, 167
198. **Neostyriaca strobeli**, 169

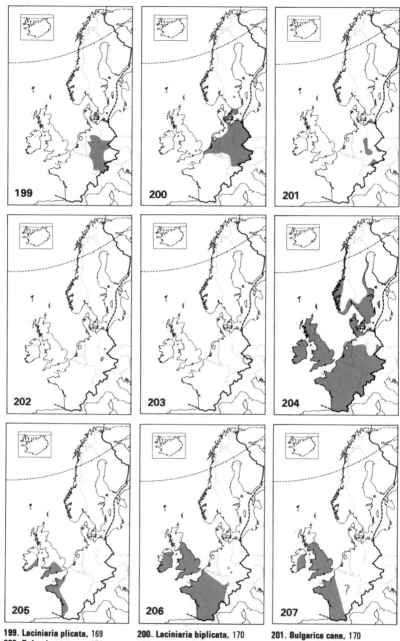

199. Laciniaria plicata, 169
202. Bulgarica vetusta, 171
205. Testacella maugei, 173, 14

200. Laciniaria biplicata, 170
203. Vestia turgida, 172
206. Testacella
     haliotidea, 173, 14

201. Bulgarica cana, 170
204. Balea perversa, 172
207. Testacella scutulum, 174, 14

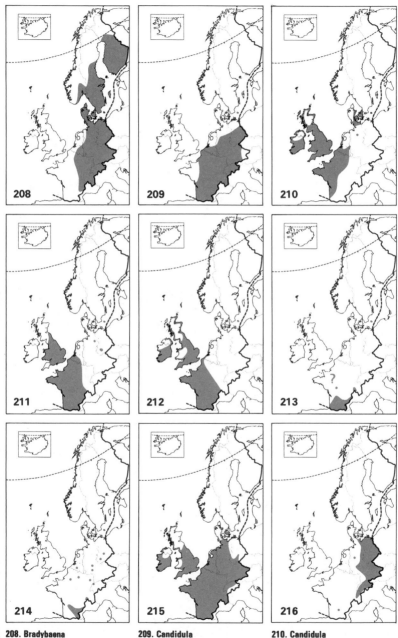

208. **Bradybaena**
     fruticum, 174, 20
211. **Candidula gigaxii**, 177, 15
214. **Cernuella neglecta**, 178, 16

209. **Candidula**
     unifasciata, 176, 15
212. **Cernuella virgata**, 177, 16
215. **Helicella itala**, 179, 16

210. **Candidula**
     intersecta, 177, 15
213. **Cernuella aginnica**, 178, 16
216. **Helicella obvia**, 179, 16

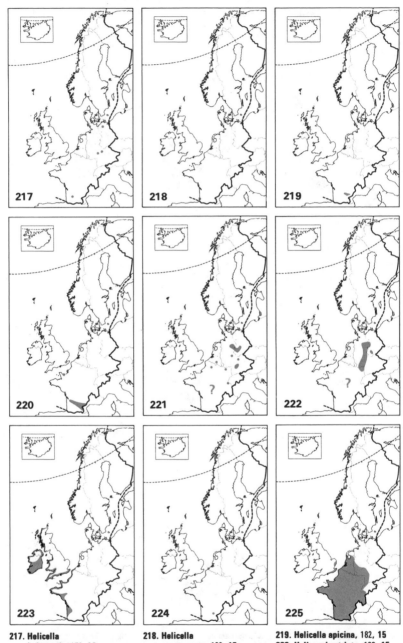

217. Helicella
  bolenensis, 179, 16
220. Trochoidea elegans, 182, 15
223. Cochlicella acuta, 183, 24

218. Helicella
  conspurcata, 182, 15
221. Trochoidea geyeri, 182, 15
224. Cochlicella barbara, 184, 24

219. Helicella apicina, 182, 15
222. Helicopsis striata, 183, 15
225. Monacha cartusiana, 184, 20

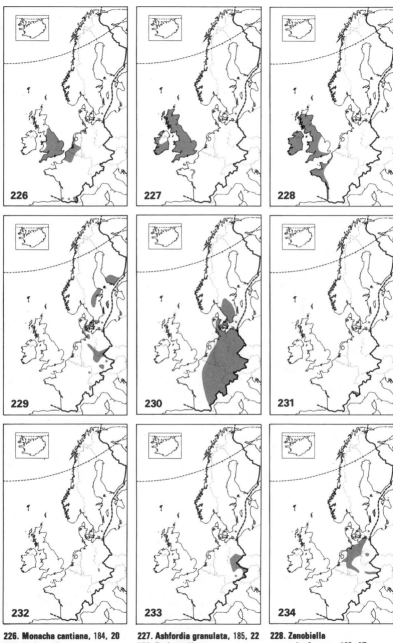

226. Monacha cantiana, 184, 20
229. Perforatella
    bidentata, 185, 17
232. Perforatella vicina, 187, 18

227. Ashfordia granulata, 185, 22
230. Perforatella
    incarnata, 186, 18
233. Perforatella umbrosa, 187, 18

228. Zenobiella
    subrufescens, 185, 17
231. Perforatella glabella, 186, 18
234. Perforatella rubiginosa, 190, 17

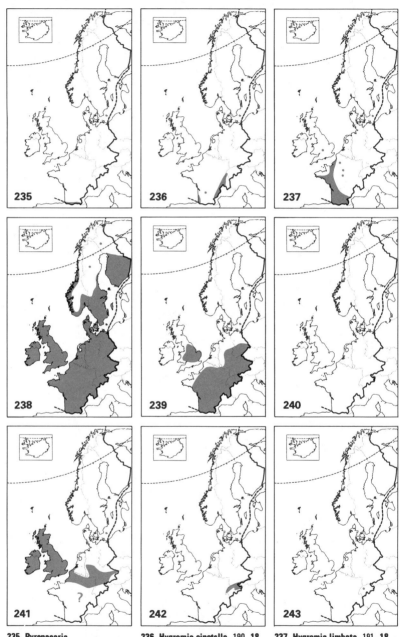

235. Pyrenaearia
      carascalensis, 190, 23
238. Trichia hispida, 191, 19
241. Trichia striolata, 194, 19

236. Hygromia cinctella, 190, 18
239. Trichia plebeia, 194, 19
242. Trichia montana, 194, 19

237. Hygromia limbata, 191, 18
240. Trichia suberecta, 194, 19
243. Trichia caelata, 195, 19

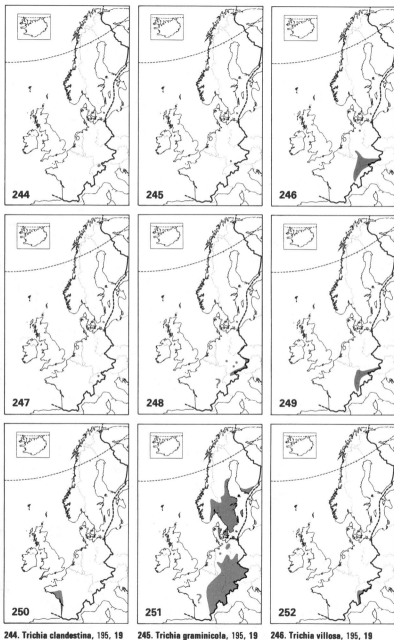

244. **Trichia clandestina**, 195, **19**
247. **Trichia biconica**, 196, **17**
250. **Ponentina**
    subvirescens, 197, **17**

245. **Trichia graminicola**, 195, **19**
248. **Trichia unidentata**, 196, **17**
251. **Euomphalia**
    strigella, 197, **20**

246. **Trichia villosa**, 195, **19**
249. **Trichia edentula**, 196, **17**
252. **Ciliella ciliata**, 197, **17**

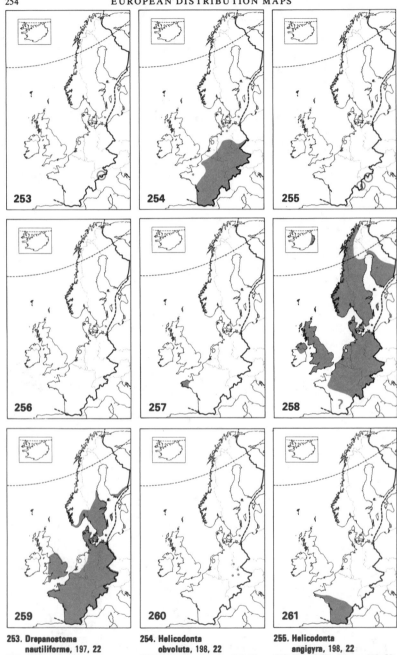

253. Drepanostoma
     nautiliforme, 197, 22
256. Trissexodon
     constrictus, 198, 22
259. Helicigona lapicida, 199, 22

254. Helicodonta
     obvoluta, 198, 22
257. Elona quimperiana, 199, 20
260. Chilostoma
     cingulatum, 199, 21

255. Helicodonta
     angigyra, 198, 22
258. Arianta arbustorum, 199, 20
261. Chilostoma
     squamatinum, 200, 21

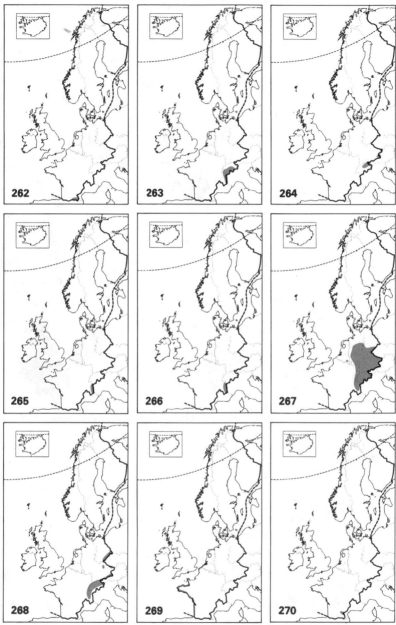

262. Chilostoma
     desmoulinsi, 200, 21
265. Chilostoma glaciale, 201, 21
268. Isognomostoma
     holosericum, 202, 22

263. Chilostoma zonatum, 201, 21
266. Chilostoma alpinum, 202, 21
269. Theba pisana, 202, 24

264. Chilostoma achates, 201, 21
267. Isognomostoma
     isognomostoma, 202, 22
270. Eobania vermiculata, 203, 24

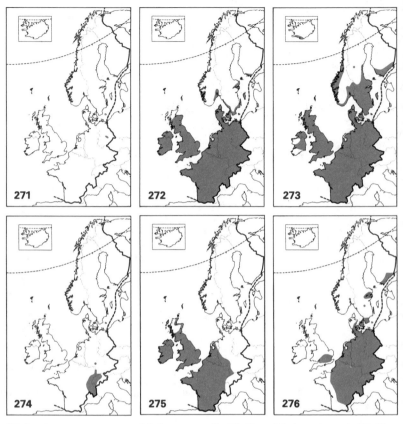

271. Cepaea
    vindobonensis, 203, **23**
274. Cepaea sylvatica, 204, **23**

272. Cepaea nemoralis, 203, **23**
275. Helix aspersa, 205, **24**

273. Cepaea hortensis, 204, **23**
276. Helix pomatia, 205, **24**

British distribution maps

The following maps are simplified versions of dot maps published in the *Atlas of the non-marine Mollusca of the British Isles* (see bibliography). The attempt to convey frequency visually by shading is necessarily somewhat subjective, especially for certain recently discovered or otherwise poorly known species.

Although a few hardy and catholic snails and slugs are nearly ubiquitous, most are geographically restricted in various ways. Clearly, many different factors are responsible.

First, there are historical reasons. Most, if not all, our species were destroyed by the intense cold of the last glacial period, so that our present 'native' fauna results from re-immigration beginning about 13,000 years ago, before a rising sea-level cut Britain off from the continental mainland. The make-up of the fauna is therefore to some extent the result of historical accident, dependent on rates of migration from refugia further south in Europe – indeed, it is known that rather different combinations of species were able to reach Britain during earlier mild interglacial periods. The absence of certain species from Ireland (e.g., *Azeca goodalli*) is probably due to the early isolation of that country by the rising sea-level. Some distributions within these islands can only be understood as the end result of complex postglacial climatic and vegetational changes; many of our rarer species with discontinuous distributions (e.g., *Abida secale*, *Vitrea subrimata*) are in this category. Such 'fossil' patterns warn us that we cannot always expect to explain distributions purely in terms of factors still operating.

Nevertheless, physiography, geology and climate are obviously important, especially in controlling the distribution of the commoner species, and the four maps overleaf offer some clues for interpretation.

Most molluscs favour calcareous soils. *Pomatias elegans*, our best example of an obligatory calcicole, is virtually restricted to the chalk and limestone tracts of southern Britain. Other clear calciphiles are *Pyramidula rupestris*, *Pupilla muscorum*, *Ena obscura*, *Cochlodina laminata*, *Cernuella virgata*, *Helicella itala* and *Helicigona lapicida*. Even the least demanding species are nearly always more common in calcareous places, and the presence of limestone or coastal shell sand may compensate for otherwise adverse factors, e.g., low temperatures. Conversely, *Zonitoides excavatus*, a rare example of a calcifuge snail, avoids calcareous areas. Soils may have other subtle effects, not always understood; for example, in the English midlands *Trichia striolata* reveals a dislike for the area of Triassic red marl.

Moisture levels are important. Some species with poor powers of surviving desiccation show distributions related to prevailing humidities. The tree slug *Limax marginatus* is a good example: it is common in moist western areas, even in exposed places, but very local in central and S.E. England, where it is found only in the dampest woods. *Leiostyla anglica* and *Zenobiella subrufescens* have similar oceanic distributions. Conversely, many xerophiles are commonest in eastern Britain. This effect is reinforced by (a) the fact that it is the climatically drier lowlands that have been most affected by drainage and cultivation, and (b) the fact that most xerophiles are also calciphiles. It is a geological accident that most of our calcareous rocks are in the lowland southeast, whereas the humid highland zone is largely non-calcareous.

Mean summer temperatures are probably important in limiting the northward range of a number of central European species which just reach the British area, e.g., *Ena montana*, *Macrogastra rolphii*, *Monacha cartusiana*, *Helicodonta obvoluta* and *Helix pomatia*. The effects of low temperatures are harder to assess. Many species can survive intense cold in hibernation, though a few are clearly frost sensitive. The garden snail *Helix aspersa*, which originated in the Mediterranean, is often killed by severe winters in British gardens, and its distribution suggests that in the north it can survive only in relatively frost-free coastal habitats. *Cochlicella acuta* is a more extreme example: in Britain it occurs only along western coasts, but in southern Ireland the mildness of the winters allows it also to penetrate inland. Few molluscs are restricted to cold regions, though *Vertigo lilljeborgi*, a late-glacial relict, is now found only in the cool north and west.

Obviously, few distributions can be explained satisfactorily in terms of single variables. For example, *Pyramidula rupestris* needs not only bare calcareous rocks or walls, but also moderate humidities, thus restricting its potential range to isolated tracts where both these requirements are met.

Apart from such natural limitations, the importance of man can hardly be exaggerated. Industrial pollution may occasionally be damaging: the absence of helicids and clausiliids from the grimy countryside of south Lancashire is partly due to this. Otherwise, man has had two overwhelming effects. First, the destruction of forests and the drainage of marshes has led to a great restriction of moisture and shade demanding species. Fossils show that the woodland snail *Spermodea lamellata* was once widespread across lowland Britain, though it has now retreated to fragments of ancient woodland mostly in the highland zone. The tiny marsh snail *Vertigo angustior*, similarly once very common, is now on the verge of extinction. Secondly, species of grassland, waste ground, gardens and other man-made habitats have been greatly favoured, e.g., *Vallonia excentrica* or *Trichia striolata*. A considerable number of these are indeed not native at all, but have been accidentally introduced from the continental mainland from Roman times onwards. Among them are probably *Oxychilus draparnaudi*, the *Milax* species, *Cecilioides acicula*, the *Testacella* species, *Candidula intersecta*, *Cernuella virgata*, *Cochlicella acuta*, *Monacha cantiana*, *Theba pisana* and *Helix aspersa*. The earliest records of some recent introductions, now well-established, are: *Trochoidea elegans* (1890), *Hygromia limbata* (1917), *Deroceras caruanae* (1931), *Hygromia cinctella* (1950) and *Boettgerilla pallens* (1972).

Our molluscan fauna is therefore not static. A few changes may be the result of continuing climatic fluctuations, but most are now humanly caused. On the whole, the effect has been to diversify the fauna. Most species are in no danger and some have benefited, but a few are clearly at risk. This is especially true of certain wetland and old woodland rarities; careful conservation of their surviving habitats is therefore important, especially as the same spots usually harbour other interesting plants or invertebrates.

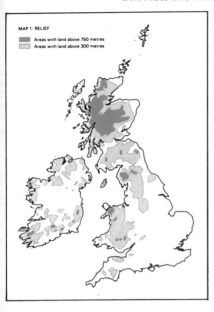

MAP 1: RELIEF

Areas with land above 750 metres
Areas with land above 300 metres

MAP 2: CALCAREOUS ROCKS

Chalk
Other calcareous rocks
Coastal shell sand

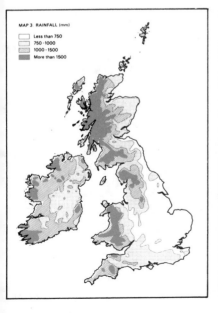

MAP 3: RAINFALL (mm)

Less than 750
750 - 1000
1000 - 1500
More than 1500

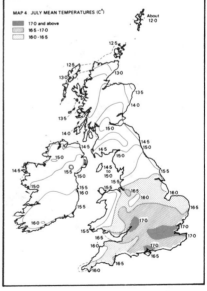

MAP 4: JULY MEAN TEMPERATURES (C°)

17·0 and above
16·5 - 17·0
16·0 - 16·5

About 12·0

8. Pomatias elegans, 53, **1**

9. Acicula fusca, 54

17. Carychium minimum, 57

18. Carychium tridentatum, 58

19. Catinella arenaria, 59, **2**

20. Succinea oblonga, 59, **2**

21. Succinea putris, 60, **2**

22. Oxyloma pfeifferi, 60, **2**

23. Oxyloma sarsi, 61, 2

24. Azeca goodalli, 62, 1

25. Cochlicopa lubrica, 62, 1

26. Cochlicopa lubricella, 62, 1

28. Pyramidula rupestris, 63

29. Columella edentula, 66

31. Columella aspera, 67

32. Truncatellina cylindrica, 68

33. Truncatellina callicratis, 68

38. Vertigo pusilla, 70

39. Vertigo antivertigo, 70

40. Vertigo substriata, 71

41. Vertigo pygmaea, 71

43. Vertigo moulinsiana, 72

46. Vertigo lilljeborgi, 74

48. Vertigo geyeri, 75

49. Vertigo alpestris, 75

50. Vertigo angustior, 75

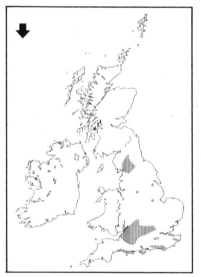

62. Abida secale, 84, 2

75. Pupilla muscorum, 90

79. Leiostyla anglica, 92

80. Lauria cylindracea, 92

83. Vallonia costata, 95

85. Vallonia pulchella, 96

87. Vallonia excentrica, 96

89. Acanthinula aculeata, 97

90. Spermodea lamellata, 98

95. Ena montana, 100, **3**

96. Ena obscura, 100, **3**

98. Punctum pygmaeum, 101

99. Helicodiscus singleyanus, 101

101. Discus rotundatus, 102, **3**

103. Geomalacus maculosus, 103, **4**

104. Arion ater, 104, **4**

105. Arion lusitanicus, 104, **4**

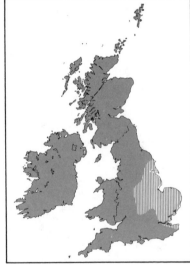

106. Arion subfuscus, 104, **5**

107. Arion fasciatus, 105, 5

108. Arion circumscriptus, 105, 5

109. Arion silvaticus, 105, 5

110. Arion hortensis, 106, 5

111. **Arion intermedius**, 106, **5**

112. **Vitrina pellucida**, 109, **6**

116. **Semilimax pyrenaicus**, 111, **6**

120. **Phenacolimax major**, 115, **7**

124. Vitrea subrimata, 118

125. Vitrea crystallina, 118, **8**

126. Vitrea contracta, 119

128. Nesovitrea hammonis, 120, **8**

130. Aegopinella pura, 120, 8

131. Aegopinella nitidula, 121, 8

138. Oxychilus draparnaudi, 123, 9

139. Oxychilus cellarius, 124, 9

142. Oxychilus alliarius, 125, **10**

143. Oxychilus helveticus, 125, **10**

149. Zonitoides excavatus, 127, **11**

150. Zonitoides nitidus, 127, **11**

151. Milax gagates, 130, **12**

152. Milax sowerbyi, 130, **12**

154. Milax budapestensis, 131, **12**

155. Boettgerilla pallens, 131, **12**

156. Limax maximus, 136, **13**

157. Limax cinereoniger, 136, **13**

158. Limax tenellus, 136, **13**

159. Limax flavus, 137, **13**

160. Limax pseudoflavus, 137, **13**

162. Limax marginatus, 138, **13**

164. Deroceras laeve, 142, **14**

166. Deroceras caruanae, 143, **14**

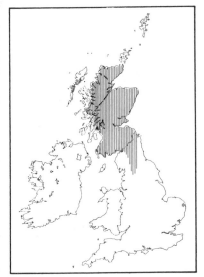

167. Deroceras agreste, 143, **14**

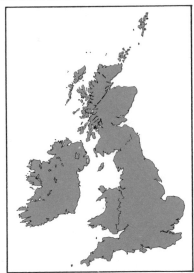

168. Deroceras reticulatum, 143, **14**

170. Euconulus fulvus, 148

170a. Euconulus alderi, 149

171. Cecilioides acicula, 149

176. Cochlodina laminata, 155, 11

191. Macrogastra rolphii, 165

193. Clausilia bidentata, 166

194. Clausilia dubia, 166

200. Laciniaria biplicata, 170

204. Balea perversa, 172

205. Testacella maugei, 173, **14**

206. Testacella haliotidea, 173, **14**

207. Testacella scutulum, 174, **14**

208. Bradybaena fruticum, 174, **20**

210. Candidula intersecta, 177, **15**

211. Candidula gigaxii, 177, **15**

212. Cernuella virgata, 177, **16**

215. Helicella itala, 179, **16**

220. Trochoidea elegans, 182, **15**

223. Cochlicella acuta, 183, **24**

224. Cochlicella barbara, 184, **24**

225. Monacha cartusiana, 184, **20**

226. Monacha cantiana, 184, **20**

227. Ashfordia granulata, 185, **22**

228. Zenobiella subrufescens, 185, **17**

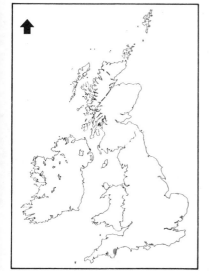

236. Hygromia cinctella, 190, **18**

237. Hygromia limbata, 191, **18**

238. Trichia hispida, 191, **19**

239. Trichia plebeia, 194, **19**

241. Trichia striolata, 194, **19**

250. Ponentina subvirescens, 197, 17

254. Helicodonta obvoluta, 198, **22**

258. Arianta arbustorum, 199, **20**

259. Helicigona lapicida, 199, **22**

269. Theba pisana, 202, **24**

272. Cepaea nemoralis, 203, **23**

273. Cepaea hortensis, 204, **23**

275. Helix aspersa, 205, **24**

276. Helix pomatia, 205, **24**